# Yahoo!® SiteBuilder For Dummies

**Cheat Sheet**

## Yahoo! SiteBuilder

Text properties

Toolbar

Open Web pages

Site Contents pane

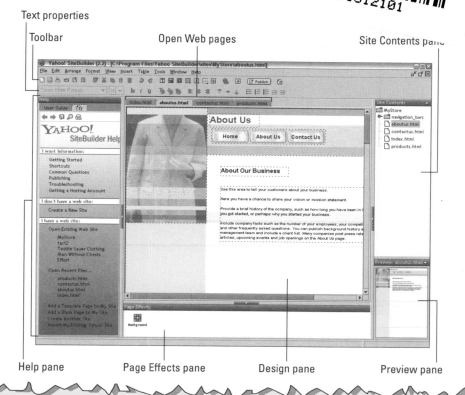

Help pane

Page Effects pane

Design pane

Preview pane

## Web Design Tips

- Get design ideas from big company Web sites, but don't be a copycat.
- Get rid of the sounds, effects, and other gadgets you don't really need.
- Update your site regularly to keep people coming back.
- Keep the size of your home page under 50K.
- Test your site using multiple browsers. Hey, they're free to use anyway.
- You don't have to become the next John Grisham, but pay attention to the quality of the text on your site.

- Ensure that your site can communicate within 10 seconds what your company is or what your products do.
- Design your site for technology laggards, but don't worry about the people lost in the Stone Age.
- Consider converting special text (such as headings) to a graphic so you can antialias the text.
- Never assume the visitor to your site has the same computer that you do.

See Chapter 16 for more design tips.

# Yahoo!® SiteBuilder For Dummies®

## Yahoo! SiteBuilder Toolbar

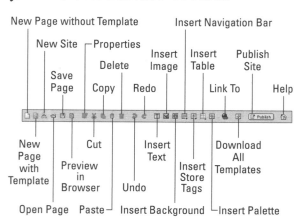

New Page without Template

Insert Navigation Bar

New Site — Properties

Insert Image

Insert Table

Publish Site

Delete

Save Page

Copy

Redo

Link To

Help

New Page with Template

Cut

Insert Text

Download All Templates

Preview in Browser

Insert Store Tags

Open Page — Paste — Insert Background — Insert Palette

Undo

---

## Buzzwords You Need to Know

**Add-Ons:** Cool elements that you can add to your Yahoo! Web site to provide helpful information for your visitors or to improve the look of the site.

**Domain name:** A unique name that identifies a Web site, such as `www.yahoo.com`. Domain names have two or more parts that are separated by dots. The last part represents the type (`.com`, `.net`, `.org`, and so on) and the further left you go, the more specific you get.

**FTP:** The method in which you transfer files between your computer and your Yahoo! Web site. FTP stands for *File Transfer Protocol.*

**HTML:** The behind-the-scenes coding language used for constructing Web pages. HTML stands for *HyperText Markup Language.*

**HTTP:** The protocol used for transferring files over the Web. Stands for *HyperText Transport Protocol.*

**Hypertext:** A link to another page on the Web.

**Meta tags:** Meta tags are "hidden" inside the HTML code of your Web page to provide information for search engines. Meta tags contain a description and keywords related to your site.

**Navigation bar:** The element on your Web site that visitors use to navigate around your Web site. The navigation bar contains links to the major sections of your site.

**Subdomain name:** A unique name to the left of the domain name that subdivides a Web site. For example, the `yahoo.com` domain contains many subdomains, including `help.yahoo.com` and `smallbusiness.yahoo.com`. You can add subdomains to your Yahoo! site.

**URL:** A unique address for a Web page or resource on the Internet, such as `http://www.dummies.com/index.html`. URL stands for *Uniform Resource Locator.*

See also `help.yahoo.com/help/us/webhosting/glossary`.

## *For Dummies: Bestselling Book Series for Beginners*

# Yahoo!® SiteBuilder

## FOR

# DUMMIES®

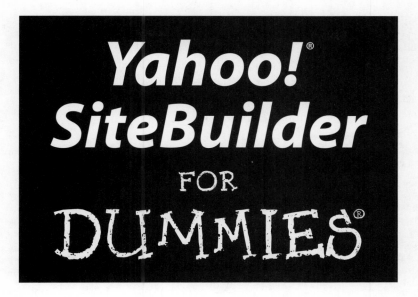

# Yahoo!® SiteBuilder FOR DUMMIES®

**Richard Wagner**

WILEY

Wiley Publishing, Inc.

**Yahoo!® SiteBuilder For Dummies®**

Published by
**Wiley Publishing, Inc.**
111 River Street
Hoboken, NJ 07030-5774
www.wiley.com

For general information on our other products and services, please contact our Customer Care Department within the U.S. at 800-762-2974, outside the U.S. at 317-572-3993, or fax 317-572-4002.

For technical support, please visit www.wiley.com/techsupport.

Wiley also publishes its books in a variety of electronic formats. Some content that appears in print may not be available in electronic books.

Library of Congress Control Number: 2005924597

ISBN-13: 978-0-7645-9800-5

ISBN-10: 0-7645-9800-7

Manufactured in the United States of America

10  9  8  7  6  5  4  3  2  1

1O/SU/QY/QV/IN

WILEY

# About the Author

**Richard Wagner** is an experienced author of over 16 technical books, including *WordPerfect 12 For Dummies, XSLT For Dummies,* and *XML All-in-One Desk Reference For Dummies*. He is also former V.P. of Product Development at NetObjects and inventor of the award-winning NetObjects ScriptBuilder. In his non-tech life, Richard is author of *Christianity For Dummies*. He lives in Princeton, Massachusetts.

# Dedication

To the Jboys.

# Author's Acknowledgments

In writing this book, I'd like to thank the following people for their contributions: Paul Levesque, for his guiding hand throughout the project and keen suggestions for improving the book; Rebecca Senninger, for her editing prowess and attention to detail; Lee Musick, for his technical perspective to ensure the book's accuracy; and Jennifer Shrauger, Sunil Saha, and others at Yahoo!, for their insights into SiteBuilder and how to best cover their Web site builder in this book. Finally, I'd like to thank my wife, Kimberly, and the J-team for their patience and grace throughout the entire writing project.

## Publisher's Acknowledgments

We're proud of this book; please send us your comments through our online registration form located at www.dummies.com/register/.

Some of the people who helped bring this book to market include the following:

*Acquisitions, Editorial, and Media Development*

**Project Editor:** Paul Levesque

**Acquisitions Editor:** Steven Hayes

**Copy Editor:** Rebecca Senninger

**Technical Editor:** Lee Musick

**Editorial Manager:** Leah Cameron

**Permissions Editor:** Laura Moss

**Media Development Specialist:** Travis Silvers

**Media Development Manager:** Laura VanWinkle

**Media Development Supervisor:** Richard Graves

**Editorial Assistant:** Amanda Foxworth

**Cartoons:** Rich Tennant (www.the5thwave.com)

*Composition Services*

**Project Coordinator:** Maridee Ennis

**Layout and Graphics:** Carl Byers, Andrea Dahl, Heather Ryan, Erin Zeltner

**Proofreaders:** Laura Albert, Leeann Harney, Joe Niesen, TECHBOOKS Production Services

**Indexer:** TECHBOOKS Production Services

**Publishing and Editorial for Technology Dummies**

    **Richard Swadley,** Vice President and Executive Group Publisher

    **Andy Cummings,** Vice President and Publisher

    **Mary Bednarek,** Executive Acquisitions Director

    **Mary C. Corder,** Editorial Director

**Publishing for Consumer Dummies**

    **Diane Graves Steele,** Vice President and Publisher

    **Joyce Pepple,** Acquisitions Director

**Composition Services**

    **Gerry Fahey,** Vice President of Production Services

    **Debbie Stailey,** Director of Composition Services

# Contents at a Glance

# Table of Contents

# Introduction

**T**he term "best of both worlds" has a nice ring to it, doesn't it? All the sugary taste without the carbs. A roomy SUV that gets great gas mileage. An all-in-one-kitchen-knife-bought-from-an-infomercial-for-just-three-easy-payments that actually works.

When you think about creating a Web site for yourself or your business, you undoubtedly want the "best of both worlds" principle to apply here as well. You want to be able to create a really cool Web site by yourself without being forced to get a graduate degree in Web programming or computer human interface design.

Yahoo! SiteBuilder is a highly popular software tool for people who want to do just that. Using SiteBuilder, you can create a Web site that looks far more sophisticated than many low-end, design-in-a-browser alternatives but without diving deep into the nitty-gritty details of something called *HyperText Markup Language* (HTML).

*Yahoo! SiteBuilder For Dummies* serves as your friendly tour guide to help you create, design, and manage your SiteBuilder Web site. It gives you just the information you need to know to create "wicked cool" sites without resorting to that geeky stuff.

Using the dynamic duo of Yahoo! SiteBuilder and *Yahoo! SiteBuilder For Dummies,* you can make the "best of both words" goal a reality. But why stop there? I have so many more euphemisms and trite sayings to conquer with this combo. You'll have your cake and eat it too. Your rolling stone will start to gather moss. Your watched pot will actually boil. Your road-crossing chicken will . . . well, you get the idea.

## Conventions Used in This Book

*Yahoo! SiteBuilder For Dummies* is one book that doesn't bow to convention or even bow at conventions (unless free food is involved). But I follow some usual practices to make life easier for you.

## Text formatting

I use the following formatting conventions:

- *Italics* are used for term definitions.

- **Boldface** is used to indicate words that you're supposed to type.

- `Monofont` text is used for Web addresses; text that you see on-screen; and, on very rare occasions, JavaScript or HTML programming code.

## Commands

When referring to a menu item inside of Yahoo! SiteBuilder, I use a shortcut. For example, I abbreviate the Copy command on the Edit menu to Edit⇨Copy. Also, when I suggest pressing two keys at the same time, such as the Ctrl key and the C key, I use a plus sign like this: Ctrl+C.

# What You're Forbidden to Read

In this book, you explore what you need to know to create great-looking Web sites with Yahoo! SiteBuilder. However, on your first reading of this book, I do cover some topics that you are absolutely, positively forbidden to read. — okay, okay, not forbidden, just topics that you can feel free to skip if you want to. The sections that you have an official waiver for skipping are

- **Any text that is marked with the Technical Stuff icon.** Paragraphs with this icon are more technical in nature. It is undoubtedly fascinating information, but you won't miss anything if you gloss over it.

- **Sidebars.** The shaded boxes that you see scattered throughout the book are like espresso bars you pass on your way home from the office: Stopping for a cappuccino or two is fine, but your trip home takes a lot longer if you stop at every one (not to mention how wired you'll be on arrival at your house).

# Foolish Assumptions

In *Yahoo! SiteBuilder For Dummies,* I assume that you have basic knowledge of how to use Microsoft Windows and get around the Web with a popular browser such as Microsoft Internet Explorer. However, I don't assume that you have any prior know-how involving the creation of Web sites when you start the book.

# How This Book Is Organized

*Yahoo! SiteBuilder For Dummies* is divided into five parts.

## Part I: Getting to Know Yahoo! SiteBuilder

As you start your tour of Yahoo! SiteBuilder, you get to know the software and the basics of creating and publishing a Web site. You also focus on how to design a site so that it looks good and is easy to navigate. I give special attention to how you can design your Web site effectively using Yahoo! SiteBuilder's built-in templates.

## Part II: Creating "Cool" Web Pages

While Part I focuses on the design of your Web site, Part II looks at the content that goes into your Web pages. You dive into the basic building blocks of Web pages: text, links, pictures, tables, navigation bars, and forms.

## Part III: Going Further: Developing "Wicked Cool" Web Pages

In Part III, you discover how to add cool functionality to your site — such as Yahoo! Search, Yahoo! Directions, and page effects — but I show you how to do so without making these features look gimmicky.

## Part IV: Managing Your Web Site

Designing and creating your Web site may be your major task at the start, but after you get your site up and running, you need to effectively manage it. Part IV looks at how to manage your Yahoo! SiteBuilder Web site through the Yahoo! Web Hosting Control Panel. Finally, you tackle the world of e-commerce, looking at how to turn your Web site into an electronic storefront.

## Part V: The Part of Tens

In the final part, you get quick tips for effective Web site design and tricks and techniques for using Yahoo! SiteBuilder.

# About the CD

The CD tucked inside the back cover of this book is loaded with a full version of Yahoo! SiteBuilder 2.2, along with a complete bundle of SiteBuilder templates. (Talk about convenient!) For more CD details — including installation stuff — check out this book's appendix.

# Icons Used in This Book

Throughout the book, you'll be bedazzled with nifty little icons that are beside important paragraphs. These pictures indicate special kinds of information that you'll find amazingly useful:

The Tip icon points you to key techniques, tidbits, or shortcuts that can save you time and effort.

The Remember icon draws attention to something in the text that is absolutely, positively, definitively, kind of, sort of important. What's more, if you have a photographic mind and love memorizing entire sections of text, I recommend focusing your mental skills on these particular paragraphs.

The Warning icon means "Pay attention, buddy! Or you will run into trouble!" Heed these warnings to save yourself from falling into the pit of Web site despair.

The Technical Stuff icon highlights nonessential but interesting stuff that no one but geeks and geek-wanna-bes really cares about.

# Where to Go from Here

My guess is that you are so mesmerized by this book's prose by now that you want nothing more than to keep reading from cover to cover. If you do, you'll find the topics are ordered logically. However, _Yahoo! SiteBuilder For Dummies_ is designed as a reference book, so you don't have to read the book from start to finish. If you have a specific topic that you want to immediately dive into, consider the following jumping-off points:

- To install Yahoo! SiteBuilder, check out Chapter 1.

- For a basic overview of the Web site publishing process, skip to Chapter 2.

- To create a Web site that will make the industry leading designers beg you for tips, check out Chapter 3 and 16.

- To create a basic Web page, see Chapter 4.

- To use the Yahoo! SiteBuilder Control Panel, check out Chapter 14.

# Part I

# Getting to Know Yahoo! SiteBuilder

The 5th Wave                                    By Rich Tennant

PLEASE

"NO INTERNET ADDRESS"

## In this part . . .

**O**ne of my least favorite activities is to go to a party or
similar gathering in which I know no one. After some
awkward introductions, I typically retreat to the corner by
myself, munching on chips, veggies, and dip, all the while
everyone around me is chatting and happily involved with
others. Many people find learning how to create a Web
site can be much like my social woes. They make an
attempt to do so, but don't like what happens, and then
become too intimidated to try again.

Part I helps you eliminate any awkwardness you may have
as you think about creating a Web site by yourself. To do
so, I guide you through how to use Yahoo! SiteBuilder and
the basics of creating and designing a Web site.

# Chapter 1

# Yahoo! Let's Go Site Building

## In This Chapter

▶ Exploring how Web site publishing works

▶ Signing up with Yahoo! Web hosting

▶ Getting Yahoo! SiteBuilder ready to roll on your computer

▶ Scoping out and sizing up SiteBuilder

*Zeitgeist. Angst. Mercedes. Porsche.* I am embarrassed to say that those four words pretty much composed the extent of my German vocabulary prior to a business trip to Zurich a few years back. Because of my lack of knowledge, I felt nervous, even inadequate, about living several weeks in Switzerland, Austria, and Germany. Oh, I'd talk to my well-traveled friends, and they'd reassure me that I could learn enough of the language to get by. I even bought a Learn-German-in-a-Day book and studied en route. But I was still tense stepping off that plane into the unknown.

As you start out your journey into Web site building, you may feel much the same way I did before my European excursion. Perhaps you know a few terms — such as *URL, domain name, JPG,* and *hypertext.* Maybe you've even talked with friends who've had success creating a business or personal Web site. Perhaps you've even created a Web site before with one of those quick and easy online Web builders out there but are ready for something better.

This chapter helps you as you "step off that plane into the unknown," so to speak. It helps you get acquainted with what Web publishing and Yahoo! SiteBuilder are all about and also helps you understand the basics about how it all works.

# Discovering How Web Publishing Works

Before you even start working with SiteBuilder, you should take a moment to explore the process of Web publishing. You can think of creating, designing, and publishing a Web site much like a director making a film. For example, consider Peter Jackson's well-documented saga of creating *The Lord of the*

*Rings*. He and his band of merry troops spent years filming and editing the Tolkien classics in New Zealand. In the process, they pulled together count-less clips from the general shoot, CGI effects, and miniature shoots to form a single, complete film. Then, for each of the three films, an original film was sent off and copied and then delivered to movie theaters across the world. Moviegoers then traveled by the millions to their local cinemas to watch the film Jackson made.

The Web publishing model has many parallels to making a film — though fortunately without Orcs and Gollum trying to mess you up along the way. You create a home Web site by pulling together information from a variety of sources. After you have the site ready, you publish the various parts as a single unit to a computer that can be accessed worldwide. Then people can flock by the millions (or the thousands or the tens) to their browsers to visit the site you made. As you can see, the basic process for Web publishing is

- ✔ Create and design in the comforts of your home or office
- ✔ Publish your site and go public
- ✔ Visit your site from anywhere
- ✔ Repeat the process for changes

Figure 1-1 illustrates the process. I describe each step in the following sections.

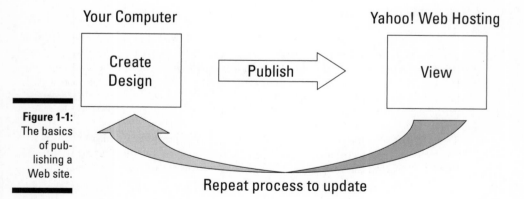

**Figure 1-1:**
The basics
of pub-
lishing a
Web site.

## *Creating and designing on your computer*

The first step is to create and design your Web site on your desktop or laptop computer (which I refer from here on out as your *local* computer). A Web site consists of several different kind of files and resources, all of which I conve-niently describe for you in this section. Your Web site building software, such as SiteBuilder, then pulls all these pieces together to form a single Web site.

### Web pages

A Web site contains one or more Web pages. A Web page is written in HTML (*HyperText Markup Language*) format and has a filename with an .htm or .html extension. An HTML file is just a normal text file, but each one contains a lot of information, such as the following:

✔ Text you want to display on-screen in a Web browser

✔ References to images, multimedia controls, and other resources that you also want to display on a Web page

✔ Links to other pages

✔ A set of instructions that tells the browser how to arrange and display all of this content

You can work with Web pages in two ways — using a "visual" editor that allows you to create and edit the page visually (in the process hiding all the complex HTML code from you) or using a "code" editor that enables you to work directly with the HTML code itself. Some editors, such as Macromedia Dreamweaver and Microsoft FrontPage, are hybrids and provide support for both visual and code editing.

SiteBuilder has a visual page editor (called the *Design pane*) built into it, freeing you from worrying about the yucky complexities of HTML. See Chapters 4, 6, and 8 for details of how to work with Web pages inside of SiteBuilder.

### Images

The Web may have started out as a text-based world, but it has emerged as an image-driven medium of communication. Go to any nice-looking site, and you see all sorts of images scattered around the text.

You can either use images you created yourself — taken with your digital camera or drawn using a software program of some kind — or images received from another source (though, as Chapter 7 discusses, you want to make sure you can freely use the image). SiteBuilder's templates, which I explore in Chapter 5, come with many nice-looking graphical elements for you to incorporate into your Web site design.

Today's Web sites often use navigation bars that incorporate both text and graphics. Chapter 9 shows you how to create navigation bars in SiteBuilder.

You don't create, edit, or manipulate images inside of SiteBuilder. SiteBuilder hands that job off to another graphics software package, such as Adobe Photoshop, Microsoft Office Picture Manager, or even Microsoft Paint. After you have a Web-ready image, you can add it to your Web page inside of SiteBuilder. Once again, Chapter 7 covers all those details.

### Interactive elements

The Web is more than just a giant bulletin board that visitors can browse. A visitor can also interact with the site, providing feedback, ordering products, or requesting more information. A Web page can contain form elements, such as edit boxes, drop-down lists, or buttons, to enable this kind of interaction. Chapter 10 explores how to create and work with forms inside of SiteBuilder. And if you're interested in selling products on the Web, check out Chapter 15.

### Embedded media

While text and images make up the bulk of the content on Web pages, you can also embed other resources in a Web page. Popular choices are video or audio clips and Java applets. Chapter 12 discusses how to add multimedia resources to your Web page. Finally, you can also embed HTML code and JavaScript scripts (see Chapter 13) in your page to add functionality and services not provided inside SiteBuilder — such as a guestbook, news headlines, and stock quotes.

### Yahoo! Add-Ons

A major benefit to using SiteBuilder and Yahoo! Web hosting is that you can incorporate Yahoo! service-oriented add-ons into your Web pages. (Add-ons let you add neat interactive features such as a Yahoo! Map or Yahoo! Search box into your page right inside of SiteBuilder. Chapter 11 has more on add-ons, including how to add features to your Web site.)

### Linked resources

A final batch of resources that can be part of a Web site are non-HTML documents and other files that a visitor can link to. Technically, these files don't appear as part of a Web page, but you link to (and open) them from other Web pages inside of your Web site. Common examples include Adobe Acrobat (PDF) files, PowerPoint presentations, and Microsoft Word documents. See Chapter 6 for more on how to link to these documents.

## Publishing your site

After you create and design your site on your local computer, it's time to go public and publish your site to the Web. Publishing is nothing more than copying the Web site files (Web pages, images, and anything else you have) from your local computer to a Yahoo! computer — the computer that's going to act as your site's *Web server.*

## Visiting your site from anywhere

After you publish your Web site, it's available for anyone in the world to access. A Yahoo! server stores your Web site files somewhere out in cyberspace for you to access them. Physically, it doesn't matter where that Yahoo! server is — it could be a facility in Sunnyvale, California; or Dallas, Texas; or Atlanta, Georgia — all that matters is that when people type your site's Web address in the Address bar of their browser or click a link that goes there, they're accessing your Web site on that particular server.

## Repeating the process

As I discuss in Chapter 16, you'll want to regularly update your Web site to ensure that it doesn't grow stale and start to grow mold. When you update your site, you make the changes and additions in SiteBuilder on your local computer and then republish the updates, overwriting the files that are on the Yahoo! Web server.

# Signing Up for Yahoo! Web Hosting

Before you can publish a SiteBuilder Web site, your first step is to sign up for Yahoo! Web hosting. Do so by following these steps:

Make sure you have a Yahoo ID before beginning this process.

1. **With your browser, go to `smallbusiness.yahoo.com`.**

   The Yahoo! Small Business home page makes an appearance (see Figure 1-2).

2. **Click the <u>Web Hosting</u> link to begin the signup process.**

   A new page appears in your browser, outlining the various Web hosting options available to you.

3. **Click the Sign Up button for the Web hosting plan that best suits your needs.**

4. **On the next page, enter the desired domain name for your Web site.**

   Your domain is a unique name that identifies a Web site, such as `yahoo.com`. Domain names have two or more parts separated by dots. The part to the right of the dot represents the general type (`.com`, `.net`, `.org`); the part to the left of the dot is meant to be the name that describes or identifies your site.

**Figure 1-2:**
Signing up
with Yahoo!
Web
hosting.

Keep the following tips in mind:

- Find a domain name that is unique to and descriptive of your business, organization, interest, or yourself as much as possible.

- Don't include hard-to-remember abbreviations. I also don't recommend using hyphens, simply because people easily forget about them.

- Be descriptive, but don't make it toooo long.

- Above all, make your domain name easy for people to remember.

Yahoo! searches to see if your choice is still available — meaning that nobody else has registered it before. If it is available, you can continue. If not, you need to search again.

5. **Continue through the registration process, providing necessary payment and contact information to complete the order.**

After your order is completed, you first receive a confirmation e-mail of your order. and then within a few hours, you receive a second e-mail letting you know that your account is active and ready to roll.

After your account is activated, you can access the Yahoo! Web Hosting Control Panel, which I discuss in Chapter 14.

# Downloading and Installing Yahoo! SiteBuilder

After you sign up for Yahoo! Web hosting, your next step is to download and install SiteBuilder onto your computer. No need to wait for your account to become active; jump right in by following these steps:

1. **With your Web browser, go to `webhosting.yahoo.com/ps/sb`.**

   The Yahoo! SiteBuilder page displays, as shown in Figure 1-3.

2. **Click the <u>Download SiteBuilder Today</u> link.**

   The Download page loads in your browser, at your service.

3. **Click the <u>Download</u> link.**

   If you're not signed into your Yahoo! account, you need to enter your Yahoo! ID and password before downloading SiteBuilder.

4. **Save the download file to an appropriate folder on your computer.**

5. **When the download completes, double-click the `ysitebuilder.exe` file in your download folder.**

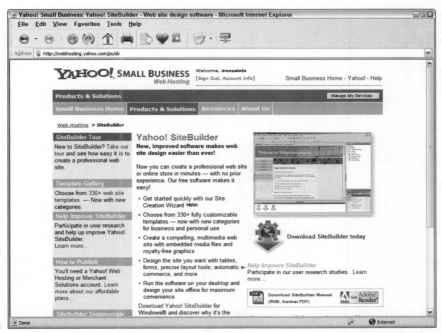

**Figure 1-3:** Down-loading SiteBuilder.

6. **After the Installer launches, follow the directions on-screen to install and configure SiteBuilder.**

   The installer places SiteBuilder into your Program Files directory and adds an icon on your Windows desktop and Windows Start menu.

# Exploring Yahoo! SiteBuilder

The rest of this book is devoted to building Web sites using SiteBuilder. But before getting into the specifics of how to do this or do that, take a moment to start up SiteBuilder and just get a feel for what the workspace looks like.

Follow these steps to launch SiteBuilder and take it through its paces:

1. **Double-click the Yahoo! SiteBuilder icon on your Windows desktop.**

   The main SiteBuilder window opens, as shown in Figure 1-4.

   You can also launch SiteBuilder by choosing All Programs⇨Yahoo! SiteBuilder⇨Yahoo! SiteBuilder from the Windows Start menu.

   For the purposes of exploring SiteBuilder, continue with the following steps. Your focus here isn't how to create a Web site just yet; you're simply exploring SiteBuilder and getting a sense of what the tool is like.

2. **In SiteBuilder, click the <u>Create a New Site</u> link in the Help pane on the left.**

   You can use the Help pane to perform several tasks, such as create a Web site, import a Web site you've already created in another program, or open a Web site you've already started.

3. **Click the Start button in the Site Creation Wizard.**

   The contents of the Help pane change, starting the wizard.

4. **In the Name of My Web Site box, enter** dummysite.

5. **Click the Next button.**

   The wizard takes you to Step 2.

6. **Click the A Blank Page option and then click the Next button.**

   As shown in Figure 1-5, SiteBuilder creates a blank, single-page Web site, enough for your exploration purposes.

With a simple site created, you can explore the different features of the SiteBuilder workspace.

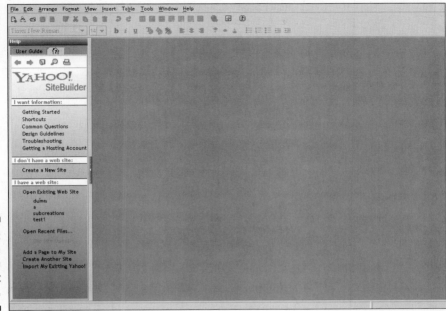

**Figure 1-4:**
Building a
Web site
starts right
here.

## SiteBuilder panes

Your main work area is the *Design pane,* the center of the SiteBuilder workspace. The Design pane enables you to create a Web page in a "point-and-click"
manner by adding different page elements to the page and then arranging them
as you wish. You can have multiple Web pages open, each one of which has a
tab at the top of the editor. See Chapters 4, 6, 7, and 8 for the full details on
working with the Design pane.

In addition to the Design pane, you can find other panes as part of the
workspace:

- ✔ **Site Contents:** The Site Contents pane shows you a folder view of your
  Web site contents, including Web pages (`.html` files), clip art graphics,
  sounds, and other files you have as part of your site. Chapter 4 shows
  you how to use the Site Contents pane to manage all your Web site
  resources.

- ✔ **Preview:** The Preview pane displays the currently selected item in the
  Site Contents pane. If nothing is selected, it displays the current page in
  the Design pane.

Toolbar          Open Web pages

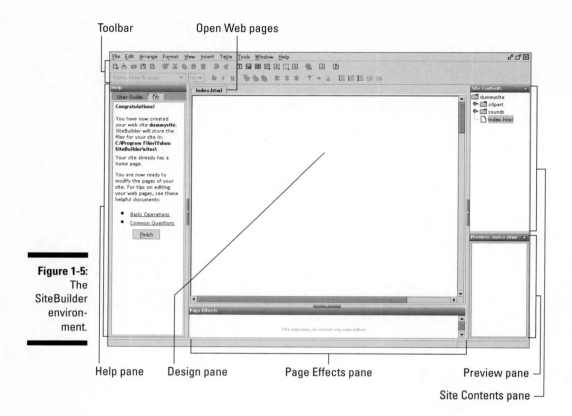

**Figure 1-5:**
The
SiteBuilder
environ-
ment.

Help pane      Design pane          Page Effects pane                Preview pane

Site Contents pane

- ✓ **Page Effects:** Some effects you can add to your page, such as a bouncing image or a background sound, don't display in the Design pane. That's because they're event-based effects that kick in when the page is being viewed "live" in the browser. Placeholders represent these effects in the Page Effects pane. Chapter 12 tells you all about how to work with page effects.

- ✓ **Help:** The Help panel serves as the go-to place within SiteBuilder, allowing you to access the User Guide and other helpful information.

## SiteBuilder toolbar

Just like in any Windows application, commands are available from the top menu, toolbar, contextual menus, and even keyboard shortcuts. In this book, I refer most often to the toolbar (see Figure 1-6), though you can use whichever of these options you prefer.

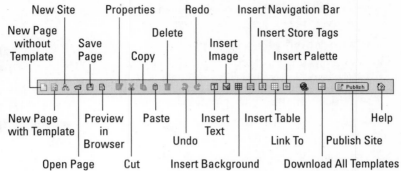

**Figure 1-6:**
The
SiteBuilder
toolbar.

The toolbar contains the commands you use most often during the Web site building process. These include the following:

- ✔ **New Page without Template** creates a new blank page.

- ✔ **New Page with Template** creates a new page based on a template you specify.

- ✔ **New Site** launches the Site Creation Wizard.

- ✔ **Open Page** allows you to open a page in your Web site.

- ✔ **Save Page** saves changes to the active Web page in your site.

- ✔ **Preview in Browser** displays the active Web page in your default Web browser.

- ✔ **Properties** shows the properties for the active page element in the Design pane.

- ✔ **Cut** deletes the selection and places it on the Clipboard.

- ✔ **Copy** adds the selection to the Clipboard.

- ✔ **Paste** inserts the contents of the Clipboard into the current page or page element.

- ✔ **Delete** removes the selection without adding it to the Clipboard.

- ✔ **Undo** undoes the last action you made.

- ✔ **Redo** redoes the action that you undid.

- ✔ **Insert Text** adds a text element to the middle of the current page.

- ✔ **Insert Image** adds an image element to the current page.

- ✔ **Insert Background** adds a background color or image to your current page and adds a Background icon to the Page Effects pane.

- ✔ **Insert Navigation Bar** displays a drop-down list of navigation bars available for your site or an option to create a new navigation bar.

- ✔ **Insert Store Tags** allows you to add e-commerce store tags to your active page.

- ✔ **Insert Table** adds a table grid to the current page.

- ✔ **Open the Insert Palette** displays the Insert palette for dropping page elements onto your page.

- ✔ **Link To** enables you to create Web links from the selected text or image.

- ✔ **Download All Templates** enables you to retrieve additional SiteBuilder templates from Yahoo.com.

- ✔ **Publish Site** uploads Web pages from your computer to Yahoo! Web Hosting.

- ✔ **Help** displays SiteBuilder Help in the Help pane.

In addition, as you explore SiteBuilder, be sure to check out Chapter 17, which provides ten important productivity tips that you should know about SiteBuilder.

# Chapter 2

# Publishing Your First Site: Around the World (Wide Web) in 16 Minutes

**In This Chapter**

▶ Creating a site from scratch and publishing it in minutes

▶ Discovering the basic processes of Web site publishing

*P*hileas Fogg is so "last century." (Or was it the century before that?) It took him 80 days to make his way around the world. That timeframe may have been impressive in his day, but you and I can take a circumnavigational supersonic flight around the world in far less than 80 hours, let alone days. So, too, in the early days of the Web, site builders would have to spend several hours or days hand-coding their Web pages and then copying these files onto a server using some geeky FTP tool. In contrast, using SiteBuilder, you can create a nice-looking Web site presence in a mere 16 minutes. In fact, I show you how to do that in this chapter.

Of course, as you work with SiteBuilder on your actual site, you'll want to spend much more time and energy thoughtfully designing, producing content, and fine-tuning your site. But you'll be glad to know that the mechanics of creating a SiteBuilder Web site are as quick as reading just a few pages from a Jules Verne classic.

In this chapter, I'm your personal valet — or, keeping with the Phileas Fogg imagery, your *Passepartout* — to help you make it around the world of Web site publishing before Big Ben strikes the stroke of midnight.

## Getting Started in Web Publishing

The purpose of this chapter is to get you comfortable with the basic mechanics of Web publishing by introducing you to each of the major steps that you take in creating and publishing a Web site. I won't explain these steps in detail; that's what the rest of the book is all about! However, I think as you go through this exercise in Web publishing, you become better equipped to get your hands around exactly what Web site publishing is all about.

Before starting your little road race, you need to have two steps done (both of which I tell you about in Chapter 1):

- ✔ Signed up for a Yahoo! Web Hosting Plan.
- ✔ Launched SiteBuilder.

After you do those two tasks, get out your stopwatch, and get ready to let out the clutch.

# Stop #1: Creating a Web Site with the Site Creation Wizard

**Estimated Time: 4 minutes**

Your first stop on your Around the Web Tour is to create a new Web site using SiteBuilder. SiteBuilder walks you through a step-by-step process using its Site Creation Wizard. After you finish your process, your Web site pages are created and ready for editing.

So go ahead and do the following to get the show on the road:

1. **From the Help pane inside of SiteBuilder, click the <u>Create a New Site</u> link, as shown in Figure 2-1.**

   The Help pane updates to display the opening page of the Site Creation Wizard.

2. **In the opening page of the Site Creation Wizard, click the Start button to continue.**

   The Help pane updates to show the next step in the site creation process, as shown in Figure 2-2.

3. **Enter** My First Site **or any other appropriate name in the Name of My Web Site text box.**

   The site you create in this chapter is for instructional purposes only, so just indicate that in the name you choose.

4. **Click the Next button to continue.**

   The Help pane once again updates, ending up with what you see in Figure 2-3.

Create a New Site

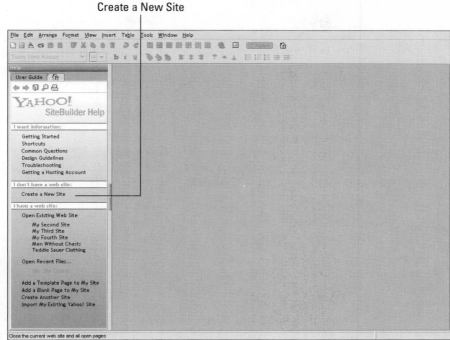

**Figure 2-1:**
Begin your
SiteBuilder
tour here.

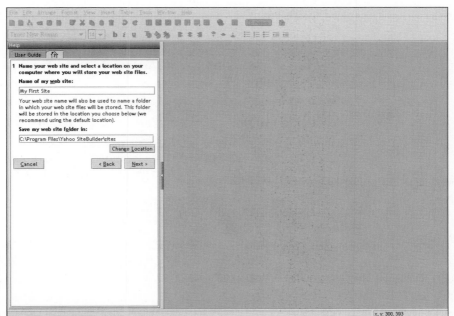

**Figure 2-2:**
Filling out
the basics.

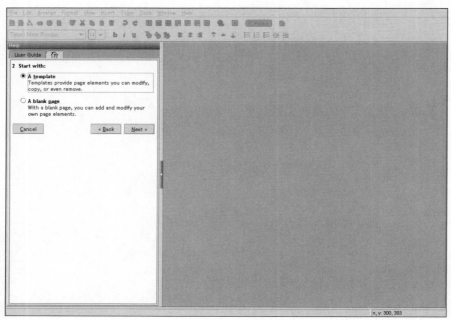

**Figure 2-3:**
Starting
with a
template.

**5. Stick with the default A Template option, and click the Next button.**

The Help pane updates to allow you to select the template of your choice. (See Figure 2-4. )

The Templates list displays the available templates, both ones that you've downloaded to your computer all ready as well as ones that have not yet been downloaded. For the Around the Web Tour, choose one that comes with SiteBuilder.

**6. Select Business from the Template Categories drop-down list.**

**7. Select the Consulting – Blue template from the Templates list box.**

Don't worry if you're not a consulting company or don't like the template design; you can always change it immediately after this exercise.

**8. Click Next to continue.**

The Help pane updates to display the last page of the wizard, as shown in Figure 2-5.

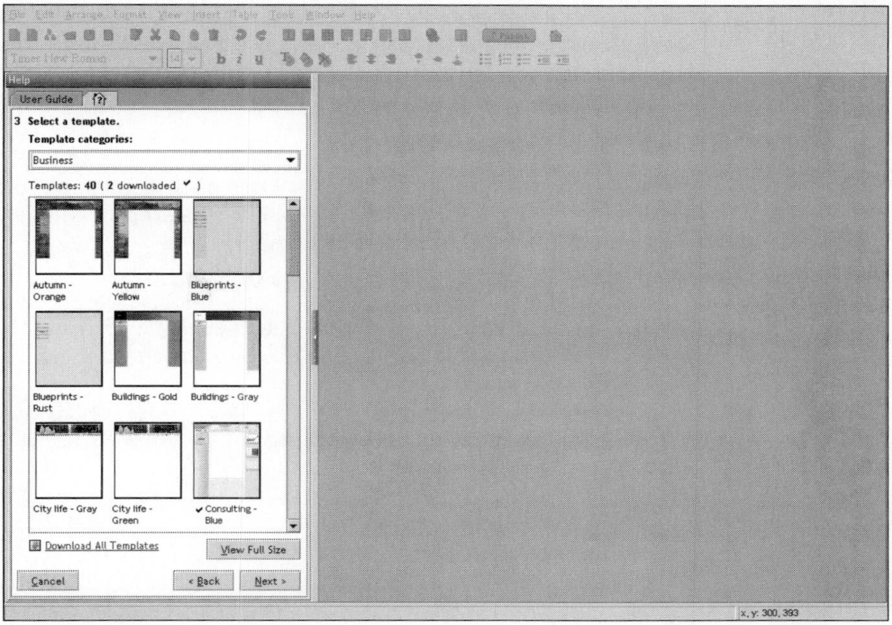

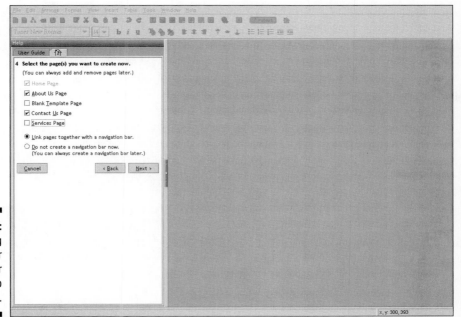

**Figure 2-4:**
Selecting
the right
template for
your Web
site.

**Figure 2-5:**
Selecting
the starter
pages for
your Web
site.

This screen helps you determine which pages of your site you want SiteBuilder to create for you at this time. For the Around the Web Tour, you can narrow it down to just three initial pages: the Home Page, the About Us Page, and the Contact Us Page.

**9. Uncheck the Services Page box.**

If you own a small business, the Services page comes in handy for describing your company's services. For this step-by-step example, however, you don't need to include this page.

**10. Click the Next button to create your Web site.**

SiteBuilder creates your Web site, opens each page inside the Design pane, and displays the Web site in the Site Contents pane. Figure 2-6 shows the final results.

For the full scoop on creating and working with your Web site, see Chapter 3.

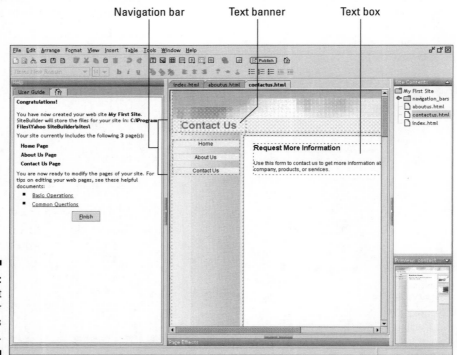

**Figure 2-6:**
The first step of your journey is complete.

# *Stop #2: Editing Your Pages*

**Estimated Time: 7 minutes**

Your second stop on the Around the Web Tour is the Design pane, where you can edit the three pages that SiteBuilder created for you as part of your Web site. You can do four basic page-building tasks here: editing text, deleting text elements, adding an image, and creating a link.

To edit your home page

1. **Click the `index.html` tab at the top of the Design pane.**

   The tabs allow you to move between your open pages. The `index.html` page is the home page for the Web site.

   Take a look around at the various elements that appear on the page, including the text banner, navigation bar, text boxes for descriptive text, and images. Figure 2-7 shows the page before you make any changes.

2. **Click the Your Company Name Here text box to select it.**

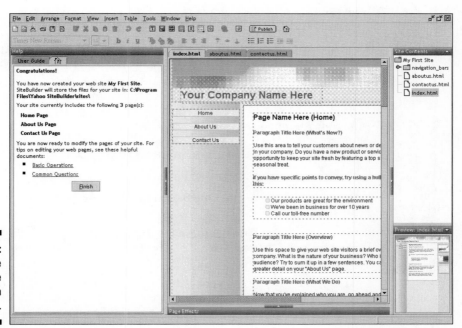

**Figure 2-7:**
Your home page in the Design pane.

3. **Select all the text with your mouse.**

   Alternatively, if you're up for it, you can triple-click inside the box to select all the text.

4. **Type** XYZ Creations **over the selected text.**

   Feel free to use your own company or personal name instead.

5. **Click the topmost text element (box) in the content area of the page to select it.**

6. **Overwrite the Page Name Here (Home) text with a welcome message, such as** Welcome to XYZ Creations.

7. **Select the Paragraph Title Here (What's New?) text, and press the Delete key. Press Delete once more to get rid of the blank line.**

   In doing so, you are deleting the extra sample text that you don't need for these simple steps.

8. **Overwrite the sample paragraph text with a "coming soon" message, such as** Coming soon. Web site under construction. Check back after I finish reading Yahoo! SiteBuilder For Dummies.

9. **Remove the rest of the sample text in the text element.**

   SiteBuilder provides sample text to help you get started on your home page. You can delete the extra text elements for this exercise.

10. **Select the text box underneath the one you just modified, and press the Delete key. Repeat this process for the other two elements.**

    Your basic vanilla home page is ready. It should look something like what you see in Figure 2-8.

To edit your About Us page

1. **Click the** `aboutus.html` **tab on the top of the Design pane.**

   The About Us page makes an appearance.

2. **Double-click the About Our Business text element to edit the text inside it.**

3. **Leave the About Our Business heading as is, and overwrite the remainder of the text with** XYZ Creations is the leading provider of XYZs in the world.

   Or, if you're describing your actual business, modify the text of this paragraph as you like. However, because your tour is on a tight schedule, I recommend keeping it to just a sentence or two.

4. **Resize the text element box to fit the amount of text inside of it.**

   To do so, first click the blue handle on the bottom middle of the text box and (while keeping your mouse button down) drag the box to the appropriate size; then release your mouse button.

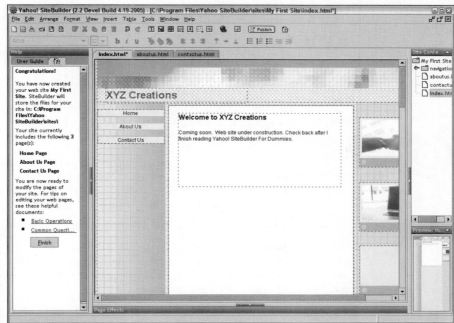

**Figure 2-8:**
Your starter
home page
is ready
to go.

**5. Click the Insert Image button from the toolbar.**

The Choose an Image dialog box appears, as shown in Figure 2-9.

**6. In the Select From section, click the Clip Art option.**

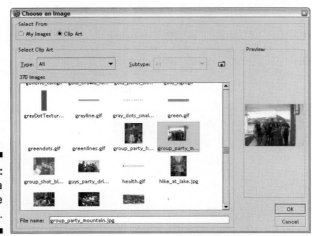

**Figure 2-9:**
Adding a
sample
image.

7. **In the Select Clip Art box, select the `group_party_mountain.jpg` image from the list.**

8. **Click OK.**

   The image is placed in the center of your page.

9. **Click the image, drag it down, and position it under the text element box.**

   Your basic vanilla About Us page is all set to go. (See Figure 2-10.)

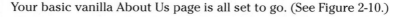

See Chapter 7 for full details on working with images.

To edit your Contact Us page

1. **Click the `contactus.html` tab at the top of the Design pane.**

2. **Double-click the Request More Information text element to edit the text inside of it.**

3. **Leave the Request More Information heading as is, and overwrite the remainder of the text with** E-mail us for more information about the best XYZs this side of Texas.

   Use this text as the basis for a link to your e-mail address. Therefore, when the link is clicked in the browser, the visitor's e-mail software opens with a new message addressed to you.

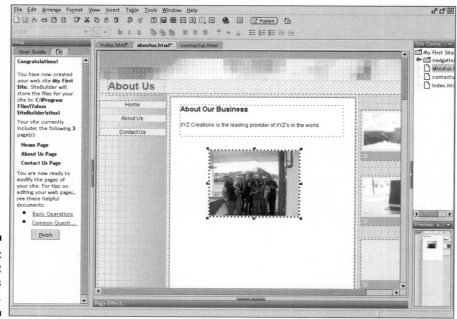

**Figure 2-10:**
The About Us page is ready to roll.

4. **Select** E-mail us **with your mouse.**

5. **Click the Link To button on the toolbar.**

   The Link dialog box appears.

6. **In the Select the Type of Link drop-down menu, choose An Email Address from the list.**

   The Link dialog box changes its options, as shown in Figure 2-11.

7. **In the An Email Address text box, enter your e-mail address.**

8. **Click the Create button.**

   Your Contact Us page is ready to go, as shown in Figure 2-12.

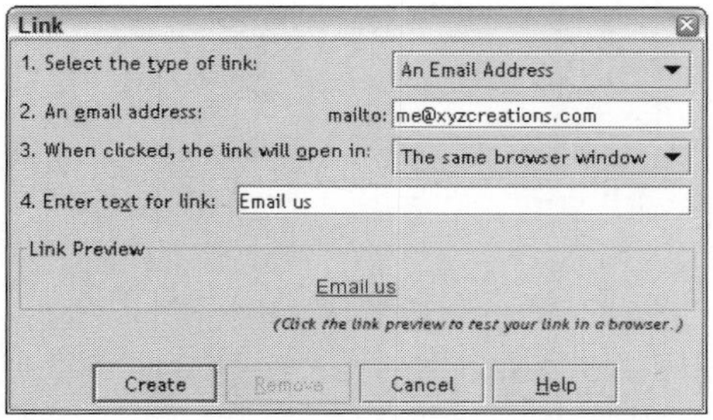

**Figure 2-11:**
Creating a
link to your
e-mail
address.

**Figure 2-12:**
The Contact
Us page is
rarin' to go.

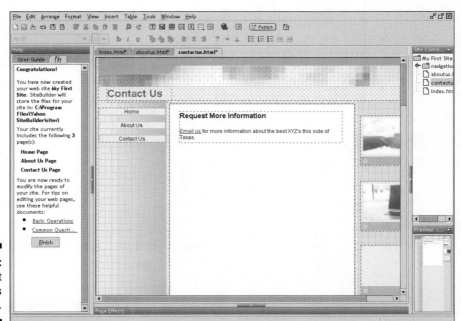

See Chapter 6 for more on creating links in SiteBuilder.

Your Web site is now ready to go. Notice that I ignored talking about the *navigation bar* (a graphical bar of links in your site) on the left-hand side of the pages. That's because SiteBuilder already set up the links for you.

Before continuing, choose File⇨Save All Pages to save all the pages in your site.

# Stop #3: Previewing Your Site

**Estimated Time: 2 minutes**

Your third stop on the Around the Web Tour is a preview of your site before you publish. SiteBuilder enables you to open your Web site inside your browser before publishing. This preview feature allows you to catch mistakes before you actually "go live" with your Web site.

To preview your site

1. **Click the Preview in Browser button on the toolbar.**

   SiteBuilder opens the current page shown in the Design pane in your default Web browser.

2. **Click each of the pages in the navigation bar to view each of them.**

Under normal circumstances, you spend a lot of time going back and forth between designing your Web site and previewing it and testing it and redesigning your Web site and previewing it and testing it and . . . you get the point.

# Stop #4: Publishing Your Site to Yahoo! Web Hosting

**Estimated Time: 2 minutes, 59 seconds**

Now that you've created your site, edited your pages, and previewed your site locally, you're ready for the home stretch of the Around the Web Tour. And looking at the clock, you've not a moment to spare! Follow these steps to complete the experience:

1. **Choose File⇨Publish to Yahoo! Site from the main menu (or just click the Publish Site button on the toolbar).**

Unless you're all ready logged into Yahoo!, the Sign In to Yahoo! dialog box appears, as shown in Figure 2-13.

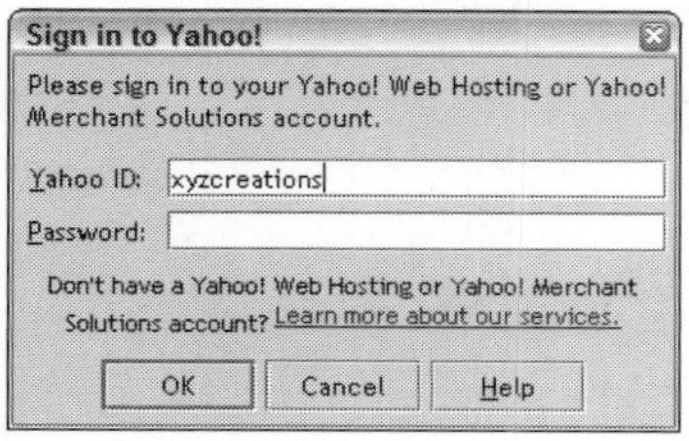

**Figure 2-13:**
Log in to
Yahoo!
before
publishing.

**Sign in to Yahoo!**

Please sign in to your Yahoo! Web Hosting or Yahoo! Merchant Solutions account.

Yahoo! ID: xyzcreations

Password:

Don't have a Yahoo! Web Hosting or Yahoo! Merchant Solutions account? Learn more about our services.

[ OK ]  [ Cancel ]  [ Help ]

2. **Enter your Yahoo! ID and password in the Sign In to Yahoo! dialog box and then click OK.**

The Publish Site dialog box appears, as shown in Figure 2-14.

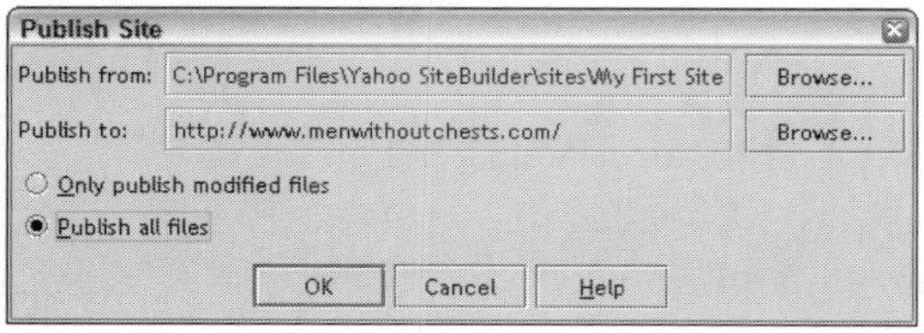

**Figure 2-14:**
Publishing
your Web
site.

**Publish Site**

Publish from: C:\Program Files\Yahoo SiteBuilder\sites\My First Site  [ Browse... ]

Publish to: http://www.menwithoutchests.com/  [ Browse... ]

○ Only publish modified files
● Publish all files

[ OK ]  [ Cancel ]  [ Help ]

3. **Click the Publish All Files option.**

4. **Click OK.**

SiteBuilder starts the transfer process and notifies you when the publish is complete. (See Figure 2-15.)

**Figure 2-15:**
Publishing
success
before the
sounds of
Big Ben.

**Success**

Publish to **Yahoo! Web Hosting** completed successfully.

Your site may now be viewed at
http://www.menwithoutchests.com/

[ OK ]

5. **Click the link in the dialog box to take you to a live view of your Web site.**

Figure 2-16 shows how the Web site looks after it's been published.

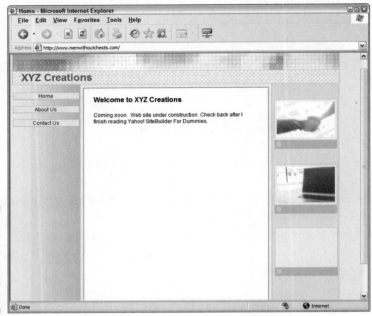

**Figure 2-16:**
Not ready
for prime
time,
perhaps, but
a good start.

See Chapter 3 for more on publishing your Web site.

# Going Forward

Congratulations! Or, as Passepartout would undoubtedly say, *"Félicitations! Magnificient!"* True, the site you published is basic; it is vanilla. But you've done it successfully in less than 16 minutes.

You've gotten the basic mechanics of what Web site publishing is all about. With that backdrop, you're ready to roll up your sleeves and get down to business — creating a genuine, killer Web site using SiteBuilder.

# Chapter 3

# Building a Purpose-Driven Web Site

*P*oor Karl Marx; the man was misdirected. He sought revolution through the political and economic systems when all along, he should have been a geek and invented the Web. Everybody knows that the Web has become the great equalizer. (Hmmm, does that make Web surfing "the opiate of the masses?")

Indeed, whether you're a "mom and pop" shop or a large global conglomerate, the Web levels the playing field. Yes, the "big boys" can spend megabucks on advertising, focus groups, and faster servers. But in spite of those advantages, you don't need that much to put together a Web site that is every bit as effective.

In this chapter, you explore some of the basic practices you should undertake as you start to build your Web site. This chapter is all about the upfront work you should think about *before* you jump in and use SiteBuilder. Then, after you have a handle on this preliminary stuff, you're ready to create something I call a *purpose-driven* Web site — one that unifies the visual design, content, site organization, and messaging to reach the people you most want to reach.

Use this chapter in combination with Chapter 16. While I cover the upfront issues to consider in Web site design here, Chapter 16 explores very practical tips that you should be aware of as you are in the midst of creating, designing, and publishing your SiteBuilder Web site.

# Creating a Purpose-Driven Site

The single most important factor to keep in mind as you work with SiteBuilder is to create a site that is driven by a specific purpose. If you just start creating a site without this upfront effort, your site (and its effectiveness) can suffer as a result. You don't have to spend a lot of time and money in research, focus groups, and the like. Instead, simply carve out a few hours from your schedule, and devote that time to exploring what you want out of your Web site. You'll be glad you put the effort into it.

As you do so, consider the following issues:

- ✔ **Identify a specific purpose:** If you're taking the time and effort to learn how to use SiteBuilder to create a Web site, you must have a reason. Identify your purpose and your goals. If you have a business site, are you trying to attract new customers? Or are you trying to better serve your existing ones? Or are you trying to provide a balance between the two?

  After you identify your site's purpose, gear every part of the Web site toward achieving that purpose — including understanding what your priorities are, what your messaging should be, and what Yahoo! add-on features and templates you want.

- ✔ **Define your target visitor:** Consider who is going to be most interested in coming to your site. Develop a list of various types of people and then narrow it down to just one or two archetypes. After you identify the kind of visitor you expect your Web site to attract, most of the questions concerning what kind of design, content, and services you want to offer simply fall into place.

  Don't forget to consider the technical expertise and technology-adoption behavior of the target visitor. Your understanding of the target visitor in this area is sure to have an impact on your site design.

  Make sure you account for people coming to your site with disabilities.

- ✔ **Give a professional feel to your site:** As Chapter 16 stresses, one of the most important objectives is to create a professional-looking Web site. But unless you're targeting stuffy old Ivy League professor types, "professional" doesn't mean stuffy and stiff-collared. Instead, professional simply means "well done."

- ✔ **Define a "presence:"** After you consider your site's purpose and target audience, identify the way in which you want your Web site to appear to visitors, and develop an aura throughout your Web site that supports that objective. Consider the following potential "tones:"

  - Conservative and traditional
  - No-nonsense and practical
  - Informal and friendly
  - Avant-garde and cutting-edge

Tailor every visual element on your Web site toward this decision, including

- The SiteBuilder template you standardize on. (See Chapter 5.)

- The graphic style. (Photos can convey a more conservative tone, while clip art and illustrations are effective in creating an informal aura.)

- The writing style.

- The visual elements. (Conservative and friendlier sites need to provide intuitive labels and navigation, while a cutting-edge site can have an aura of mystery by taking a more abstract approach.)

✓ **Evaluate competing sites:** As you consider your own purpose-driven site, take a look around the Web at sites that directly or indirectly compete with yours. How effective are they at communicating to a similar target visitor? What mistakes do they make that you can avoid?

Bookmark these sites you find, and see how their Web sites evolve over time.

# Organizing Your Site

Web sites can be logically thought of as hierarchies or as pyramid-like structures. Your home page is at the top of the heap, with three to six second-level sections, and subsections within each of these. Therefore, as you begin planning your Web site, you need to give forethought to the hierarchical structure of your Web site. The hierarchy helps you determine which pages to include on your navigation bar, what pages to bundle together in separate sections, and how the visitor can navigate through your Web site.

For example, consider the following structures of two basic sites, shown in Figures 3-1 and 3-2.

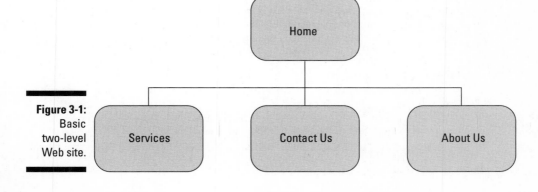

**Figure 3-1:**
Basic
two-level
Web site.

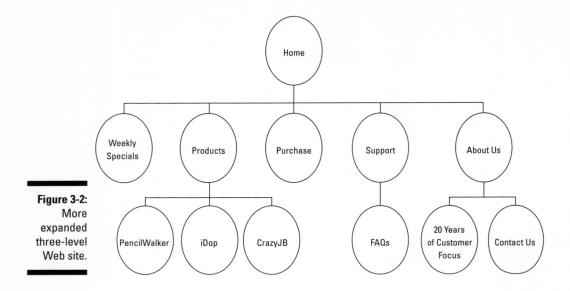

**Figure 3-2:**
More
expanded
three-level
Web site.

Pictures are sometimes worth a thousand words, but now and then the best way to grasp a concept is to read some solid prose. For some solid ideas on how best to organize your site, read on to the end of this section.

## Mocking up your site structure

The best way to define your Web site structure is to develop a list of all potential pages, topics, or services you wish to include. As you brainstorm, ask yourself what the target visitor should expect to find when arriving at your home page.

After you have a working list of ideas, mock up your site, using either a low-tech or high-tech option:

✔ **Old-fashioned index cards.** Get a stack of 4 x 6 index cards, and write down these major topics or pages you wish to include in your site. Then spread them out on a table, look for logical groupings, and begin to organize them into a hierarchy. A natural hierarchy begins to develop as you see the various pages and topics presented to you in this manner.

✔ **Charting software.** If you just can't imagine the thought of doing a creative task away from your computer, then use any charting software you may have to create a hierarchical chart. Visio is a popular package, but that's really overkill. Instead, if you have Microsoft PowerPoint, use its built-in Organization Chart tool. This easy-to-use tool (see Figure 3-3) gives you an ideal visual aid to assist in creating your Web site structure.

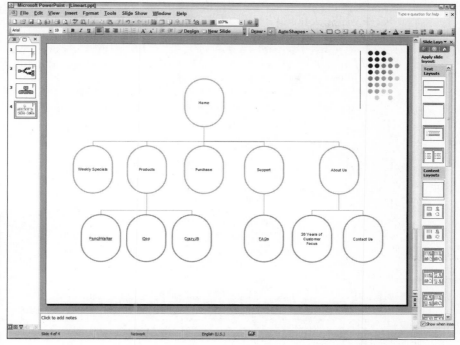

**Figure 3-3:**
Taking
advantage
of the built-
in charting
tool of
PowerPoint.

## Filling in the missing pieces

After you define the basic structure, you want to identify additional Web site pages or features that may not immediately show up. These include

- **Section pages.** As you visually group your pages into clusters, you often encounter the need for a section-level page — one that doesn't provide much content in and of itself but is needed as a centralized starting point for a subsection.

- **Links.** You also want to sketch out the links that you want to include across your site's pages. Remember, while Web sites are hierarchical, links are positively nonlinear. Sketching or printing the site structure and drawing lines to identify these links is helpful.

## Avoiding deep hierarchies

Be careful not to make the hierarchy too deep. If you have a lot of topics, it is better to be broad at the higher level than to have many layers of pages. Studies have shown that visitors easily get lost when they descend more than three layers deep in a site. For example, suppose you have an About Us section in which you'd like to include the following Web pages: `aboutus.html`, `companyhistory.html`, `investors.html`, `contactus.html`, `maps.html`, `directions.html`, and `phonelist.html`. Logically, the purest hierarchy is shown in Figure 3-4, but its added layers will make it more difficult for visitors. (I even added two extra grouping pages — `background.html` and `visitus.html`.) In contrast, Figure 3-5 shows an alternative site hierarchy, which flattens the structure levels and avoids deep nesting.

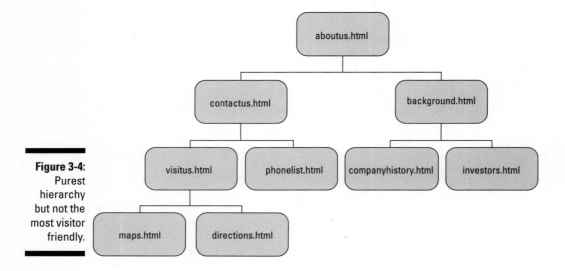

**Figure 3-4:**
Purest
hierarchy
but not the
most visitor
friendly.

## *Planning for effective feedback*

In addition, you should provide feedback on your Web pages that indicates where the visitor is on your site. Fortunately, some of the SiteBuilder navigation bars change the button state of the active page. In this way, visitors can quickly discern their location.

Another handy technique is to include a listing of the hierarchy just under the page header. For example, consider the following heading for a feedback page:

### Sound Off to Us

Home \ Contact Us \ Sound Off to Us

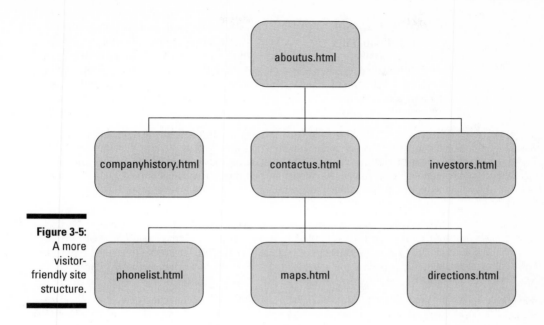

**Figure 3-5:**
A more
visitor-
friendly site
structure.

As you can see, underneath the page header's Text element is a second Text element that visually shows where the visitor is in the site's hierarchy. It even includes links to each of the pages above the current one. Used in combination with a SiteBuilder navigation bar, a visitor can never get lost in your Web site.

# Writing Content for Your Web Site

Many people find developing a site's structure to be an almost intuitive process — the pages naturally start to group themselves into a tree-like hierarchy. However, to many Web site builders, "intuitive" is not a term that comes to mind when you talk about what content should be on a page and how to best present it.

Writing content for a page is one of those tasks that you often have to slog through a few times before you really feel like you got it right. Even if content development is more "art" than "science," keep in mind these general principles as you work your way through this book:

✔ **Write descriptive headings.** Make sure visitors can quickly scan the text heading of your page and instantly know exactly what they can expect on it. Don't be cute; be clear.

✔ **Avoid forced scrolls.** In general, avoid developing pages that require too much scrolling. However, in cases where scrolling is possible, you can still inform visitors what they are going to read on this page rather than force them to scroll down the page to see it. You can create a mini table of contents at the top that highlights section headings of a lengthy page. You can also provide a quick summary that highlights what the visitor can expect.

✔ **Place key content at the top.** Within the main text on a page, consider writing the text like a newspaper article — placing the key information first and then providing details in subsequent sections. This technique doesn't force readers to read all the page in order to understand what you're trying to communicate.

✔ **Avoid "link-itis."** As Chapter 6 discusses, links are the primary driver of the Web and add power to your Web site. At the same time, if you're writing a page that has multiple paragraphs of text, don't feel obligated to add a link at every possible place within that content. Too many links within a body of text can be disruptive to the flow of reading. So use them, but recognize the trade-offs. Also, placing links at the start or end of paragraphs is better for the reading flow.

✔ **Be concise.** Don't add content just because you feel like you need to beef up your Web site. As you proofread through your Web site, get rid of any fluff. Say more with less. Period. End of story. That's exactly my point. (Ooops, perhaps I should follow my own advice.)

✔ **Avoid "pixel cramming."** Along the same lines as the previous point, make sure you don't place too much content on a given page. A page should have plenty of white space and should not — I repeat, should not — be cluttered. White space makes for a much more inviting Web site to come to rather than going to a place that has every pixel of a page crammed with information.

✔ **Create an aura of accessibility.** If you're a business trying to sell products and services, make sure you seem accessible to your site visitor in case of questions or concerns. Provide contact information at the bottom of each page (an e-mail link or page link to your Contact Us page). Also, the Yahoo! Presence Indicator add-on (see Chapter 11) is another way to let visitors know if you are available online for your visitors.

✔ **Emphasis your trustworthiness.** Unless the site visitors know you already, they're going to be on guard, wary of buying something from an unknown company or even fearful of giving you an e-mail address or other personal information. Therefore, in those parts of your site where a level of trust is needed, such as submitting a feedback form or purchasing a product, tackle that issue head on, and put your visitors at ease. Take a look around at some of the way other sites handle trust and then come up with a solution that best meets your site's needs.

✔ **Be informative on downloads.** If you have any PDF documents, PowerPoint presentations, large graphics, or software programs that visitors can download from your site, be sure to indicate the size of the download. A major frustration for visitors, particularly those who use a dialup Internet connection, is to not know the size of a file that they wish to download. What's more, if your download requires a program or separate reader (such as Adobe Acrobat Reader) in order to access the document or file, be sure to inform the readers and provide a link to a Web site from which they can download it.

# Evaluating Your Site

As you develop your Web site, you should constantly be evaluating it. As you do so, ask yourself the following questions:

✔ Is the purpose of my site clear?

✔ Do all the pages of my site focus on that one purpose?

✔ Am I effectively targeting my audience?

✔ Is the content interesting and relevant?

✔ Is my site professional looking? Would a visitor know my skill level by the look of the Web site?

✔ Is the content well written and easy to read? Is the content written appropriately for my target visitor?

✔ Do I always know where I am throughout every page of the Web site? Or do I find myself lost or in a dead end?

✔ On a dialup connection, do the pages load fast enough?

✔ Is my site accessible to visitors with disabilities? (Test how your Web site looks when you use extra-large fonts in the browser. Also, print your Web site in black and white on your printer, and see if it's readable by color-blind people.)

# Chapter 4

# Trickle-Down Site Building: Working with Sites, Pages, and Elements

- - - - - - - - - - - - - - - - - - - - - - - - - - - - - - - - - - - - - - - - - - - -

## In This Chapter

▶ Creating and working with your Web site

▶ Publishing your Web site

▶ Handling the basics of page editing

▶ Working with elements on a Web page

- - - - - - - - - - - - - - - - - - - - - - - - - - - - - - - - - - - - - - - - - - - -

*B*y and large, the software programs that you work with on your desktop or laptop computer are file-based applications. For instance, when working in Microsoft Word, you'll edit a document (.doc file); in Excel, calculate a spreadsheet (.xls file). Or, if you listen to music in iTunes or Window Media Player, you'll play .mp3 or .wmf media files. In fact, as if to underscore this point, open virtually any Windows program, and check out the name of its first menu. Chances are you see a certain word that rhymes with Gomer Pyle.

Within this file-based world, SiteBuilder has a different take: You work with both a group of files (a Web site) as well as individual Web pages (.html files) with the help of SiteBuilder's Design pane (where you do most of your editing). Therefore, from its File menu, you can actually create, open, and save a Web site as well as a Web page. That might be enough to get Gomer to say *golllllly!*

In this chapter, you explore how to use SiteBuilder to perform basic tasks associated with your Web site and individual pages within it. You also discover how to use SiteBuilder to work with various elements on pages — the text, images, and links that make up any decent Web page.

# Working with Your Web Site

A Web site in SiteBuilder is kind of like the titles of the classic fantasy series *The Lord of the Rings* and *The Chronicles of Narnia*. These titles refer to a series of books, but you never, for example, read a book with those specific titles. Instead, you read individual books, such as *The Fellowship of the Ring* or *The Lion, the Witch, and the Wardrobe,* within that collection. In the same way, a SiteBuilder Web site serves as an organizing device for a collection of individual Web pages. You perform basic site-related tasks to organize and manage the pages, but you never really *edit* your Web site as a whole. Instead, you create and edit Web pages within the site.

In this section, you explore the major tasks you perform when working with your Web site.

## Creating a new site

In order to build a Web site, you need something to work with. So you either need to create one from scratch or start with one that you've built using another Web site building tool. (See the "Importing a Web site you've previously created" section, later in this chapter, for more on that course of action.) Using SiteBuilder, however, you'll normally want to start from scratch to take advantage of SiteBuilder's templates.

After you start the Site Creation Wizard, you can't access the SiteBuilder menu or toolbar. You either need to complete the site creation process or cancel out of the wizard to enable the full functionality.

To create a site using SiteBuilder's templates, follow these steps as you go through the Site Creation Wizard:

1. **Click the <u>Create a New Site</u> link in the Help pane. (The Help pane is on the left side of the SiteBuilder main window.)**

   You can also choose File⇨New Site from the main menu or press Ctrl+Shift+N.

   The Help pane updates to display the opening page of the Site Creation Wizard, as shown in Figure 4-1.

2. **Click the Start button to continue.**

   The Help pane updates to show the next step in the creation process. (See Figure 4-2.)

**Figure 4-1:**
Step on up
and create
your own
Web site.

**Figure 4-2:**
Gathering
information
for your
Web site.

3. **Enter the name of your Web site in the text box provided.**

   The name you pick never shows up on your public Web site but is used to name the Web site folder on your hard drive.

4. **If you wish to change the base location in which SiteBuilder stores the Web site, enter a new folder in the Save My Web Site Folder In box.**

   Normally, you'll want to simply stick with the default location (typically `c:\Program Files\Yahoo! SiteBuilder\sites`), because that's where SiteBuilder naturally assumes all your stuff is kept — and sometimes old assumptions die hard.

   However, if you are a rebel, then you can create a My Web Sites subfolder in your My Documents folder to use as a home base for your Web site.

5. **Click the Next button to continue.**

   The Help pane once again updates, as shown in Figure 4-3.

6. **Determine whether you wish to use a SiteBuilder template for your Web site design or not.**

   If you want to use a SiteBuilder template — the optional resource that gives you predefined page designs and graphics — then choose the Template option.

**Figure 4-3:**
Your choice: Start with "the works" or "the bare bones?"

If you do not want to use a template at all, then choose the Blank Page option.

**7. Click Next to continue.**

If you chose a blank page, then the Site Creation Wizard ends and your site, containing one blank Web page, is ready to roll. You can ignore the remaining steps in this list.

If you're using a template, then the Help pane updates to allow you to select the template of your choice, as shown in Figure 4-4.

**8. Select the template that you want to base your site design on.**

The Templates list displays the available templates, both ones that you've already downloaded to your computer as well as ones that are available but you haven't downloaded. Downloaded templates have a check mark beside their name.

If you select a template that isn't available on your local computer, SiteBuilder asks if you want to download the template from the Yahoo! Web site as you continue the process. (For more on downloading templates, see Chapter 5.)

Click the View Full Size button to see a full-size thumbnail in a separate window.

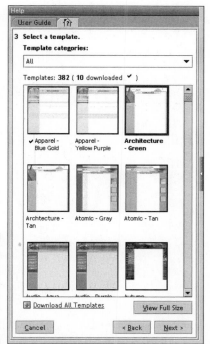

**Figure 4-4:**
Selecting the right template for your Web site.

Picking a template is one of the most important — and long-reaching — decisions you make when it comes to your Web site. First, your selection dominates the look of your site, so make sure it's something you'll want to live with on a day in, day out basis. Second, it is also not a decision you can easily turn back from — switching to another template after you already create your site is not simply done. Third, the template provides a starting point for you, but SiteBuilder templates are customizable so you can make a site that meets your unique needs. Again, check out everything you need to know about templates in Chapter 5 before making your final decision.

9. **Click Next to continue.**

   If you need to download the template you select, SiteBuilder prompts you at this point to download it before continuing and gives you the approximate time it will take to do so. You can continue or cancel the process.

   After the template is ready, the Help pane updates one final time, as shown in Figure 4-5.

10. **On the last page of the wizard, check the boxes beside each standard page you want in your Web site.**

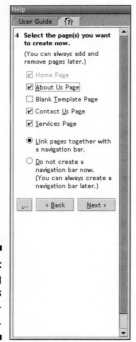

**Figure 4-5:** Determining your site's organization.

You must include a home page, but you can decide whether you want to start out with other typical pages, such as an About Us page, Contact Us page, or a Services page. Checking the Blank Template Page box creates a page without any starter text, but it still has the overall visual template style.

If you don't add these page types now, you can always decide to add them later on. See the "Creating a new Web page" section, later in this chapter, for more details.

11. **If you want to add a navigation bar, select the Link Pages Together with a Navigation Bar radio button. (If not, select the Do Not Create a Navigation Bar Now radio button.)**

    As Chapter 9 discusses, the navigation bar provides an easy way for people to get around on your Web site.

12. **Click the Next button to create your Web site.**

    SiteBuilder creates your Web site, opens each page inside of the Design pane, and displays the Web site in the Site Contents pane. Figure 4-6 shows the final results. (Note that each page now has its own tab at the top of the Design pane.)

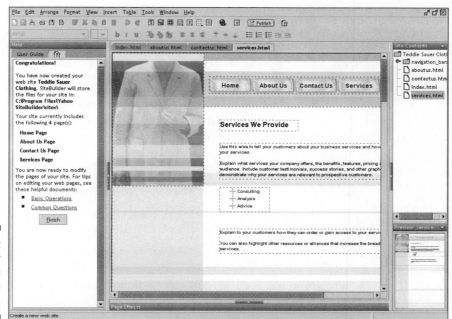

**Figure 4-6:** Presto! Your Web site is ready to begin.

## *Importing a Web site you've previously created*

If you've never created a Web site before or had an old one that could be a candidate for the Web's Ten Ugliest Sites list, then you can simply start from scratch, following the instructions in the "Creating a new Web site" section. However, perhaps you are now just turning to SiteBuilder after you've already poured a lot of blood, sweat, and tears into a site that you don't want to simply throw away.

You can import your previous work into SiteBuilder, with two important qualifications:

✔ Your Web site must be on your Yahoo! Web server. If you have a Web site that exists elsewhere, you need to transfer it first to your Yahoo! host and then import it.

✔ Importing into any Web site builder is usually an imperfect process, so don't expect perfect results. If you did not use SiteBuilder or Yahoo! PageBuilder to create the site before, your original pages may need tweaking and redesigning after you import them. Some Web site builders may use complex formatting techniques that are difficult for SiteBuilder to interpret correctly.

My own personal caveat: Importing a Yahoo! Web site into an existing SiteBuilder Web site is possible. However, because of the potential for confusion and unexpected complications, I recommend you don't do it. If you still decide to go through with it, at least be sure you have any opened Web sites closed before proceeding by choosing File⇨Close Site. (This menu item is disabled if you don't have a site opened.) This ensures that you don't accidentally import pages into an existing Web site that you are working on.

To import a Web site into SiteBuilder, follow these steps:

1. **Choose File⇨Import Yahoo! Site from the main menu.**

   A dialog box may display, letting you know what I already told you — don't expect perfect results. Click OK to continue.

   If you are not signed in with Yahoo! Web Hosting for this session, SiteBuilder prompts you for your Yahoo! ID and password.

   You're prompted whether you wish to import the files into a new or existing Web site. (See Figure 4-7.)

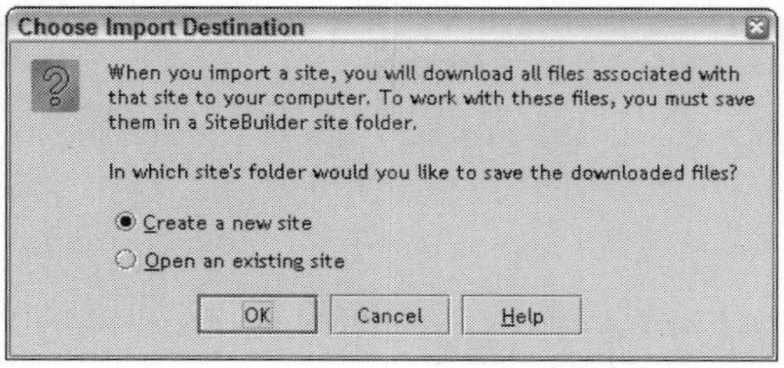

**Figure 4-7:**
Deciding the
destination
of the
imported
files.

> **Choose Import Destination**
>
> When you import a site, you will download all files associated with that site to your computer. To work with these files, you must save them in a SiteBuilder site folder.
>
> In which site's folder would you like to save the downloaded files?
>
> ● Create a new site
> ○ Open an existing site
>
> OK    Cancel    Help

2. **Click the Create a New Site radio button and click OK.**

   The Choose a Name and Location dialog box displays, as shown in Figure 4-8.

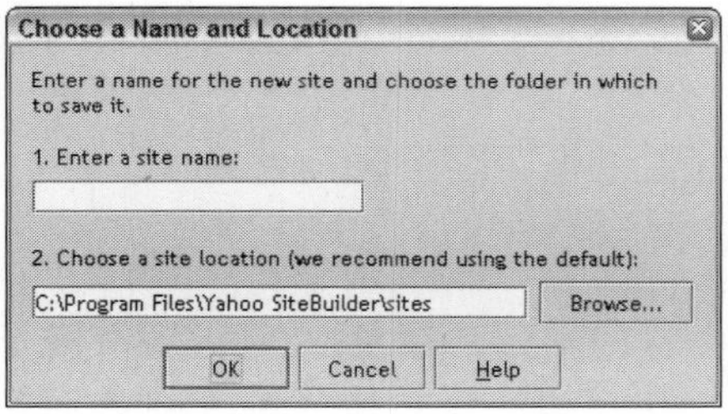

**Figure 4-8:**
Creating a
comfy new
home for
your
incoming
files.

> **Choose a Name and Location**
>
> Enter a name for the new site and choose the folder in which to save it.
>
> 1. Enter a site name:
>
> 2. Choose a site location (we recommend using the default):
>
> C:\Program Files\Yahoo SiteBuilder\sites    Browse...
>
> OK    Cancel    Help

3. **Enter a name for your site in the box provided.**

4. **Choose a location on your hard drive to put your imported Web site.**

   As the dialog box recommends, you'll usually want to stick to the default folder provided.

5. **Click OK in the Choose a Name and Location dialog box to continue.**

   The Import Site dialog box, shown in Figure 4-9, displays.

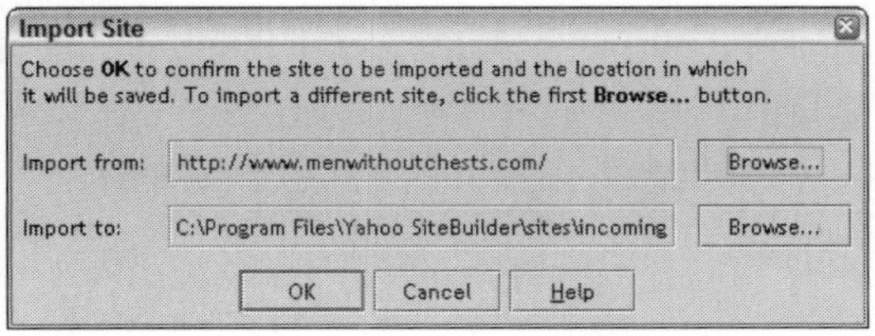

**Figure 4-9:**
An all-
*import*ant
task:
importing
your Web
site.

> **Import Site**
>
> Choose **OK** to confirm the site to be imported and the location in which it will be saved. To import a different site, click the first **Browse...** button.
>
> Import from:    http://www.menwithoutchests.com/    Browse...
>
> Import to:    C:\Program Files\Yahoo SiteBuilder\sites\incoming    Browse...
>
> OK    Cancel    Help

6. **Confirm the Import From and Import To locations in the Import Site dialog box and then click OK.**

   SiteBuilder begins the importing process, copying each of the files located on your Yahoo! host to your new Web site.

## Opening an existing site

Just like Rome wasn't built in a day, so too you'll be working on your Web site in more than one sitting. Therefore, each time you want to work on creating or update your Web site, you first need to open it. Follow these steps to open a site you've already created:

1. **Choose File⇨Open Site from the main menu.**

   The Open Site dialog box, shown in Figure 4-10, displays.

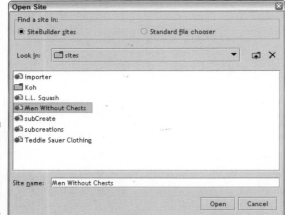

**Figure 4-10:**
Open
sesame and
Web sites
too!

2. **Select your Web site from the list displayed.**

   If your Web site is stored in the SiteBuilder Sites folder, then select your Web site from the list.

   Or, if it is located elsewhere, such as in your My Documents folder, then click the Standard File Chooser radio button at the top, navigate to your Web site folder using the Look In box, and then select the root folder of your site.

3. **Click the Open button.**

   SiteBuilder opens up the site.

# Saving your site

You may create, open, and publish a Web site, but SiteBuilder has no equivalent Save Site command. However, you can perform the same task by choosing File⇨Save All Pages from the main menu.

# Closing a site

When you are ready to close your Web site, choose File⇨Close Site from the menu. Before closing, you will be prompted to save any changes you've made to the Web pages.

# Deleting a site

You can delete a site by opening the Open Site dialog box (accessible by choosing File⇨Open Site from the main menu). In the dialog box, select the Web site and click the Delete button. (Refer to Figure 4-10 for a peek at the Delete button; it's at the top right and has an "X marks the spot" look.) SiteBuilder asks you to confirm the deletion process.

# Previewing your site before you publish

One of the advantages of using a desktop-based Web site builder like SiteBuilder is that you can preview, test, and *debug* (fix any problems) the site on your own computer before you go live with it for the world to see. When you preview your site locally, SiteBuilder launches your default Web browser and points to the local file version of your home page. Previewing allows you to

- ✔ See how the design and look of your Web site appears in the actual browser.

- ✔ Click through the links on your Web site to make sure they work as you expect.

- ✔ Test page effects and other functionality on your page to ensure their proper operation. However, not all functionality, such as form processing, is available when you preview your Web site locally. So if you have a site with a lot of bells and whistles, you probably need to publish to your Yahoo! host first if you really want to check out every aspect of your site.

Follow these steps to preview your site:

1. **Click the Preview in Browser button on the toolbar.**

   Or choose File⇨Preview in Browser from the menu.

2. **Test your Web site design and functionality in the browser.**

You don't need to save your open files before previewing them. This capability is handy, enabling you to test different ideas without actually having to save your changes first.

Within SiteBuilder itself, you can only preview your Web site using the default browser. However, if you have more than one browser on your system and want to preview your site in a nondefault browser, then perform the following trick:

1. **Preview your Web site in the default Web browser.**

   This process ensures that you've properly prepared all the site files for previewing.

2. **In your default Web browser, copy the URL in the Address box to the Clipboard.**

3. **Open your nondefault browser.**

4. **Paste the URL into the Address box and press Enter.**

   The nondefault browser displays the preview Web site.

# *Ready for the Big Leagues: Publishing Your Web Site*

After you create, design, and preview your Web site offline on your local computer, you're ready to "go public" with it. However, before doing so, make sure your site passes two critical tests:

- ✔ Make sure that you've fully debugged the Web site, as I describe in the "Previewing your site before you publish" section, earlier in this chapter. Thorough debugging before you go live ensures that your visitors don't run into potentially embarrassing problems with your site.

- ✔ Make sure the home page of your Web site is named `index.html` in the Site Contents pane. If not, your published Web site won't display properly.

You need to be connected to the Internet before starting this process. Otherwise, you receive an error message from SiteBuilder.

After you pass these two sanity tests, transfer your files to your Yahoo! Web server by following these steps:

1. **Choose File➪Publish to Yahoo! Site from the main menu.**

   *Note:* You need to save all your Web pages before you can publish — otherwise, SiteBuilder can't copy your latest changes. If all of your files aren't saved, SiteBuilder prompts you to save first.

   The Publish Site dialog box displays, as shown in Figure 4-11.

**Figure 4-11:**
Publishing your Web site takes just a couple easy steps.

2. **Make any necessary changes in the Publish From and Publish To boxes. (You will rarely need to adjust these default settings.)**

   The Publish From box displays your current Web site folder on your local computer.

   The Publish To box shows the Web site domain that the files will be published to. You'll almost always want to publish to the root domain folder (the default). However, if you want to publish to a subfolder on your site, click the Browse button next to the Publish To box and select a different folder.

   Under most circumstances, you can ignore this step, because you'll usually want to publish your Web site to the root folder of your domain (for example, www.anysite.com). But if you have a Web site that you want to start from a subfolder (such as www.anysite.com/myothersite), then change this value before publishing.

3. **Determine which files you want to publish.**

   If you wish to update just the files you updated since the last time you published, click the Only Publish Modified Files radio button. You'll normally want to use this option as a timesaver.

If you wish to publish or republish all the contents of your Web site, then click the Publish All Files button.

**4. Click OK.**

SiteBuilder starts the transfer process and notifies you when the publish is completed. (See Figure 4-12.)

**Figure 4-12:**
Publishing
success,
even
without a
*New York*
*Times*
bestseller.

# Working with Web Pages

"No sense reinventing the wheel" is what I always say. You'll soon discover that you can perform several file-based tasks inside of SiteBuilder that operate surprisingly like the file-based tasks you'd perform in a word processor program like Microsoft Word. This section highlights these tasks.

## Creating a new Web page

When you use the New Site Wizard (see the "Creating a new site" section, earlier in the chapter), you begin with a Web site containing a basic set of four or five pages. Or, if you import a Web site, you start off with the number of pages transferred from the Web server. However, your Web site doesn't stay static. As your needs change, so too do the pages on your site. You add some, edit others, and remove old ones that you no longer need.

When you add a new Web page to your Web site, you have two choices. You can

- Add a blank page
- Add a template-based page

A blank page is useful if you want to fully customize the design and overall look of your Web page. Otherwise, you want to choose the template-based page option. The following two steps of instructions tell you how to add these two types of new pages.

To create a new blank page

1. **Click the New Page without Template button on the toolbar.**

   Or you can choose File⇨New Page⇨Without Template from the main menu or just press Ctrl+N.

   SiteBuilder adds an empty Web page to your site.

To create a new template page

1. **Click the New Page with Template button on the toolbar.**

   Or you can choose File⇨New Page⇨With Template from the main menu or just press Ctrl+Shift+N.

   The Add New Page dialog box appears, as shown in Figure 4-13.

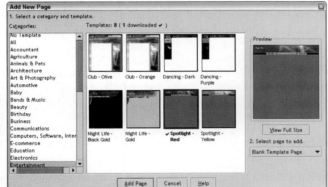

**Figure 4-13:**
Adding a
new
template-
based page.

2. **Select the template you want to use for the new page from the Template list box.**

   Be careful. This is one of those places where Yahoo! gives you too many choices for your own good. Mixing and matching templates in a single Web site is *always* a bad idea. Therefore, avoid the glamour and allure of all of those pretty templates, and plunk down the same template you already picked for the rest of your Web site. If you find yourself so enamored of one of these templates, then consider making that template the look for your entire site.

3. **Select the type of page you wish to add:**

   • **Blank Template Page:** Provides the basic page design of the template but without any canned text.

   • **About Us, Contact Us, Home Page,** and **Services Page:** All provide template-specific versions of these SiteBuilder basic page types.

  • **Store Products Wizard:** Creates an e-commerce products page for your Yahoo! Merchant Solutions Web site. See Chapter 15 for more details.

4. **Click the Add Page button.**

A new page named Untitled is added to the SiteBuilder Design pane, and a new tab is added to the top of the page editor display.

When you create a new Web page, it isn't officially part of the site itself until you save it with a real name. After you save it (see the "Saving a Web page" section, later in this chapter), then it's added to the Site Contents pane.

## Saving a Web page

As you design and edit your Web page, you should save it periodically inside of SiteBuilder just like any file-based Windows application.

### Saving an untitled page

The first time you save an untitled page, you're prompted to both enter a file-name in the Save As dialog box and specify the location of the file. Normally, you want to give the file a descriptive name, such as directions.html (for a Directions page) or news.html (for a Latest News or What's New page). The name you choose is the one used on the Web site. For example, if I have a page called booklist.html on my domain, the URL for accessing that file would be www.menwithoutchests.com/booklist.html.

### Saving a titled page

If you've already titled and saved the file before, simply click the Save Page button on the toolbar to save your latest changes. You can also choose File⇨Save Page or press Ctrl+S.

### Saving a file with a new name

If you wish to save the Web page with a new name, then choose File⇨Save Page As from the main menu. In the Save As dialog box, enter a new name and click OK.

When you save a file with a new name, SiteBuilder adds the new page to your Web site but keeps the original file and all its link associations intact. In this way, you can think of the Save As process as duplicating your original Web page instead of renaming it.

## Opening a Web page

When you wish to edit a Web page already in your site, you can open it in various ways.

To open the page immediately, double-click the name of the Web page in the Site Contents pane. (Refer to Figure 4-6.)

To open up a page through the Open dialog box:

- ✔ Click the Open Page button on the toolbar.
- ✔ Choose File➪Open Page from the main menu.
- ✔ Press Ctrl+O.

In SiteBuilder, you can open an HTML file on your computer that is not part of your Web site. However, when you do so, SiteBuilder treats it essentially as a file import process: SiteBuilder copies the file into your Web site and renames it `untitled`. As a result, you are working off a copy, not the original file.

## Closing one or more Web pages

When you are done with a Web page, close it by choosing File➪Close Page. Or, if you're through with the whole lot of pages you have open in your Design pane, choose File➪Close All Pages. SiteBuilder closes them suckers quicker than you can say "Barney Fife."

## Deleting a Web page

An old Web page that needs to be put out to pasture. The page design experiment that went horribly awry. A page that you look at and suddenly scream at the top of your lungs: *I am sick of it, and I'm not gonna take it anymore!* When circumstances like these spring up, sometimes you just have to take drastic measures and delete a Web page from your site.

To do so, find the doomed file in the Site Contents pane, and press the Delete key. (Alternatively, you can choose Delete File from the right-click menu.) SiteBuilder, after asking you to confirm your drastic action, not only removes the page from your site, but also deletes the file from your computer.

## Copying a Web page

If you'd like to make a copy of a Web page, you can duplicate it by performing one of two tasks:

- ✔ Right-click the Web page inside of the Site Contents pane, and choose Copy File from the contextual menu that appears. Provide a new name in the Destination box, and click Save As.

- ✔ Choose File⇨Save As from the menu. (See the "Saving a file with a new name" section, earlier in this chapter.)

## Renaming a Web page

You can rename a Web page that you've already created by selecting it inside of the Site Contents pane and pressing F2 (or right-clicking and choosing Rename File from the contextual menu that appears). You can then make a name change inside of the Site Contents pane. Press Enter to save your changes.

If the Web page is linked or part of the navigation bar, you're asked to confirm your changes.

# Modifying Page Properties

While most of your time is spent adding, editing, and arranging elements (such as text blocks, images, and links) on a page, you can also modify certain attributes of the page as a whole. You can perform these operations from the Page Properties dialog box (see Figure 4-14), which you can access by choosing Edit⇨Page Properties from the main menu.

You can also right-click the page and choose Page Properties from the contextual menu that appears. However, depending on your page layout and template, selecting the page as whole with your mouse — rather than just an image or other element on top of the page — can be tricky. If you don't see Page Properties in the right-click menu, it means you've selected another object.

The following sections discuss how you can work with the Page Properties dialog box to modify the page.

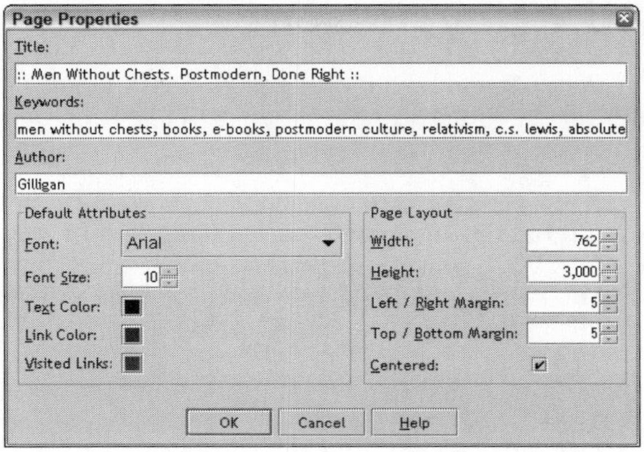

**Figure 4-14:**
Modifying
page level
properties.

# Specifying meta data

Each Web page can optionally contain *meta data,* a techie term that refers to information that is maintained "behind the scenes" of your Web page to describe the content of the document. Your page's meta data is accessible from the top section of the Page Properties dialog box. (Refer to Figure 4-14.) The three pieces of information include

- **Title:** The title provides a descriptive name for the Web page. Most Web browsers, such as Microsoft Internet Explorer, place the title of the Web page in the title bar of the browser window as well as use it as the name when a page is saved as an item in a Favorites (or bookmarks) list. Search engines also use the title when they display results from a search.

- **Keywords:** The words you provide as a comma-delimited list enable search engines to index your Web page according to these keywords. For example, if you ran a travel agency specializing in selling mountain-climbing adventure travel packages, you could include such words as *travel agency, adventure travel, Mount Everest, Alps, Himalayas, mountain climbing, adventure tours, extreme sports,* and *sport tourism.* Then, when a potential customer uses a search engine to find a travel agency specializing in alpine adventure packages, your site may pop up as one of the first hits on the list, due to your excellent choice of keywords.

- **Author:** The author meta tag is useful for your personal use. It can be especially helpful if you have multiple people working on your Web site.

Enter the meta data information that best describes your Web page in the spaces provided in the Page Properties dialog box.

# Modifying the page layout

You can also modify the physical layout of the page from the Page Properties dialog box. The following sections show you how to make these modifications.

### Resizing a page

The default size of a SiteBuilder Web page has a fixed width of 762 x 3000 — 762 pixels in width and 3,000 pixels in height. (A *pixel* is the measuring unit of screen resolutions.) You can tweak the size by changing the values of the Width and Height boxes in the Page Properties dialog box.

The width of your page is the most important design consideration in terms of physical size. Visitors coming to your site will be using a variety of screen resolutions. The most popular resolution today is 1024 x 768, but other popular resolutions include 800 x 600 and 1280 x 1024. Given this resolution range, it is a wise idea to ensure that the width of your page is 790 pixels or less, guaranteeing that the visitor can view the entire contents of the page width-wise without needing to scroll horizontally. A few stragglers are still out there using 640 x 480 resolution, but as Chapter 16 indicates, you don't need to design your site for *really* old technology.

### Specifying page margins

You can specify left/right and top/bottom page margins from the Page Properties dialog box. A small margin of 5 pixels or less can offset your page nicely from the browser window. Experiment with a variety of values, and see what looks best for your Web site.

If you center your page (see the next section), left/right page margins have little effect unless the width of the browser window is the same size as or smaller than the width of the page.

### Centering your page inside of the browser

You can have your page centered inside of the browser window by checking the Centered check box in the Page Properties dialog box. Therefore, instead of being left aligned, your page is always centered smack dab in the middle of the browser window.

If, for example, your Web page is 762 pixels in width, and you view the page at 800 x 600 resolution, you won't notice much difference. But centering is especially attractive for visitors coming to your site who use a high resolution, such as 1280 x 1024. For example, Figure 4-15 shows a noncentered page at 1280 x 1024, while Figure 4-16 displays the same page with the centered option turned on.

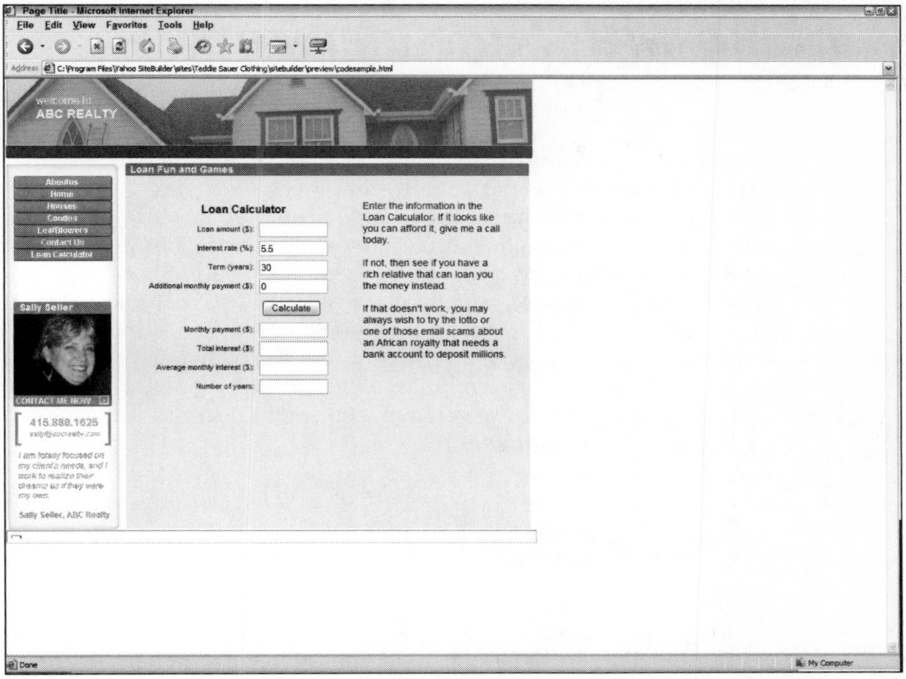

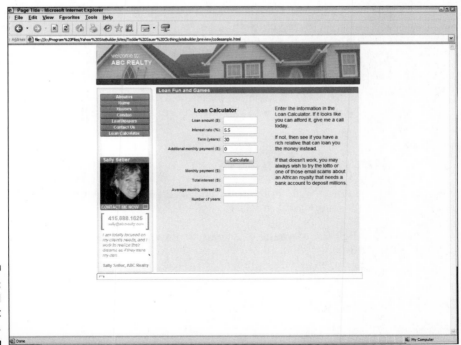

**Figure 4-15:**
Uncentered
page at
1280 x 1024.

**Figure 4-16:**
Centered
page at
1280 x 1024.

# Working with Page Elements

So far in this chapter, you've been looking at how to work with the Web site as individual Web pages. Important work, to be sure, but for the most part it's work that involves relatively simple tasks you can take care of rather quickly. The bulk of the work you actually do on your Web site — the stuff that really eats up your time — deals with what's inside your Web pages: its content. In SiteBuilder, when you talk about content you're talking about page elements such as text boxes, images, tables, forms, navigation bars, and all the other doohickeys you can physically place on a Web page. Most of the remaining chapters deal with how to work with each of these specific page elements. For now, though, think of this section — the one you have in your hot little hands right now — as your (relatively brief) introduction to how you organize and arrange all these various page elements onto the page itself. Read on and become enlightened!

## Selecting elements

Inside of the SiteBuilder Design pane, you can select any page element by clicking inside its borders with your mouse. When you do so, a flashing blue border displays by default around your selection. When selecting elements, keep the following in mind:

- ✔ To select multiple elements on a page, press the Ctrl key while you click each element you wish to select. SiteBuilder adds the element you click to the overall selection.

- ✔ To select all the elements on a page, choose Edit➪Select All from the main menu.

- ✔ To unselect all the elements on a page, choose Edit➪Select None from the main menu or click somewhere on the page itself.

## Moving elements

You can move elements around on your page and place them wherever you want to. To do so

1. **Click the element you want to move, keeping your mouse button down.**

   The element shows a flashing blue border around it.

   If you wish to move more than one element at a time, press the Ctrl key while you select each element with your mouse.

2. **Drag the page element(s) to the desired new location.**

3. **Release the mouse button.**

You can also use your arrow keys to move any page elements you've selected one pixel at a time. This technique is useful when you wish to precisely position your element.

If you want to line up a page element based on x, y coordinates, you can right-click the element and choose Properties from its contextual menu. Click the Coordinates tab and adjust the x, y values as desired. Click OK to reposition the element.

## *Other common element-based tasks*

You can perform several other common tasks on any element on your page. If you've worked with Windows applications before, these tasks should be old hat to you. Select one or more elements and then perform one of the following:

✔ **Cut:** To cut an element, click the Cut button on the toolbar. (Or choose Edit⇨Cut from the main menu or press Ctrl+X.) SiteBuilder moves this element to the Clipboard. You can then paste it into the current page or any other page inside your Web site.

✔ **Copy:** You can copy an element by clicking the Copy button on the toolbar. Alternatively, you can choose Edit⇨Copy or press Ctrl+C.

✔ **Paste:** Once you cut or copy an element, you can paste it into another page on your Web site by clicking the Paste button on your toolbar (or choosing Edit⇨Paste or pressing Ctrl+V). SiteBuilder inserts it in the same position (x, y coordinates) that it had when it was cut or copied. Therefore, if you paste an element onto the same page you copied it, the new element is on top of the original.

✔ **Duplicate:** If you'd like to duplicate an element, you can perform a two-step copy-and-paste process. However, you can save a step by choosing Edit⇨Duplicate from the menu. SiteBuilder adds the duplicate copy right on top of the original.

Because Duplicate adds elements to the same page, use the traditional copy-and-paste process if you wish to use the duplicate element on a different page.

✔ **Delete:** To delete an element, click the Delete button on the toolbar (or press the Delete key or Edit⇨Delete).

## Layering elements

In the early days of the Web, every page element that you added to a Web page had its own rectangular sandbox where it could play to its heart's content but would throw everyone else out of if they ventured inside of its borders. The only exception was a background image, which could cover the entire page regardless of what was on top of it.

This meant that if you tried to put one image on top of another, the browser wouldn't know how to display the combination properly, and so it would force one image to move downward, outside of the sandbox of the other. But, in so doing, it would skew the intended look of the page — not exactly what the doctor ordered.

If you've ever needed proof that, every day and in every way, things are getting just a little bit better, the newer browsers allow for you to overlap images and other page elements, one on top of the other. (Cause for celebration, I think.)

The vast majority of your Web site visitors will have browsers capable of displaying layered images just as you intended when you designed the page. However, there are some exceptions. For example, a text element overlapping a navigation bar doesn't display properly in the current version of Firefox. In addition, a few old-time dinosaur browsers may also prove incapable of displaying your page properly. Keep that in mind as you design your site.

To layer elements, simply drag one element over the rectangular sandbox of another. As you do so, you see that one of them has to be "on top" of the other, taking precedence in what's displayed on-screen. Ultimately, for all of the elements on your page, there's a "king of the mountain" — the image or other page element that is on top of all other elements. Each of the other elements then fit in somewhere farther down the line. This relative ranking order among page elements is maintained by SiteBuilder and passed along to the Web browser for keeping track of the overlapping of page elements.

Some of the elements are transparent, but other elements may have all of its area filled in. For example, a text element with no background color or graphic will be transparent except for the text that is contained in it. As a result, any image or element underneath the text element will show through the transparent regions of the element.

You can't layer all page elements. Several of the Add-Ons, such as the Yahoo! Map Add-On, need their own sandboxes. SiteBuilder displays a flashing red border around these elements when they overlap with another page element, letting you know that the page won't display properly unless corrected.

As you work inside of SiteBuilder, you can determine where the elements rank in that list by following these steps:

1. **Select the page element with your mouse.**

2. **Determine the relative display order of the selected element to other, overlapping elements.**

   - If you'd like to make it the "king of the mountain" and appear on top of any other element, choose Arrange⇨Bring to Front from the main menu (or press Ctrl+Shift+F).

   - If you'd like to send it spiraling downward to the bottom of the display order, choose Arrange⇨Send to Back (or press Ctrl+Shift+B).

   - If you'd like to move it up one level, choose Arrange⇨Bring Forward.

   - If you'd like to move it down one level, choose Arrange⇨Send Backward.

   SiteBuilder then updates the display order based on your choice. Figures 4-17 and 4-18 show how changing the order of the layers impacts what's displayed on-screen.

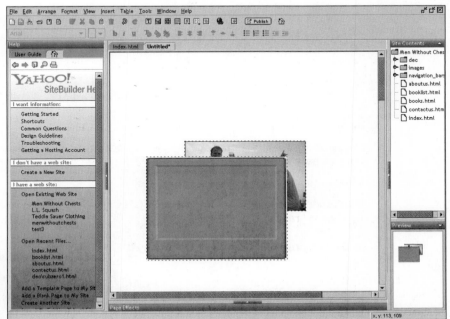

**Figure 4-17:** Option 1 of layer order.

**Figure 4-18:**
Option 2 of
layer order.

## *Aligning and spacing page elements*

You can move page elements around anywhere you want on the page, but getting all your elements aligned with each other or evenly spaced is tricky. To align and space multiple page elements, follow these steps:

1. **Select each of the page elements you wish to align.**

   *Remember:* To select multiple elements, press the Ctrl key as you make your individual selections.

2. **Choose Edit⇨Align from the main menu.**

   If you like keyboard shortcuts, press Ctrl+Shift+A.

   The Align dialog box displays, as shown in Figure 4-19.

3. **In the Alignment box, select the desired type of alignment.**

   Choose one of your six alignment choices (left, vertical center, right, top, horizontal center, and bottom). Or, if you are going to adjust the other settings in the dialog box and not the alignment, then choose None.

**Figure 4-19:**
Align this
way and
that.

**4. If you wish, check one or both boxes in the Match Largest box.**

The Height box sets the height of each element to be the same size as the largest selected element.

The Width box adjusts the width of each element to be the same size as the widest selected element.

**5. If you wish, select the desired spacing option in the Space Items box.**

To space the elements evenly based on your alignment direction, click the Space Evenly option.

To arrange the elements flush next to the other, click the Space Edge to Edge option.

To keep the spacing as is, click the No Change option.

**6. Click OK to align.**

# Chapter 5

# Designers At Your Beck and Call: Using SiteBuilder Templates

*Y*ou've probably seen those "home makeover" shows on TV. The typical scenario is the following: A professional designer comes into a couple's home and transforms it from "this old house" to "this spectacular house." Invariably, the homeowners cry in joy at the grand unveiling and thank the designer profusely for the great work. Perhaps it's just the ornery side of me, but I secretly wish, just once, a couple would despise the changes — and with such a ferocity that they throw the designer into their pool!

In some ways, SiteBuilder templates are reminiscent of those home makeover shows. As a Web site builder, you get to utilize the expertise of a professional designer and have them make over your site. Your Web site look can go from "drab and dull" to "rockin' and stylin'." Best of all, unlike those homeowners, you don't have to wait a week before being surprised by the results. You get to pick and choose the exact style that best fits your needs *before* you actually create your Web site in the first place.

Sound like something you might be interested in? Then read on, for this is the chapter where you get to explore SiteBuilder templates, those "virtual" designers always at your beck and call.

If you have your own custom design that you wish to use instead of a SiteBuilder template, feel free to move on to Chapter 6.

# Exploring SiteBuilder Templates

SiteBuilder gives you access to over 380 professionally designed templates right inside of the product itself. The SiteBuilder template designs are grouped into over 40 categories, such as Real Estate, Beauty, Baby, Computers, E-Commerce, Medical, and Wedding. You can either take the time to install all these templates right onto your local computer, or you can view thumbnail versions of templates online and then download just the ones you need on demand.

## What is a SiteBuilder template?

Many software applications that you use every day — applications such as Microsoft Word or Microsoft PowerPoint — make use of "templates" or "master" pages. Yet a template means something different to each of these applications, and the SiteBuilder templates are no exception.

SiteBuilder templates are page designs that serve as the backbone for your Web site. A template includes most or all of the following components, which combine to create a unified look and feel for your site:

- A graphical theme, including coordinated graphics, background image, customized navigation bar, and custom image bullets.
- Text colors coordinated to match the template graphics.
- Pre-designed "boilerplate" pages tailored for a specific purpose. The pages that are available depend on the actual template.

  Business-oriented templates often include About Us, Contact Us, and Services pages. Real Estate templates include many pages specific to that vertical market, such as Calculator, Listing Details, and Neighborhoods pages. Personal- or activity-oriented templates usually include About Us, Contact Us, Calendar, and Photo Album pages.

- A predefined layout area on each page to place your content.
- Clip art specific to the template design.

Figure 5-1 displays a sample template page with several of these components.

## Avoiding "template remorse"

You select the template you are going to use *before* you create your Web site. After you create your site and start adding your own content, you can't simply switch over to another template. Instead, you have to start all over again and create a new site. Therefore, avoid "template remorse" by making sure you explore all the possible templates that you may be interested in before you hone in on one to use:

✔ Download all the possible templates that you are considering using. (See the "Need More? Downloading Additional Templates" section, later in the chapter, for instructions on how to download additional templates.)

✔ Create a dummy site for each of these templates. (Chapter 3 gives you the lowdown on creating Web sites.) You don't need much, if anything, on a test site. You just want the basic site created to the get the flavor of the template.

✔ Evaluate each candidate.

After you narrow your template list and make a final selection, you're ready to create your Web site.

You may not be able to change templates after you create your site, but as Chapter 3 explains, you can always add new pages based on the template to your site after the initial site creation.

Graphics      Coordinated Navigation bar       Text color          Template pages added

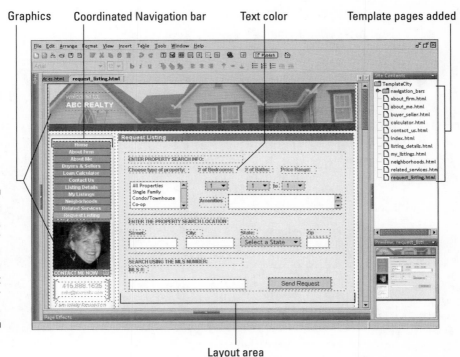

**Figure 5-1:**
A SiteBuilder template does all the upfront work for you.

Layout area

# *Need More? Downloading Additional Templates*

To minimize the time it takes to download the SiteBuilder program files, Yahoo! includes just a handful of templates in the initial SiteBuilder installation. However, you can download additional templates — even all of them, if you want — so you can have them ready to go at a moment's notice.

You must be connected to the Internet, of course, in order to download SiteBuilder templates. (Ahh, details, details. . . .)

The following steps show you how to download a single template "on demand:"

1. **Choose File⇨New Site from the main menu.**

   The Help pane updates to display the opening page of the Site Creation Wizard.

2. **Proceed through Steps 1 and 2 of the Site Creation Wizard.**

   See Chapter 3 for a complete details on the site creation process.

   After completing these steps, Step 3 displays. (See Figure 5-2.)

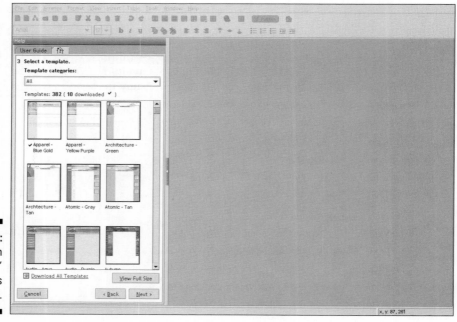

**Figure 5-2:** "High definition" templates on demand.

3. **Select the desired template from the Template list box.**

You have a couple tools that help in your template selection process, including

- The Template Categories list box, great for filtering templates by category.
- The View Full Size button, which lets you look at a normal-size preview of the template.

*Note:* If you've all ready downloaded a template, a check mark is beside its name.

4. **Click Next to continue.**

If you select a template that is not yet installed on your computer, SiteBuilder downloads the template for you automatically and makes it available for use.

5. **Proceed through the remaining steps of the Site Creation Wizard.**

When your site is created, it's based on the specified template.

You can also download a template "on demand" from the Add New Page dialog box (see Figure 5-4, shown later in the chapter). You access the Add New Page dialog box by clicking the New Page with Template button on the toolbar.

Follow these steps to download SiteBuilder templates in advance:

1. **Click the Download All Templates button on the toolbar.**

The Download More Templates dialog box displays, as shown in Figure 5-3. SiteBuilder then contacts the Yahoo! server and retrieves information on any template packages available for download. If you have a dialup connection, this process may take a few minutes.

**Figure 5-3:**
Download
More
Templates in
one big
swoop.

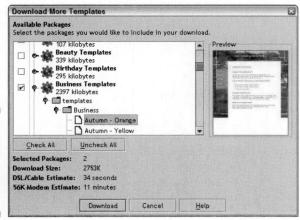

---

## Tweaking a SiteBuilder template

After you put your template to its intended use — creating your Web site — don't hesitate to tweak the look of the SiteBuilder template elements on your pages. If you are creative, this kind of tweaking can help ensure that your Web site's design is truly unique and different from other Web sites that use SiteBuilder.

For example, suppose you like some aspects of a given template but want to remove the background color, change the font from Arial to Verdana, and set the navigation bar to be vertical instead of horizontal. If so, you could make these changes on your first page and then update all other pages to give your entire Web site the same unique look.

---

2. **In the Download More Templates dialog box, check the templates you want to download or click the Check All button to download all templates.**

3. **Click the Download button to start the download process.**

   When SiteBuilder is done downloading, you can begin using the templates and clip art with your Web site.

You can also view the SiteBuilder Templates Gallery inside your browser — just go to `webhosting.yahoo.com/ps/sb/templates`.

# Creating Your Own Template Page

While you cannot make your own SiteBuilder templates, you can create your own template page and reuse it within your site.

In some software applications, such as Microsoft PowerPoint, you can make one change to the "template," and the changes ripple throughout every page based on that template. Not so with SiteBuilder: After you create a custom template page, it no longer contains any "linkages" to the pages that were created from it. As a result, make sure you are satisfied with the design and look of your custom template page *before* you create pages from it.

You can create and use a customized template page by following these steps:

1. **With your Web site open, click the New Page with Template button on the toolbar.**

   The Add New Page dialog box appears, as shown in Figure 5-4.

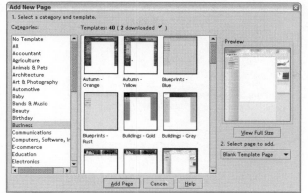

**Figure 5-4:**
Choosing
the template
when
creating a
new page.

2. **In the Add New Page dialog box, select the template you are using from the list.**

   The current template is selected in the list.

3. **From the Select Page to Add drop-down menu, choose Blank Page.**

4. **Click the Add Page button at the bottom of the Add New Page dialog box.**

   The new page is added to your Web site.

5. **Within the Design pane, set up the page layout exactly as you want it to.**

   Continue until you are satisfied with the results. See Chapter 3 for more on working with pages in the Design pane.

6. **Click the Save Page button on the toolbar.**

   The Save As dialog box appears.

7. **In the File Name box, give the template page a name that reflects its usage, such as** `template.html` **or** `basic.html`.

8. **Click Save.**

   Your custom template page is now ready to go. You can see it in the Site Contents pane, as shown in Figure 5-5.

Create a new page based on your custom template with these steps:

1. **From the Site Contents pane (refer to Figure 5-5), right-click the template page and choose Copy File from the menu that appears.**

   The Copy File dialog box displays.

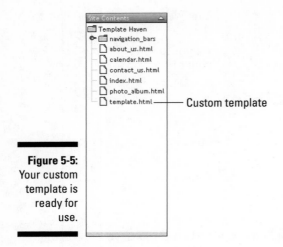
———— Custom template

**Figure 5-5:**
Your custom
template is
ready for
use.

2. **Enter the new page name in the Destination box, and click Save As.**

   SiteBuilder creates a new page based on your template page.

   Your new page is added to the site and is displayed in the Site Contents pane.

# Using Templates or Going Solo?

The site templates that come with many Web site builders are often not too impressive. They can look tacky, cookie cutter, and give your site a very amateurish look. Not so with SiteBuilder. The templates that are included are nicely designed and creatively packaged. Therefore, many people who use SiteBuilder are going to want to simply go with a template to design their Web site. At the same time, just because you can use templates doesn't mean that you necessarily should. Instead, you should consider the advantages (and disadvantages) of using templates versus striking out completely on your own.

The advantages to using SiteBuilder templates are

✔ Templates give you a professional-looking site oriented toward your business type or interest.

✔ You can create a template-based site in SiteBuilder in mere seconds and be productive with it immediately.

✔ You can get a well-designed site without needing to know how to use Adobe Photoshop or any other graphics software.

✔ You are freed from doing any design work yourself. As a result, you can focus purely on the content and messaging of the site.

The advantages to doing it yourself are

✔ You don't have to base your Web site design on someone else's ideas.

Your blank page is an open canvas. Whatever you can dream up and produce visually, you can do.

✔ You can rest assured that your design is going to be unique and not used by another Yahoo! SiteBuilder user.

In the end, it comes down to three factors: productivity, design skills, and the level of control you want. Most SiteBuilder users will opt for templates, as they provide a healthy balance among each of these factors.

# Part II
# Creating "Cool" Web Pages

The 5th Wave                    By Rich Tennant

"Awww jeez- I was afraid of this. Some poor kid, bored with the usual chat lines, starts looking for bigger kicks, pretty soon they're surfin' the seedy back alleys of cyberspace, and before you know it they're into a file they can't 'undo'. I guess that's why they call it the Web. Somebody open a window!"

## In this part . . .

**Y**ou can create a vanilla, run-of-the-mill Web site in many ways. I'm guessing you're using Yahoo! SiteBuilder because you want to do something extraordinary, to create a site that looks good and is easy to use. If so, check out the chapters in Part II, which cover the building blocks you need for cool Web pages. You discover how to work with text, links, pictures, tables, navigation bars, and forms.

# Chapter 6

# Nuts and Bolts: Working with Text and Links

*In This Chapter*

▶ Adding and editing text on your page

▶ Checking your spelling on your Web site

▶ Changing the font and style of your text

▶ Working with links

The underappreciated, not-so-glamorous, yet-oh-so essential sidekick. It seems like most films with a hero has one. For every Maverick, there's a Goose. For every Frodo, there's a Samwise Gangee. For every Batman, there's a Robin.

This sidekick principle holds true in the Web design world as well. Graphics and other visual elements are the "Mavericks" of the Web world. They're the top guns, the show-offs, and the prima donnas. Heck, some have even witnessed them singing "You've Lost That Lovin' Feeling" off-key to other graphics. But even if visual elements are the most glamorous part of a Web page, text is what makes the Web go round. You use visual elements to create an atmosphere and paint broad messages for your visitors, but text is what you'll use to interact and communicate most information to them.

In this chapter, you explore how to add the "nuts and bolts" of any page to your Web site — text and links. But I'll make a guarantee: After you understand how to work with the various Text and Link tools, your pages won't suffer the crash-and-burn fate of poor ol' Goose.

## Working with Text

When you work with words and paragraphs inside of Yahoo! SiteBuilder, it's much different from working within Microsoft Word, WordPerfect, or another word processor. In a word processor, your document is much like an ever-expanding container that grows in length as you add more text. The physical area that the text occupies on a page is defined by its page margins. When you can add graphics to a page, the word processor usually treats these as foreign objects that the flow of the document ignores and just wraps around.

In contrast, Yahoo! SiteBuilder is much more like a desktop publisher, such as Microsoft Publisher. You don't work with a single document spread over multiple pages. Instead, you work with multiple independent pages that you organize yourself.

This type of software doesn't work with words and paragraphs so much as rectangular objects that contain text, graphics, or video. In terms of page layout, it wants to know how big these objects are and how to arrange them on the page.

In a word processor, when you want to add text to a document, you just start typing. But in SiteBuilder, you can't just start typing on a page. You first have to add a text box on a page and then type in the box you just created.

In this section, you explore the basic text-editing tasks, including

- ✔ Adding text to your page
- ✔ Copying text from Microsoft Word or another application to your page
- ✔ Editing your text
- ✔ Positioning the text where you want it
- ✔ Resizing the text container

Sounds like a lot, I know, but take things a step at a time and you'll do all right. Ready to get started?

## Adding text to a page

To add text to a page, follow these steps:

1. **Click the Insert Text button on the toolbar. (See Figure 6-1.)**

   You can also choose Insert⇨Text from the menu or press Ctrl+Shift+T.

   In the smack dead center of the current page, a blue text box is created.

2. **Click and drag the text box to the approximate position on the page you want.**

Insert Text button

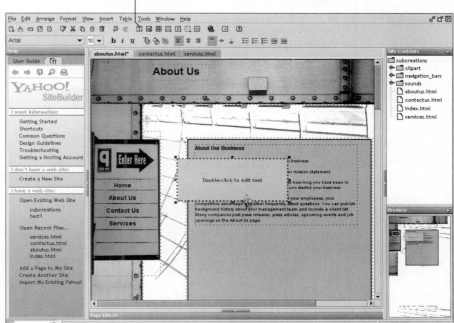

**Figure 6-1:**
Adding text
to your
page.

3. **Resize the text box to an approximate size that can hold your text.**

   To do so, position your mouse cursor on top of one of the eight *resize handles* — the tiny squares you see spaced along the borders of your new text box. Click and drag the box boundary to the desired size and then release your mouse button.

4. **Double-click the blue text box and begin typing.**

   After you start typing, if you find that you miscalculated on the text box size, see the "Resizing your text container" section later in this chapter.

## Adding text from another source to your page

When you create a Web site, you'll want to have some original text that is specifically written for your Web site visitors. However, oftentimes you'll have some information to put on your Web site that you have used for other purposes — stuff that's already hanging around somewhere on your computer. Perhaps you have text from a paper brochure you had printed up, or an e-mail you sent to a customer, or maybe just an old Microsoft Word document.

Rather than retyping it, simply follow these instructions to add it to a fitting Web page:

1. **Open your word processor or other application and copy the desired text to the Clipboard.**

2. **Add a text box to your SiteBuilder page.**

   Follow directions in the "Adding text to a page" section, earlier in this chapter.

3. **Double-click the blue text box.**

   A text cursor displays.

4. **Right-click in the text box, and choose Paste from the contextual menu that appears in order to insert the copied text into the text box.**

   You can also click the Paste button on the toolbar, choose Edit⇨Paste from the menu, or press Ctrl+V.

   The text is added to the text box at the spot the text cursor is.

   You'll quickly notice that any formatting that you had assigned to the text in the other application is stripped when you paste it into SiteBuilder. Therefore, you need to reformat the text as appropriate.

## _Editing text on a page_

To edit existing text on a page, simply follow the steps:

1. **Double-click the text box containing the text you wish to edit.**

   The text box you select displays with a flashing blue border around it. *Note:* The text cursor shows up right at the location where you double-clicked.

2. **Modify the text as desired.**

   While Yahoo! SiteBuilder is not a word processor, many text editing capabilities of your word processor are built in for you. See Table 6-1 for a list of keyboard commands.

| Table 6-1 | Basic Text Editing Shortcuts | |
|---|---|---|
| | *Task* | *Command* |
| ✄ | Cut | Ctrl+X |

| | Task | Command |
|---|---|---|
| | Copy | Ctrl+C |
| | Paste | Ctrl+V |
| | Undo | Ctrl+Z |
| | Redo | Ctrl+Y |
| | Delete | Delete key |
| | Select All | Ctrl+A |
| | Select None | Ctrl+D |

## *Moving text around a page*

One benefit of having all your text contained inside text boxes is that moving big chunks of text around is pretty easy. Just reposition the text box containing the stuff you want to move, and the content inside the text box dutifully follows along. Here's a blow-by-blow account:

1. **Click the text box you wish to move, keeping your mouse button down.**

   A flashing blue border appears around the selected text box.

2. **Drag the text box to the desired new location.**

3. **Release the mouse button.**

You can also use your arrow keys to move text boxes one pixel at a time. This technique is useful when you wish to precisely position your text.

Yahoo! SiteBuilder allows you to move the text box anywhere on the page — and I mean anywhere. You can overlap other text boxes, graphics, or whatever, so be sure to position your box carefully to avoid unwanted overlap.

## *Resizing your text container*

When you add a text element onto your page, SiteBuilder always sets the rectangular container to a standard size. However, you will usually want to resize the text box to account for the text you are adding to it. Follow these steps to resize:

1. **Click the text box you wish to resize.**

   A flashing blue border appears around the selected text box.

2. **Click one of the blue handles on the outside of the text box, and keep your mouse button down.**

   • If you wish to expand or shrink the width, click a left or right handle.

   • If you wish to expand or shrink the height, click a top or bottom handle.

   • If you wish to expand or shrink both the height and width at the same time, click a corner handle.

3. **Drag the mouse to the appropriate size.**

   Figure 6-2 shows a text box being expanded.

4. **Release the mouse button.**

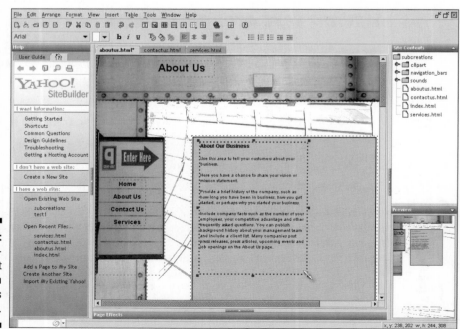

**Figure 6-2:**
Made-to-
order text
boxes can
be sized as
you wish.

# Caught Ya: Checking Your Spelling

*Win u r tring two preesent yurself professhunally, theerz feeew thinz wurse wers then havwing splling earors.* Fortunately, Yahoo! SiteBuilder comes with a built-in spell checker, so you can clean out those spelling gotchas before you publish them to your Web site. You can check your spelling both automatically — letting SiteBuilder watch your words as you type them — or manually — activating the spell checker yourself.

## Automatically alerting you of spelling mistakes

If you use Microsoft Word or WordPerfect, you know what that ubiquitous squiggly red line means resting underneath a word — *Hey, look at me! I'm spelled wrong!* Not to be outdone, Yahoo! went to the U.N. Commission on Squiggly Red Lines and got permission to include their own squiggly red line inside SiteBuilder. Therefore, when Automatic Spell Checking is on, SiteBuilder lets you know of any spelling problems. By default, Automatic Spell Checking is enabled.

To enable or disable the Automatic Spell Checking option:

1. **Choose Tools⇨Check Spelling from the main menu to display the Spell Checking submenu.**

   If already enabled, the Automatic Spell Checker option is checked.

2. **Click the Automatic Spell Checker option to toggle the current setting.**

The logic that SiteBuilder uses to determine whether a word is or is not misspelled is based on your preferences. See the "Setting spell checking preferences" section that's coming up.

Figure 6-3 shows what you see when a word you enter is marked as being spelled incorrectly.

The Automatic Spell Checker feature lets you know that a word is unrecognized, but you can't use the checker to correct the mistakes themselves — you can't simply right-click the misspelled word and see a list of suggested spellings. If you really want help on how to spell something — rather then just being notified of a spelling boo-boo — you're going to need to check your spelling manually, as I spell out (pun intended) in the next section.

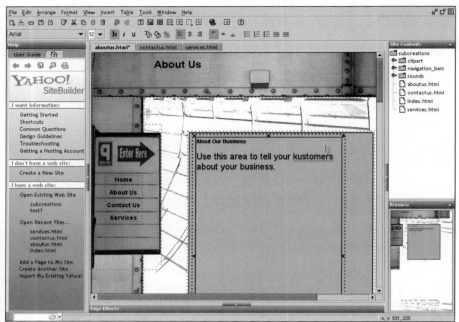

**Figure 6-3:**
Our little
squiggly red
friend.

# Checking your spelling manually

You can manually check the spelling of the text on your Web site in a variety of ranges — checking a selection of text, a page, all the open pages, or your entire site.

To manually check your spelling

1. **Determine the scope of your spell check and then choose the appropriate menu command:**

   - If you have text selected with your mouse and want to check this text but not the entire page or site, choose Tools➪Check Spelling➪ Selected Text from the main menu.

   - To check all text on the current page, choose Tools➪Check Spelling➪Current Page.

   - To check all pages you currently have open in SiteBuilder, choose Tools➪Check Spelling➪Opened Pages.

   - To check the entire "kit and caboodle," the whole Web site, then choose Tools➪Check Spelling➪Entire Site.

The Check Spelling dialog box (see Figure 6-4) appears, with the first potential spelling error shown in the Unknown Word box. A suggested replacement word is shown in the Replace By box, along with other possible choices in the Suggestions list.

**Figure 6-4:** No matter which type of manual spell checking you do, you always end up here.

2. **Decide what action you wish to take for this flagged word:**

   • **Replace this instance of the spelling error:** To replace the misspelled word with the one shown in the Replace By box, click the Replace button.

   To choose a different word from the Suggestions list, select the word with your mouse and then click Replace.

   If SiteBuilder doesn't suggest the word you need, type the correct spelling for the word in the Replace By box and then click Replace.

   • **Replace all instances of the misspelled word:** Misspelling the same word multiple times is common. For example, I habitually misspell *separate* as *seperate* and *calendar* as *calander*. If this happens to you, you can replace all instances of the misspelled word in the range you are checking by selecting the word and clicking the Replace All button.

   • **Add an unrecognized word to the Yahoo! SiteBuilder dictionary:** If you have a word that is not understood by the spell checker, but you'd like to add it to the dictionary, click the Learn button.

   • **Ignore misspellings:** If you have a word that SiteBuilder doesn't recognize but you don't want to add the word to the dictionary, you can click the Ignore button (to ignore this single instance of the word) or Ignore All (to ignore all instances of the word).

After you take an action, the spell checker moves to the next misspelling (or punctuation error, if you have that option enabled).

When you finish, SiteBuilder informs you that the spell check has completed successfully.

You can also switch spell-checking dictionaries. To do so, click the Dictionary drop-down box and select the desired language choice.

3. **Click Close to finish spell checking.**

## Setting spell checking preferences

The text you have on your Web site may not always be like a high school English paper. It can contain some words, such as Web addresses, that aren't in a standard dictionary but that are proper for the Web nonetheless. Rather than having SiteBuilder's spell checker flag lots of items that are perfectly fine in the world of the World Wide Web, you can set the spell checking preferences in order to limit the number of such "false positives." Here's how:

1. **Choose Tools⇨Preferences.**

   The Preferences dialog box makes an appearance.

2. **Click the Spell Check tab.**

   The various spell checking options display, as shown in Figure 6-5.

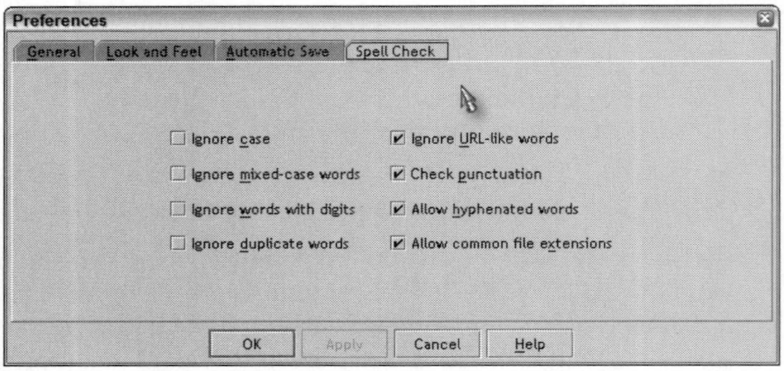

**Figure 6-5:**
Setting your
spell
checking
options.

| Preferences | | | | ☒ |
| --- | --- | --- | --- | --- |
| General | Look and Feel | Automatic Save | Spell Check | |

☐ Ignore case    ☑ Ignore URL-like words

☐ Ignore mixed-case words    ☑ Check punctuation

☐ Ignore words with digits    ☑ Allow hyphenated words

☐ Ignore duplicate words    ☑ Allow common file extensions

[ OK ]  [ Apply ]  [ Cancel ]  [ Help ]

3. **Check or uncheck the desired options.**

   See the following descriptions of each option.

4. **Click OK or Apply to save these changes.**

The spell checking options you can set are as follows:

- **Ignore Case:** Ignores lowercase words that start a sentence.

- **Ignore Mixed-Case Words:** Turns a blind eye to words that have upper- and lowercase characters, such as WordPerfect, JavaScript, and even SiteBuilder.

- ✔ **Ignore Words with Digits:** Overlooks words that contain fingers . . . oops, I mean, numeric digits.

- ✔ **Ignore Duplicate Words:** Ignores those times where you list the same word more than once.

- ✔ **Ignore URL-Like Words:** Bypasses any word that looks, smells, behaves, or in some way resembles a URL or a Web address — such as `http://www.yahoo.com` or `www.yahoo.com`.

- ✔ **Check Punctuation:** Puts on its English Teacher hat and checks for simple punctuation errors, such as having a space prior to a comma or a period at the beginning of a word, that sort of thing.

- ✔ **Allow Hyphenated Words:** Ignores two or more words attached by a hyphen, such as *sub-menu* or *venti-one pump-soy-extra whip-mocha*.

- ✔ **Allow Common File Extensions:** Doesn't flag filenames with common file extensions, such as `.doc`, `.html`, or `.zip`.

# Tweaking the Look of Your Text

The days of boring monospaced text are long gone — relics of the days of the typewriter. People nowadays, whether they read a document you created or visit your Web site, expect to see spiced-up text that looks attractive and readable.

Text formatting in Yahoo! SiteBuilder has three scopes:

- ✔ **Character:** Character formatting applies to any range of characters — from individual characters to words to sentences and even to one or more paragraphs. The Font, Style, and Text Color settings are all character formats. I discuss these in this section.

- ✔ **Paragraph:** Paragraph formatting is formatting associated with an entire paragraph — things like justification, lists, and indents. Find my discussion of these settings in the "Stylin' Your Paragraphs" section later in this chapter.

- ✔ **Text box:** Text box formatting is applied to the contents of the entire text box, whether the text contains one word or several paragraphs. See the "Formatting Your Text Boxes" section later in this chapter for more on these settings.

## Deciding which font style to use

The font style (or typeface) that you use is one of the most basic decisions you'll ever make when creating a Web page. Chapter 3 describes the specific design considerations you'll want to think about when deciding on which fonts to use. But in general, remember two rules:

✔ **Pick a font that you know people will have on their system.** When you create a printed document, newsletter, or Adobe Acrobat file, you can pick any font you have and be certain that your reader will be looking at the formatting that you intended. However, on the Web, the font you define on your Web page may or may not be on the visitor's computer. If the font is missing from the system, then the browser looks for a substitute font. However, you don't always know how the page is going to look.

Therefore, I recommend picking Arial, Verdana, or Times New Roman as fonts. You can be fairly confident using Tahoma or Georgia, too, as most users will have these fonts or at least the browser can substitute a standard font quite close to these. You can also use Courier New in specific instances where you want to display a monospaced font.

✔ **Pick one to two font styles for your site and go with them.** You'll want to pick a default font style and use it predominately across your site. For sans serif (smooth) fonts, use Arial, Verdana, or Tahoma. For serif (curvy) fonts, stick with Times New Roman or Georgia.

You may want to have a second font for headings to add some variety. But if you do so, pick the opposite font style. For example, if you use Verdana as your primary font, pick a serif font for your headings. Or if you have Times New Roman as your main font, use any of the sans serif fonts for your heading text.

## Setting the font style and size

When you work with a Web site that you created using a template, SiteBuilder already gives you a recommended font. However, if you'd like to change the font style, follow these instructions:

1. **Click the text box that contains the text you wish to modify.**

   If you wish to change the font style for all the text within the box, then keep the box selected. Or if you wish to modify a portion of text, then select just that portion with your mouse.

2. **Select the desired font style or size from the drop-down lists on the toolbar.**

   Your text updates to show the new font setting.

You can also change the font style or size for two or more text boxes on a single page. To select multiple text boxes, simply click each text box while pressing the Ctrl key. Then set the desired font style from the drop-down list on the toolbar.

## Color me beautiful

You can express colors on computers in different ways. SiteBuilder provides support for three of the most popular methods today:

**Hex color codes:** Each color is represented within the Web world with a very techie-looking hex color code, which is a six-digit code prefixed with a # sign. For example, black is #000000, white is #FFFFFF, and bright blue is #0000FF. If you ever look at the HTML source code for a Web page, you'll see the colors expressed as hex color codes.

**HSB values:** *HSB* stands for Hue, Saturation, and Brightness. Hue values range from 0 to 360 degrees — like points on the circumference of a large colorized circle. Saturation and Brightness are percentages, ranging from 0 to 100.

**RGB values:** *RGB* stands for Red, Green, and Blue. A color is created by combining the Red, Green, and Blue values — each of which range from 0 to 255. Many Windows applications, such as Microsoft Paint and Microsoft Word, support the use of RGB values.

## *Giving your text some style*

You can make parts of your text stand out by assigning the old formatting bold, italic, and underline standbys to your text:

- ✔ **Bold** is helpful for headings.
- ✔ *Italic* is useful for emphasizing certain words or phrases within a paragraph.
- ✔ Within the Web world, the <u>underline</u> style has become synonymous with Web links. Therefore, under most circumstances, I don't recommend using underline formatting. You'll find your visitors clicking the word assuming it's a Web link. (To set links, see the "Getting Jumpy: Adding Links to Your Text" section, later in the chapter.)

To set a character style for your text, follow these steps:

1. **Double-click the text box that contains the text you wish to modify.**
2. **Select the text you wish to style with your mouse.**
3. **Click the Bold, Italic, or Underline button on the toolbar.**

    You can also choose Format⇨Bold, Format⇨Italic, or Format⇨Underline from the menu or use the following key shortcuts: Ctrl+B (Bold), Ctrl+I (Italic), or Ctrl+U (Underline).

If you'd like to set a character style for all the contents of a text box, click the box and then click the appropriate button on the toolbar.

In word processors, you can toggle character style formatting on or off as you type. You can do the same here. You can turn on Bold, Italic, or Underline by clicking its toolbar button. The toolbar button is darkened to signify its "on" state. You can then turn it off by clicking the button once more.

## Changing text color

You can modify the color of your text to any color shade on the color dial. But SiteBuilder doesn't stop there: You can also use any color on the color spectrum, the color wheel, or even the color palette. (Okay, all these terms mean the same thing, but you get my drift.)

Follow these steps to change the color of the text:

1. **Double-click the text box that contains the text you wish to change its color.**

2. **Select the text you wish to color with your mouse.**

3. **Click the Text Color button on the toolbar.**

   Alternatively, you can choose Format⇨Text Color from the menu.

   The Choose Text Color dialog box displays, as shown in Figure 6-6.

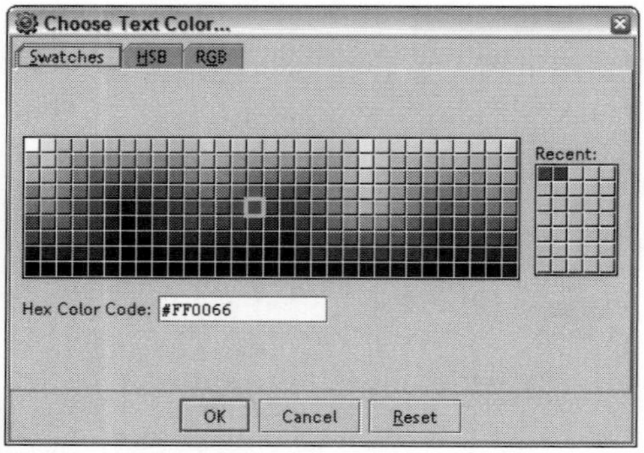

**Figure 6-6:**
Coloring
your text
without
crayons.

4. **Select the color you want to use.**

   The Swatches tab displays the common colors, along with a box of the most recent colors you've chosen before.

   Or if you don't see the exact color you want to use on the Swatches tab, you can more precisely define the color using the HSB or RGB tabs. (See the "Color me beautiful" sidebar for a discussion of what these acronyms mean.)

In the past, you wanted to be careful to use only "Web safe" colors, which are a set of 216 colors common to most browsers. Web safe colors helped ensure that the colors you picked would display reliably on monitors that display only 256 colors. However, now that the vast majority of your visitors will be using a monitor with thousands of colors, you can feel confident using any color.

5. **Click OK to save your settings.**

   The text you selected displays with the new color.

# Stylin' Your Paragraphs

Most text formatting inside of SiteBuilder is done at the character or text box level. SiteBuilder has just two paragraph-level formats that you can set — lists and indents.

## Making lists

Whether it is a to-do list, a grocery list, or a list of points covered in a lecture or sermon, people just seem to think in lists. Lists are popular on Web sites as well because they enable people to quickly read and process "sound bites" of information much more quickly than if they were forced to plow through paragraph upon paragraph of dense text. The designers behind SiteBuilder recognized that fact and came up with software that allows you to create a broad spectrum of lists, including bulleted lists, numbered lists, and even image bulleted lists.

### Adding bulleted and numbered lists

A *bulleted list* is used to offset a bunch of related sentences or bits of information on your Web page. A *numbered list* is sequential list of steps or other items that SiteBuilder automatically numbers for you. To add bullets or numbers to one or more existing paragraphs, follow these steps:

1. **Double-click the text box containing the paragraph or paragraphs you've targeted for a bulleted or numbered list makeover.**

2. **Select one or more paragraphs that you want to transform into a list.**

3. **Click the Bulleted List or Numbered List button on the toolbar.**

    You can also choose Format➪Bulleted List or Format➪Numbered List from the menu.

You can also customize the bullet or number format SiteBuilder uses. See the "Customizing bulleted and numbered lists" section later in this chapter.

### *Adding image bulleted lists*

If you are sick of the normal round or square bullets that SiteBuilder uses, you can use your own image as the bullet instead. Image lists are an attractive and professional-looking alternative to normal bullets. You'll notice that many of the SiteBuilder templates use image lists.

To create an image bulleted list

1. **Double-click the text box where you're planning to place the image bulleted list.**

2. **Select a paragraph (or paragraphs) to transform into such a list.**

3. **Click the Custom List button on the toolbar.**

   The Choose Bullet dialog box appears, as shown in Figure 6-7.

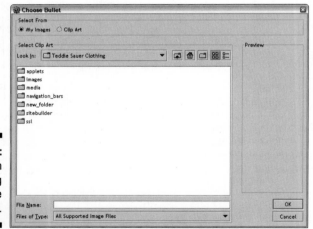

**Figure 6-7:**
Faster than
a speeding
image
bullet.

4. **Determine whether you wish to choose a bullet from your own images or from the SiteBuilder Clip Art library.**

   If you wish to use your own image, use the Select Clip Art pane to navigate to the image file.

   If you wish to use SiteBuilder Clip Art, click the Clip Art radio button in the Select From pane and then use the Select Clip Art pane to pick your bullet.

   Be sure the image you use is 12 pixels or less in height. (And remember, the point here is to look professional, so no images of Socko the Clown.)

5. **Click OK to create the image bulleted list.**

### Removing list items

If you want to remove an item from a bulleted, numbered, or image bulleted list, simply position the text cursor at the left margin to the right of the bullet or number and press the Delete key.

### Customizing bulleted and numbered lists

SiteBuilder also enables you to more precisely define your lists using the Bullets and Numbering dialog box.

Here's how to get your list to look exactly like you want it:

1. **Double-click the text box that contains the list you are going to customize.**

2. **Select each of the paragraphs that make up your list.**

3. **Choose Format⇨Bullets and Numbering from the main menu.**

    The Bullets and Numbering dialog box appears, as shown in Figure 6-8.

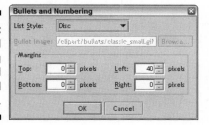

**Figure 6-8:** Bullets and Numbering command and control center.

4. **Customize the list as desired.**

    Use the List Style drop-down menu to choose the bullet or numbering style you want.

    • For bullets, you can choose Disc (the default), Circle, Square, or Image.

    • For numbered lists, you can choose normal 1, 2, 3, 4 order or else jazz it up with roman numerals (I, II, III, IV or i, ii, iii, iv) or use alphabetical order (A, B, C, D or a, b, c, d).

    • For an indented list with blank bullets, select Blank.

    In the Margins box, you can specify any custom margins for the list. Usually, the only value you want to modify is the Left margin.

    The Top and Bottom margins can be helpful if you are using an extra-large image bullet.

5. **Click OK to save changes.**

## *Indenting your text*

*Indenting* moves the left margin for a paragraph several spaces to the right. You can indent a paragraph within your text box when you want to offset a specific piece of text for emphasis, including a lengthy quotation, or simply to make an unnumbered list.

To indent a paragraph

1. **Double-click the text box that contains the paragraph you are going to indent.**
2. **Position your cursor anywhere inside of the desired paragraph.**

3. **Click the Increase Indent button on the toolbar.**

   You can also choose Format⇨Increase Indentation from the main menu.
4. **If you'd like to increase the indentation more, click the Increase Indent button again.**

You can unindent a paragraph to reverse the indent settings as well by following these steps:

1. **Double-click the text box that contains the paragraph you are going to unindent.**
2. **Position your cursor anywhere inside of the desired paragraph.**

3. **Click the Decrease Indent button on the toolbar.**

   Alternatively, you can choose Format⇨Decrease Indentation from the main menu.
4. **If you'd like to decrease the indentation more, click the Decrease Indent button again.**

   When you unindent all the way to a normal paragraph, SiteBuilder ignores the Decrease Indent command.

# *Formatting Your Text Boxes*

Within SiteBuilder, you can apply certain text formatting commands to everything inside of a text box. These include

- Background color
- Justification and alignment

# Changing the background color of your text box

While you can't change the background color of individual pieces of text within your text box, you can change the background color of the entire text box by following these steps:

1. **Click the text box whose background you wish to change.**

2. **Click the Text Background button on the toolbar.**

   You can also choose Format⇨Text Background from the main menu.

   A dialog box appears almost identical to the one shown in Figure 6-6, except this time it's called the Choose Text Background dialog box.

3. **Select the color you want to use.**

   See the "Changing text color" section, earlier in this chapter, for details on how to change the settings in this dialog box.

4. **Click OK to save your settings.**

   The background of the selected text box updates with the new color.

# Resetting the text background

You can call it "coloring remorse" or "backgrounder's regret." But whatever label you want to put on it, sometimes you'll decide that changing the text box background wasn't such a good idea after all. SiteBuilder allows you to reset the background color with a touch of a button:

1. **Click the text box that has the really horrid, awful color scheme that you can't stand the sight of.**

2. **Click the Remove Text Background button on the toolbar.**

   You can also choose Format⇨Remove Text Background from the main menu.

   Whew! The colorizing experiment is over. You're back to where you started from.

# But Your Honor . . . I was justified!

Within the printed world of documentation, paragraph justification is a big thing. For example, for standard letters, you often right-align the sender's mailing address while left-aligning the rest of the letter. For reports, you usually center titles on the front page. Within the Web world, justification is used less often as a formatting technique. By and large, Web designers usually stick to left-aligned text. It just seems to work better. However, you may have specific text boxes that need different alignment, such as a page title or the text inside of a navigation bar.

Moreover, there's another level of alignment that isn't thought about in the word processing world but is important when working with SiteBuilder's text boxes: vertical alignment. Because you're working with the entire text box, you may want to align the text vertically within the boundaries of the text box.

When you need to change the horizontal or vertical justification for a text box, follow these steps:

1. **Click the text box that contains the text you wish to justify.**

2. **Click the appropriate justification button on the toolbar.**

   For horizontal alignment, click the Left Justify, Center Horizontally, or Right Justify button.

   For vertical alignment, click the Top Justify, Center Vertically, or Bottom Justify button.

   Alternatively, you can choose the corresponding command from the Format part of the main menu.

   The text box alignment updates based on your selection.

# Getting Jumpy: Adding Links to Your Text

Links are the backbone of the Internet — the very reason that the Web came to be what it has become today. A link (also called a *hypertext link* or *hyperlink*) is an element on a Web page that you click with your mouse to jump to another Web page or another destination. A link can be a bit of text you click, but it can also be a clickable graphic. (You can explore how to set graphic links in Chapter 7.)

In SiteBuilder, you can create links to several different types of resources on the Web, including

✔ Another page on your Web site

✔ A page on another Web site

    ✔ An e-mail address

    ✔ A file, such as a Microsoft Word or an Adobe Acrobat document

In this section, you explore how to add links to each of these types of resources.

## Linking to another page in your site

Probably the most common link that you want to add is a link to another page on your Web site. To do so, follow these steps:

1. **Double-click the text box that contains the text that you want to use as the link.**

2. **Select the word or words that you want to use as the link text.**

3. **Click the Link button on the toolbar.**

    The Link dialog box appears, as shown in Figure 6-9.

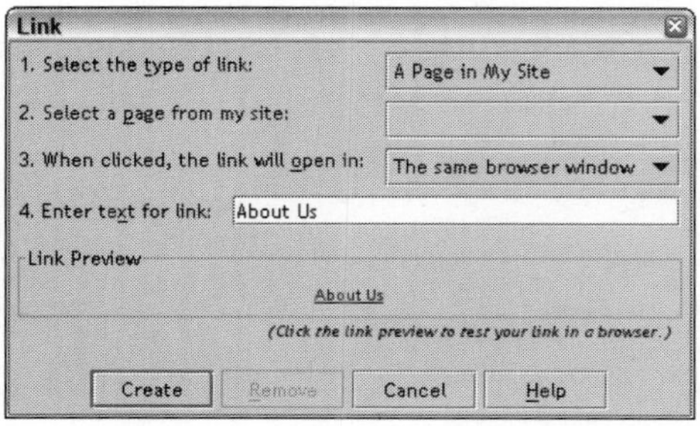

**Figure 6-9:**
Linking to
another
SiteBuilder
page.

| Link |
| --- |
| 1. Select the *type* of link:    A Page in My Site ▼ |
| 2. Select a *page* from my site:    ▼ |
| 3. When clicked, the link will *open* in:    The same browser window ▼ |
| 4. Enter text for link:    About Us |
| Link Preview |
| About Us |
| *(Click the link preview to test your link in a browser.)* |
| Create    Remove    Cancel    Help |

4. **In the Select the Type of Link drop-down list, keep the default option (A Page in My Site).**

5. **Choose a page from the Select a Page from My Site drop-down menu.**

    The list displays all the pages that are part of your Web site.

6. **If you wish to modify the hyperlink text, do so in the Enter Text for Link box.**

7. **Click the link inside the Link Preview pane if you wish to test the link before creating it.**

8. **Click the Create button.**

You can set the link to open in a new browser window by adjusting the When Clicked, the Link Will Open In setting. However, for pages within your site, you almost always want to simply use the same browser window, the default option. Multiple browser windows can be annoying for users, and so you only want to use this option if you have a compelling reason to do so.

## Linking to a page elsewhere on the Web

If you want to refer your visitors to another Web site, create an external link by following these instructions:

1. **Double-click the text box that contains the text that you want to use as the link.**

2. **Select the word or words that you want to use as the link text.**

3. **Click the Link button on the toolbar.**

    The Link dialog box appears.

4. **Choose the Another Web Site option from the Select the Type of Link drop-down menu.**

    The Link dialog box changes its options, as shown in Figure 6-10.

**Figure 6-10:** Linking to another Web site.

5. **In the Enter the Destination URL text box, enter the URL (Web address) of the Web page you want to link to.**

    To ensure accuracy, I recommend locating the Web page in your browser and then copying and pasting the URL from your browser's Address box.

6. **Decide whether you wish to have the destination page open in the same window (replacing the existing page) or else in a new browser window. Select the desired option from the When Clicked, the Link Will Open In drop-down menu.**

For Web links that take visitors off of your Web site to another destination, using a new browser window is often a good idea. Otherwise, they may leave your site and forget to come back.

7. **If you wish to modify the hyperlink text, do so in the Enter Text for Link box.**

8. **Click the link inside the Link Preview pane if you wish to test the link before creating it.**

9. **Click the Create button.**

## Linking to an e-mail address

Not only can you link to Web pages, but you can also enable a visitor to send you an e-mail message by clicking a link on your site.

To link to an e-mail address, do the following:

1. **Double-click the text box that contains the text that you want to use as the link.**

2. **Select the word or words that you want to use as the link text.**

   This text is usually your e-mail address (such as `info@digitalwalk.net`) or perhaps something like Contact Us.

3. **Click the Link button on the toolbar.**

   The Link dialog box displays.

4. **Choose the An Email Address option from the Select the Type of Link drop-down menu.**

   The Link dialog box changes its options, as shown in Figure 6-11.

5. **In the An Email Address box, enter the e-mail address you wish to link to.**

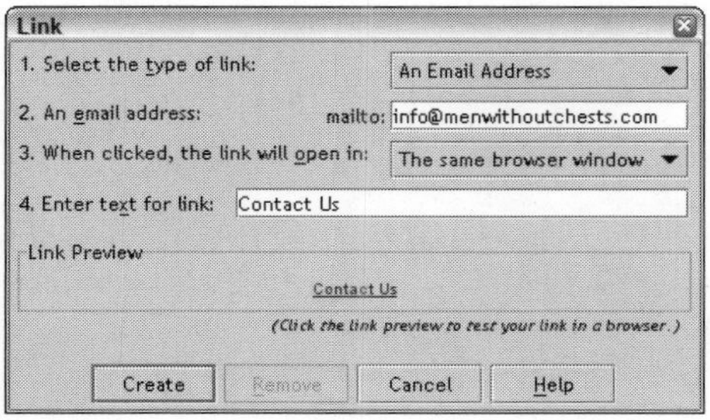

**Figure 6-11:**
Faster than
snail mail,
slower than
a Web link.

| Link | |
|---|---|
| 1. Select the type of link: | An Email Address ▼ |
| 2. An email address: | mailto: info@menwithoutchests.com |
| 3. When clicked, the link will open in: | The same browser window ▼ |
| 4. Enter text for link: | Contact Us |
| Link Preview | |
| | Contact Us |
| | *(Click the link preview to test your link in a browser.)* |
| | Create   Remove   Cancel   Help |

6. **If you wish to modify the hyperlink text, do so in the Enter Text for Link box.**

7. **Click the link inside the Link Preview pane if you wish to test the link before creating it.**

8. **Click the Create button.**

## Linking to a file

On occasion, you may refer your visitors to a file that is not a Web page. Perhaps you have a 50-page case study in a Microsoft Word document that you'd like prospective customers to download. Or perhaps you have a user's manual that you created as an Adobe Acrobat (PDF) file that you want visitors to reference. If so, then you can set up a link to these files — make sure they're available on your local computer — and SiteBuilder uploads these to your Web site when you publish.

To link to a file, follow these steps:

1. **Double-click the text box that contains the text that you want to use as the link.**

2. **Select the word or words that you want to use as the link text.**

3. **Click the Link button on the toolbar.**

   The Link dialog box displays.

4. **In the Select the Type of Link drop-down menu, choose the A File in My Site option.**

   The Link dialog box changes its options, as shown in Figure 6-12.

5. **Enter the path of the file you wish to link to into the Select a File in My Site text box.**

   Click the Browse button to navigate to the file.

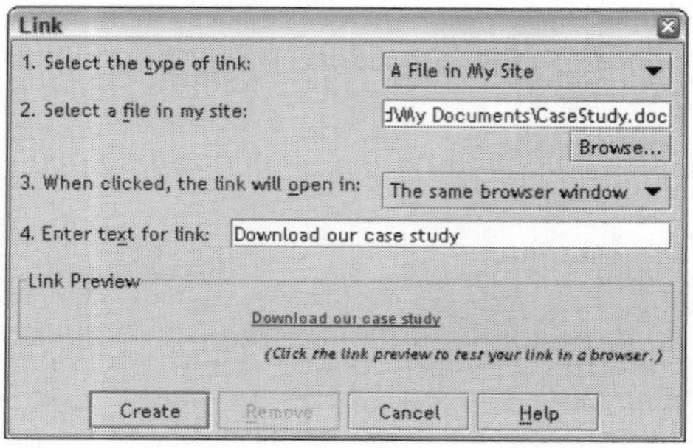

**Figure 6-12:** "Heavens to linkatroids," yet another type of link.

| Link |
|---|
| 1. Select the type of link: — A File in My Site ▼ |
| 2. Select a file in my site: — :\My Documents\CaseStudy.doc — Browse... |
| 3. When clicked, the link will open in: — The same browser window ▼ |
| 4. Enter text for link: — Download our case study |
| Link Preview |
| Download our case study |
| *(Click the link preview to test your link in a browser.)* |
| Create — Remove — Cancel — Help |

6. Decide whether you wish to have the destination page open in the same window (replacing the existing page) or else in a new browser window and then select the desired option from the When Clicked, the Link Will Open In drop-down menu.

7. If you wish to modify the hyperlink text, do so in the Enter Text for Link box.

8. Click the link inside the Link Preview pane if you wish to test the link before creating it.

9. Click the Create button.

# Editing and Removing a Link

After you create a link, you can always edit or remove it.

To edit a link

1. Double-click the text box that contains the text that you want to use as the link.

2. Position your text cursor anywhere inside of the link.

3. Click the Link button on the toolbar.

The Link dialog box displays with the current settings.

4. Make any changes you wish and then click the Create button.

To remove a link

1. Double-click the text box that contains the text that you want to use as the link.

2. Position your text cursor anywhere inside of the link.

3. Click the Link button on the toolbar.

The Link dialog box displays.

4. Click the Remove button to blow that link to kingdom come.

# Chapter 7

# Picture Perfect

· · · · · · · · · · · · · · · · · · · · · · · · · · · · · · · · · · · · · · · · · · · · · · · · · · · · · · · ·

## In This Chapter

▶ Knowing which graphics to use
▶ Adding clip art and images
▶ Moving and resizing images
▶ Creating a background

· · · · · · · · · · · · · · · · · · · · · · · · · · · · · · · · · · · · · · · · · · · · · · · · · · · · · · · ·

*W*ith great power comes great responsibility. Those memorable words are spoken by Uncle Ben to Peter Parker in the hit film *Spider-Man*. Yet they also are a fitting motto to keep in mind when you think about using graphics on your Web site. The power and effectiveness of images and visual communication are amazing. Just by glancing at the major sites around the Web, you'll see not only large numbers of images, but also the many creative ways in which to use them. Yet if you're going to use the power of images on your Web site, you need to use them responsibly. The reason is that every graphic you use can "weigh down" your Web page and make it longer to download, especially for those visitors using dialup access.

Smart Web site designers take Uncle Ben's advice and make sure that the graphics they use on their Web pages both serve an important purpose and are relatively "lightweight." This combination smacks of "Spidey Sense:" powerful.

In this chapter, you explore the balance of using the power of graphics effectively and responsibly. As you aim for that balanced approach, you explore the types of graphics you should (and should not) use on your Web site. Then you dive into the nitty-gritty of how to work with pictures inside of SiteBuilder.

## Be Choosy: Why All Graphics Aren't Created Equal

When you begin adding pictures to your Web site, keep in mind these two important factors that can help you decide what kinds of pictures to use and what not to use: the type and size of the graphic. Getting a solid grasp of these issues goes a long way in achieving that "power and responsibility" balance for your Web site.

# Choosing the best Web graphic types

Generally, graphic files are identified by their file extension: GIF graphics have a .gif extension, JPG graphics have a .jpg extension, and PNGs have a .png extension. These three formats are popular because they are *compression-based formats* — meaning that they take up less space and require much less time to download than other uncompressed formats, such as Windows BMP files.

JPG and GIF graphics are the two most widely used image formats on the Web. PNG is a third format that's becoming popular for Web use, but it still lags behind in overall support across browsers.

You can think of JPG, GIF, and PNG formats as something like trash compactors. They take a normal-size image and compress all the "extra air" out of them so that they take less space. For example, a BMP file of 1.5MB can be reduced to a JPG of just 2.4K!

## JPG omelet: A photo's "breakfast" of choice

JPG (short for JPEG, or *J*oint *P*hotographic *E*xperts *G*roup) is an ideal format for photo-quality and other high-resolution images containing millions of colors. JPG is what is known as a *lossy* compression format, because it works to remove redundant and unneeded graphical data that doesn't impact the look of the image. However, as good as JPG is for photo-like images, it doesn't do nearly as good a job on simple line graphics, clip art, and text.

## Choosy mothers (with simple graphics) choose GIF

GIF (*G*raphic *I*nterchange *F*ormat) can often be shrunk to a smaller size than JPG, though its compression ratio is dependent on the colors used in the image. GIF also supports only a maximum of 256 colors (far less than JPG), but it provides support for transparency (clear portions of the image) and animation (which JPG does not).

GIF is known as a *lossless* method of compression, meaning that it squishes the original image but doesn't throw out any of data in the process. As a result, simple graphics that include text and line drawings are often ideally represented in GIF.

# Understanding bitmap and vector graphics

You can work with two major types of graphics on your computer: bitmap and vector graphics. Understanding their differences is important in order to know which are useful for the Web and to better understand how you can use them.

**Bitmap graphics:** The most common type of picture, a *bitmap graphic* is a pattern of colored dots (called *pixels*) that are combined to form an image. When you take a digital photo or download a wallpaper for your desktop, you are working with bitmap graphics. If you happened to magnify these pictures a whole bunch in a graphics editor, you'd see that the image is actually composed of thousands of individually colored dots that form a mosaic.

Bitmap images are the type of graphics almost always used on Web pages. And if you download a picture from the Web or receive one via e-mail from another person, it's probably a bitmap. Bitmaps are used for any purpose for which you need sharp, clear photo-like pictures and thousands of colors. The disadvantage to bitmap graphics is that you lose quality the moment you resize them. You can usually shrink a bitmap image without much trouble. But the moment you enlarge a bitmap, you'll quickly notice that the quality of the picture suffers.

The two standard types of bitmap graphics for the Web are GIF and JPG. PNG is another popular format, though some older browsers do not support it. BMP is a popular format for Microsoft Windows but is not supported across the Web. (However, as mentioned in the "Deciding the right format to use" section, SiteBuilder automatically converts a BMP image to a JPG image.)

**Vector graphics:** Vector graphics are composed of a pattern of lines and curves (called *vectors*) that together form the shape of the picture. The graphic is generated by math calculations (don't ask me how) instead of pixels. The result is that you can shrink or expand all you want, and those little math geeks inside of the graphic resize it without any loss in quality. Now, before you throw up your arms as to why the Web doesn't use these geeky graphic types more, there's a catch. Vector graphics never look as realistic or have the detail that bitmaps do. Instead of looking like photos, they look like sketches or hand drawings.

The most common vector file types on Microsoft Windows is WMF. However, vector graphics have no standard support in browsers, so *don't* use them.

## PNG pong

PNG (*P*ortable *N*etwork *G*raphics) is a third compression format that has started to become popular over the past few years. It also uses a lossless method of compression but does so at a higher quality, with more colors, and at a smaller size than does GIF. PNG supports transparency (like GIF) and opacity adjustment (which neither GIF nor JPG handles). *Opacity adjustment* is the percentage to which the image is visible relative to image or background underneath it. A 100 percent value would show the image normally, but 10 percent would show the image faintly.

### Deciding the right format to use

So which format is better? As good as PNG is, the format is still not universally supported by all browsers, so it's not the best choice at this time for your Web site. When you examine the other two, each has advantages and disadvantages to think about when you're deciding which format to use.

GIF is often the best option for graphics with text; graphics that require transparency; and diagrams, clip art, and other line-based images that have a small number of colors. JPG, on the other hand, is top down the best choice for true color photos, as well as images with shadows or gradations.

Fortunately, SiteBuilder takes much of this decision making process off your hands. If you use any other graphics format besides GIF, SiteBuilder automatically converts the image to JPG format for you. As a result, you can even insert BMP and TIFF images into your Web site. SiteBuilder handles all the details of conversion.

## Sizing your images appropriately

Choosing the right graphics format is only half the battle. You also need to consider the file size of the graphic you wish to use. There's no hard-and-fast rule concerning the maximum file size, but you should generally aim to keep each graphic as small as possible. You should work to keep each Web page — both the text and the graphics on the page — under 80K or less. Therefore, if you know that you want to use several graphics on a single page, you need to make sure that your graphics/text combination still fits within that allowance.

If you find your images "weighing down" your Web page — which could mean longer download times for your Web visitors — try experimenting on the best graphic format to use. (See the "Choosing the best Web graphic types" section, earlier in this chapter.) In addition, you can often crop your pictures in a graphics program to eliminate unneeded parts of the picture to save download time.

If you plan on using pictures from a digital camera, keep in mind that most digital cameras save high-resolution pictures that are far too big for Web use — both in terms of screen size (width and height dimensions) and "weight" (amount of disk space). Therefore, never slap a digital photo on your Web site and publish it without shrinking it first.

In terms of screen size, make sure the picture is 640 x 480 pixels or smaller in screen resolution. For the photo's "weight," most digital cameras use the JPG format to store digital photos in an uncompressed state. Therefore, if you have graphics software or a tool such as Microsoft Office Picture Manager, you can compress the files before putting them on your Web site. You can usually shrink a JPG as much as 40 percent and maintain essentially the same image quality as before. And you can often shrink a file as much as 60 to 80 percent and still have acceptable results.

# Adding a Picture to a Page

If a picture says a thousand words, then you can save a lot of real estate on your Web page with a well-chosen image. This section explores how to add a picture to your page.

## Using SiteBuilder clip art

SiteBuilder comes with a variety of stock clip art that you can incorporate into your Web site.

SiteBuilder divided its clip art into several categories, including

- **Backgrounds:** These images serve well as background images. See the "Turning a Picture into a Background Image" section, later in the chapter, for more on background images.

- **Bars:** Separate certain parts of your Web page with vertical or horizontal lines.

- **Bullets:** Use these in image bulleted lists, which I discuss in Chapter 6.

- **Buttons:** Button clip art enables you to use image buttons on your forms. See Chapter 10 for instructions on using these images.

- **Frames:** Use the Frames images as images that frame your Web page content.

- **Images:** The Images group contains a variety of different types of images: *frame images* (sidebars used in conjunction with navigation bars; see Chapter 9) on the left side of your page and other image varieties.

- **Photos:** The Photos group contains a variety of different photos that you can add to your Web site.

Follow these steps to add a clip art image to your Web page:

1. **With your Web page open, click the Insert Image button on the toolbar.**

   The Choose an Image dialog box is displayed.

2. **Click the Clip Art radio button in the Select From pane.**

   The Choose an Image dialog box is updated, as shown in Figure 7-1.

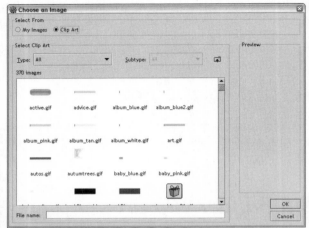

**Figure 7-1:**
Choosing
clip art for
your Web
page.

3. **Navigate to the desired clip art image using the Type and Subtype drop-down menus in the Select Clip Art pane.**

4. **Click OK.**

   The image is added to the center of your open Web page, as shown in Figure 7-2.

   You can also click and drag the image from the Site Contents pane and drop it anywhere on your Web page.

5. **Click and drag the image to move it anywhere on the page.**

Keep in mind that not all of the clip art images SiteBuilder supplies are specific to your template design. Use care to ensure you don't clash or mix and match visual designs as you use them.

## Using your own images

While the SiteBuilder clip art can be useful for many purposes, you'll very likely want to add your own images to your Web site. Perhaps you want to add your company logo as the header of each page. Maybe you created a picture in an image software package to be the highlight of your home page. Or perhaps you took unforgettable digital photos at your sister-in-law's aunt's nephew's brother-in-law's wedding.

**Figure 7-2:**
Adding the "man at the afternoon BBQ" clip art, sure to add flair and sophistication to any Web site.

Whatever image your sights are set on, here's how you add it to your Web page:

1. **With your Web page open, click the Insert an Image button on the toolbar.**

   You can also choose Insert⇨Picture from the main menu.

   The Insert dialog box displays, as shown in Figure 7-3.

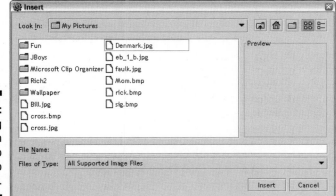

**Figure 7-3:**
Inserting your own picture into your Web page.

2. **Navigate to the image you want to add, select it, and then click the Insert button.**

   The image is added to the center of your open Web page.

3. **Click and drag the image to move it anywhere on the page.**

   SiteBuilder adds the picture to your Web page and also copies the picture file to the Images folder of your Web site. You can access the copied file by expanding the images folder in the Site Contents pane.

You can also drag an image from your Windows Explorer window and drop it on top of your Web page in SiteBuilder. This technique is the quickest way to add an image to your Web site.

## Moving a Picture Around the Page

Moving a picture is just like moving any object on a page. You can do it by following these steps:

1. **Click the picture you want to move, keeping your mouse button down.**

   A flashing blue border appears around the selected picture.

2. **Drag the image to the desired new location.**

3. **Release the mouse button.**

Or, if you want pixel-level precision when you move the image, you have two alternatives:

- Press your arrow keys to move the selected picture one pixel at a time.

- Double-click the picture to display the Picture Properties dialog box and then click the Coordinates tab. (See Figure 7-4.) Enter new x, y coordinates in the text boxes, and click OK.

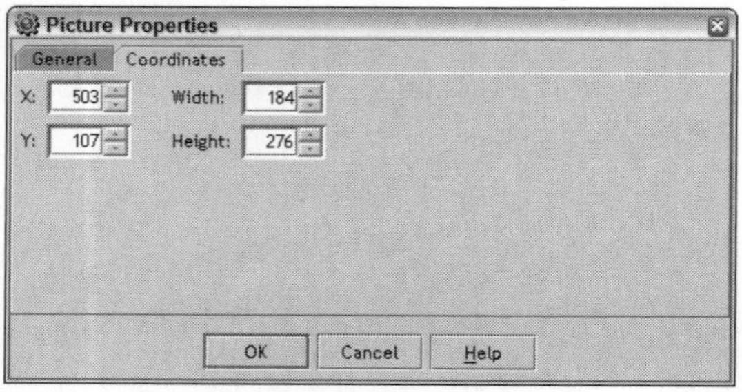

**Figure 7-4:**
And you thought you could forget that x, y coordinates stuff when you left high school math.

Picture Properties

General | Coordinates

X: 503    Width: 184

Y: 107    Height: 276

OK    Cancel    Help

# Changing the Properties of Your Picture

Each picture on your page has certain properties — filename, alt text, and target window, for example — associated with it. You can access and modify these properties through the Picture Properties dialog box, as shown in Figure 7-5.

You can access the dialog box in one of three ways:

- ✔ Double-click any image on your page.
- ✔ Select the picture and press the Enter key.
- ✔ Right-click the picture and choose Properties from the contextual menu that appears.

The next sections describe the various functions you can perform using the Picture Properties dialog box, including changing the image, supplying Alt Text, and setting up a mouse-over effect. You can also set up Web links, resize the picture, and change its x, y coordinates (which I describe later in the chapter).

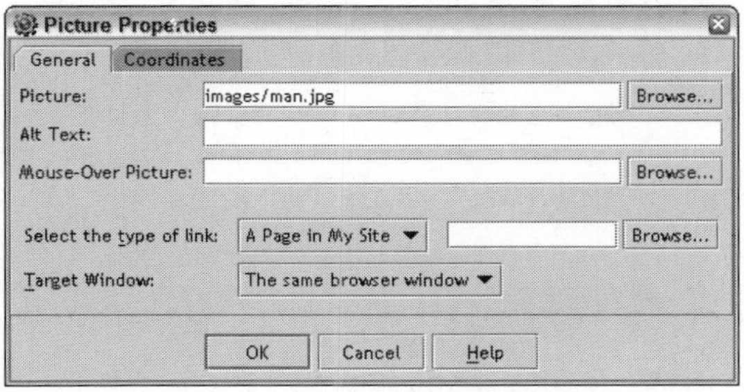

**Figure 7-5:**
Tweaking
the
properties
of your
image.

## Changing the image

The Picture text box in the Picture Properties dialog box shows the filename of the selected image. If you'd like to replace the current picture with another, click the Browse button, select another image, and click OK.

## Assigning Alt Text

While visitors to your site will almost always be able to view the images on your Web site, you need to be prepared to handle the rare occasions in which images do not display properly. For example, suppose a dialup visitor to your site has disabled images in her Web browser.

# Alt Text mistakes

People make two common mistakes when using Alt Text:

✔ **Ignoring Alt Text.** Some people are confused about what Alt Text is or why it is needed, so they simply ignore it. For the vast majority of visitors, ignoring Alt Text is fine. But when you have an occasional person who comes to your site but can't handle pictures, then you make it difficult for him or her to navigate or understand your Web site.

✔ **Describing your images.** Other people use Alt Text to simply describe the image rather than provide a text-based substitute. For example, suppose you have a graphic that displays your recommended product for the week. If you simply describe the image, you might say `Photo of Recommendation`, which would be of no help to the text-only visitor. However, if you instead use `Our Weekly Recommendation: The Sunlight Squiggly, by Maple Stirdale`, then you can be sure you are communicating to all visitors of your site rather than most of them.

The Alt Text (short for *alternate text*) property allows you to use words to express the same idea your picture does visually. Add a text-based alternative for your image in this text box.

Even more important, Alt Text is used quite extensively by the visually impaired, who may have systems configured to "read" this text to them.

## Specifying a mouse-over image

A mouse-over is the most common visual effect on the Web and, if done effectively and for the right purposes, can enhance the overall experience of your Web site. A *mouse-over* involves an image changing to another image when the mouse pointer moves over it. This technique is usually achieved by using JavaScript to do the image swapping process.

You can define a mouse-over image in the Picture Properties dialog box by entering the filename in the Mouse-Over Picture text box. SiteBuilder adds the appropriate image swapping code behind the scenes for you.

Figures 7-6 and 7-7 demonstrate the changes that occur when a visitor hovers the mouse over the picture.

If you define a mouse-over image, make sure it is the same dimensions as the original image to ensure a smooth transition.

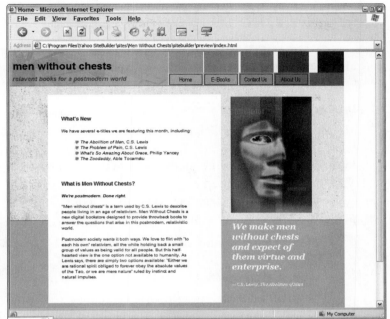

**Figure 7-6:**
Normal
state of the
mouse-over
image.

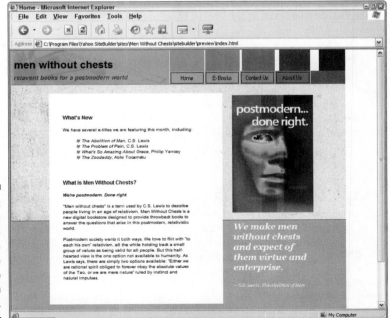

**Figure 7-7:**
Mousing
over the
image
causes the
browser to
switch
images.

# Assigning a Link to Your Picture

While Chapter 6 discusses how to add text-based links to your Web page, you may also want to use a picture as the jumping-off point to another Web page, an e-mail address, or other document. To do so, follow these steps:

1. **Double-click the image you want to link.**

   The Picture Properties dialog box makes an appearance. (Refer to Figure 7-5.)

2. **In the Select the Type of Link drop-down menu, choose the desired type of link.**

   For details on each of these link types, see Chapter 6.

3. **Provide the link specifics for the type of link you're creating:**

   - **Another page in your site:** Click the Browse button and select the appropriate file.

   - **Another Web site:** Enter the URL in the space provided.

   - **An e-mail address:** Enter the e-mail address.

   - **A file in your site — a Word or PDF file, for example:** Click the Browse button and select the desired file.

4. **Choose the desired destination from the Target Window drop-down menu.**

   As Chapter 6 discusses, except for links to other Web sites, you'll usually want to keep the link in the same browser window.

5. **Click OK.**

You can also assign a link to your image by right-clicking an image and choosing Link To from the contextual menu that appears (or by pressing Ctrl+L). The Link dialog box that displays is nearly identical to the text Link dialog box.

# Sizing Up a Picture

After you have the picture on your Web page, SiteBuilder allows you to tweak, fiddle, tug, yank, and twist the image so that it fits into the exact space you have available for it.

Because you can resize images inside of SiteBuilder, you don't have to get the dimensions perfectly right inside your graphics program before adding it to your Web site. As long as you use a format other than GIF, SiteBuilder automatically creates a new JPG copy of your image sized according to the sizing dimensions you specify. Therefore, if you place a large digital photo image on your Web page and resize it to a smaller size that fits on the page, SiteBuilder makes a smaller copy of the larger original for you.

However, you should keep in mind that when you resize an image (primarily enlarge), you are invariably going to deteriorate the quality to some extent. (See the "Understanding bitmap and vector graphics" sidebar, earlier in this chapter, for all the details.) If the size change is proportionally small to the overall size, then the quality loss very well may be invisible to the human eye, but the greater the change, the greater the loss in quality.

## Resizing a picture

Okay, if you've considered all the caveats about resizing that I outline in the preceding section, and you *still* want to do it, here's how you can do it with your mouse:

1. **Click to select the picture you want to resize.**

   A flashing blue border appears around the selected image.

2. **Click one of the blue handles on the outside of the picture, and keep your mouse button down.**

   - To expand or shrink the width, click the left or right handle.

   - To expand or shrink the height, click the top or bottom handle.

   - To expand or shrink both the height and width at the same time, click a corner handle.

   To ensure that your picture width and height stay in proportion to each other, be sure to only resize using the corner handles.

3. **Drag the mouse to the appropriate size.**

4. **Release the mouse button.**

You can also resize to a precise pixel size by modifying its Width and Height properties. Here's how:

1. **Double-click the picture to display the Picture Properties dialog box and then click the Coordinates tab. (Refer to Figure 7-4.)**

2. **Edit the Width and Height values and then click OK.**

## Returning a picture to its original size

I can be dangerous with resizing. I get a brilliant idea as to how good a picture will look on a different part of the page, and so I resize the image to fit into this new position. But something's not quite right, so I tweak some more. When that idea doesn't pan out, I try a different idea, resizing more and more and more. But before long, I realize I've so screwed up the dimensions of the image that I don't know what it should look like or what its original size even was.

If you get into a spot like I find myself in frequently, SiteBuilder has just the tool for you and me. You can reset the picture to its original size with just a couple of steps:

1. **Right-click the picture to reset.**

2. **Choose the Original Size item from the contextual menu that appears.**

   SiteBuilder restores your original width and height values.

# Creating a Thumbnail Picture

SiteBuilder enables you to easily create thumbnail pictures on your Web site. A *thumbnail* is a small image that is linked to a larger version of the same image. You can see this technique being used on many real estate sites, in which you click a small thumbnail image of a house to see the normal-size picture. But it also comes in handy for product photos, photo albums, and so on.

The major benefit of using thumbnails is that you can pack a lot of pictures onto a single page that might otherwise spread out over several pages. Yet when a visitor needs to see the details of one or more of those images, they can do so with a single click. Neat, huh?

To create a thumbnail

1. **Right-click the picture you want to transform into a thumbnail.**

2. **Choose the Thumbnail submenu from the contextual menu that appears and then choose the size of the thumbnail picture: Very Small, Small, Medium, Large, or Very Large.**

   SiteBuilder resizes the picture to the desired size and adds a link to the full-size image of the original.

   When a visitor clicks the thumbnail image, the image is shown in its original size inside of a blank browser window, as shown in Figure 7-8.

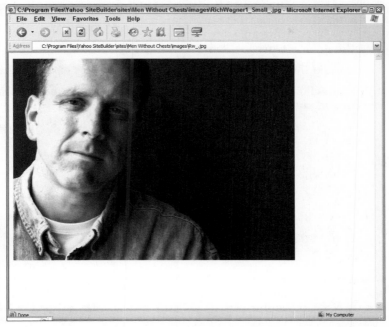

**Figure 7-8:**
Viewing the
destination
of a
thumbnail.

# Turning a Picture into a Background Image

A *background image* is one that displays behind everything else on your Web page. You can use background images to add a finishing touch to your overall Web site design.

Keep in mind these considerations when using background images:

- **Tiling effect:** No matter the size, the background image is always tiled behind the page to fill up the entire contents of the browser window. So if you use a background that shows up once when viewed on a 800 x 600 screen, the tiling effect causes the background to show up multiple times for a visitor with a high-resolution screen, such as 1600 x 1280.

- **Readability:** When you select a background image, make sure that it doesn't become a distraction for visitors and doesn't make the text that displays on top of the image hard to read.

Follow these steps to add a background picture to a Web page open in SiteBuilder:

1. **Have the picture available inside of SiteBuilder.**

   See the "Adding a Picture to a Page" section, earlier in the chapter.

2. **Right-click the image, and choose Set as Background from the contextual menu that appears.**

   If you're working with an image inside of the Site Contents pane, you don't need to add it to page first. You can right-click the item right within the pane.

   Two things happen after this step:

   • Your image appears as the background on your page.

   • A Background placeholder is shown in the Page Effects pane.

   Figure 7-9 shows the results in SiteBuilder.

Background image

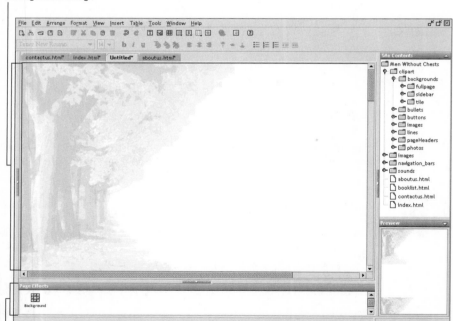

**Figure 7-9:**
Adding a background image to your site.

Page Effects pane

After you add the background picture to your Web page, you can't select it inside of the page, as you can with other pictures or other page elements. Instead, you use the Page Effects pane for modifying or deleting the background.

To modify a background picture

1. **Double-click the Background placeholder in the Page Effects pane.**

   The Choose a Background dialog box appears, as shown in Figure 7-10.

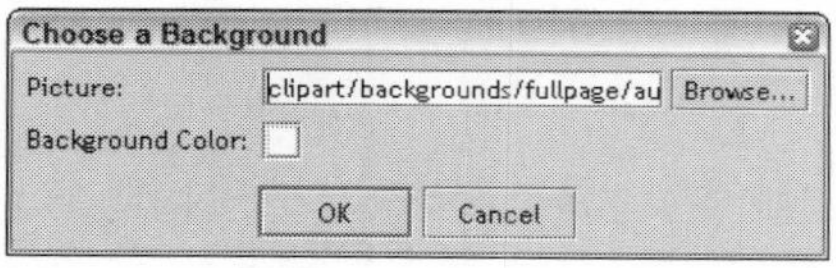

**Figure 7-10:**
Behind-the-scenes work on your Web page.

2. **Click the Browse button and select the new background image you want to use, and then click OK.**

To delete a background picture

1. **Select the Background placeholder in the Page Effects pane.**
2. **Press the Delete key.**

   Your background image is removed, quicker than you can say "Green Goblin."

# Chapter 8

# Off to the Woodshop: Building Tables

*T*echnology progress is often overrated, but sometimes innovation just makes life a heck of a lot easier. Before visual tools such as SiteBuilder and other HTML innovations came along, table creation was at the very heart of Web page design; all the page layout had to be done within the invisible grids of tables. Therefore, in order to arrange text, images, and other page elements beside and around each other, you had to develop an elaborate, messy, and wickedly complicated system of tables within tables within tables. Yucksville!

Using SiteBuilder, you are indeed fortunate: You have no need to use tables simply for arranging page elements beside each other, because you can do that far easier by simply moving page elements around your page with your mouse. Instead, you're now free to use tables for what they were designed for — stuff such as displaying tabular, spreadsheet-like information, lists, or side-by-side labels and text boxes in a data entry form. In this chapter, you explore how to work with tables in SiteBuilder.

# Inserting a Table on a Page

SiteBuilder provides two separate ways of adding a table to your page. You can add a quick table using the toolbar or set up a table more precisely using the menu. I discuss both approaches in this section.

# The quick-and-easy approach: Using the toolbar

The quickest and easiest way to create a table in SiteBuilder is by using the toolbar button. Using it, you can add a basic table to your page without worrying about formatting the settings of the table up front.

If you've used Microsoft Word's Insert Table toolbar button to add a table, SiteBuilder follows a similar process.

To add a table using the toolbar, follow these steps:

1. **Click the Insert Table button on the toolbar.**

   A table grid drops down from the toolbar, as shown in Figure 8-1.

2. **Specify the number of rows and columns of the table by sliding your mouse to the cell that will serve as the bottom-right cell of your table.**

   As you move your mouse to a new cell, SiteBuilder updates the table dimensions (specified as number of columns x number of rows — 3x5, for example) inside of the active cell.

3. **When you have selected the desired dimensions of the table, click the active cell.**

   The new table is added to the center of your Web page (see Figure 8-2).

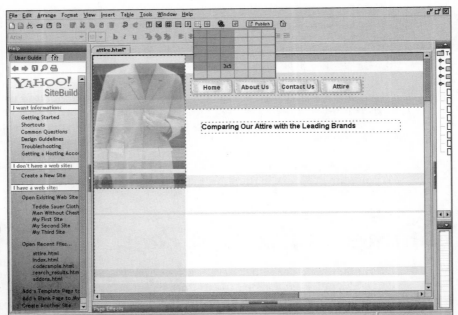

**Figure 8-1:**
Adding a
quick table
to your
page.

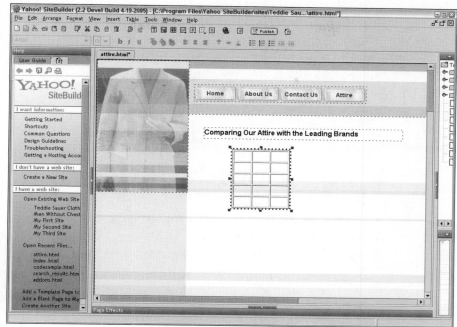

**Figure 8-2:**
Your new
table, made
to order.

Your table is now ready to go.

You'll want to stretch the table to the appropriate width and height before adding content. You can resize the table just as you would any other page element (see Chapter 3 for resizing).

## The detail-oriented approach: Using the Create New Table dialog box

You can also set up a table more precisely by using the Create New Table dialog box. While you specify more formatting property settings up front, you can always change them later. (See the "Adjusting the Table Formatting Properties" section, later in the chapter.)

Add a table using the Create New Table dialog box with these steps:

**1. Choose Table⇨Insert Table from the main menu.**

Or, if you have a real love for the Insert menu, choose Insert⇨Table. This command takes you to the same place.

The Create New Table dialog box makes an appearance, as shown in Figure 8-3.

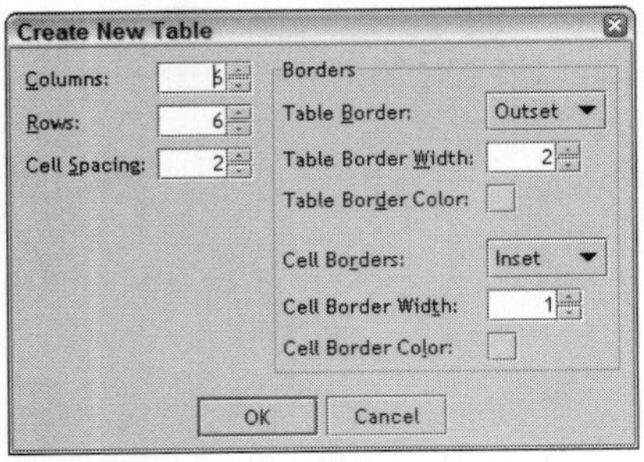

**Create New Table**

| | | | Borders | |
|---|---|---|---|---|
| Columns: | 5 | | | |
| Rows: | 6 | | Table Border: | Outset |
| Cell Spacing: | 2 | | Table Border Width: | 2 |
| | | | Table Border Color: | |
| | | | Cell Borders: | Inset |
| | | | Cell Border Width: | 1 |
| | | | Cell Border Color: | |

OK    Cancel

**Figure 8-3:**
Creating a
table more
precisely.

2. **Specify the dimensions of the table grid by adjusting the Columns and Rows boxes.**

3. **Specify the amount of spacing (in pixels) that you want to separate each cell.**

4. **Adjust the table and cell border style, width, and color.**

   Tinker with the border properties to get the table looking just right. So start with what you think works; you can always tweak it later.

5. **Click OK.**

   The table is added to the center of your page. Resize your table to the approximate size of your content.

# Filling Your Table with Content

You can add text to a table simply by double-clicking a cell. A text cursor shows up inside of the cell, ready, willing, and able to help you type some text. Follow the same procedures I discuss in Chapter 6 for working with text.

You don't need to add a text element to a table cell in order to enter text.

While text is the most common type of content that you can add to a table, you can also insert other page element types in a cell. To do so, double-click a cell and then add the desired element as you normally would on the page itself. For most elements, the cell dimensions are automatically expanded to fit the contents of the element. However, for image elements, the image shrinks to fit the size of the existing dimensions of the cell.

One of the great things about the Design pane is its drag-and-drop-capability. You can drag any element on a page you're working on and drop it into a table cell.

Because you can freely position and arrange different page elements inside of a SiteBuilder page, you normally don't need to insert nontextual page elements inside a table cell. For example, if you want an image to be next to a paragraph of text, simply arranging a text element and an image element side by side is the easier way to go, rather than using the table for alignment.

# Adjusting the Table Formatting Properties

You can adjust the formatting properties of a table to get the borders and spacing looking exactly as you want them. To do so, follow these steps:

1. **Click a table with your mouse to select it.**

2. **Position your mouse cursor over the table border (not inside a cell), right-click, and then choose Properties from the contextual menu that appears.**

   The Table Properties dialog box displays, as shown in Figure 8-4.

3. **Adjust the Spacing and Border properties as desired.**

4. **Click OK.**

   Your table updates to reflect your changes.

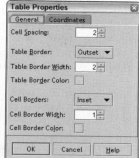

**Figure 8-4:** Tweaking the formatting of your table.

When adjusting the properties of an individual cell (such as background color or justification), you can treat the cell just like a text element. See Chapter 6 for modifying the properties of text elements.

Experiment with borderless tables (with invisible table and cell borders), distinguishing as needed between rows and columns with background color. You'll notice that most of the top sites on the Web never use standard table borders because they look unprofessional.

# Selecting Table Cells

You can select a single cell simply by clicking it. However, you can select multiple cells inside your table in two different ways:

- ✔ Click a single cell and then drag your mouse into each of the other cells you want to select.
- ✔ Click a single cell and then press the Ctrl key while you click each additional cell you want to select.

If you're used to working with tables in Microsoft Word, here's one difference between Word and SiteBuilder: You can't select an entire row or column by clicking its edge. Instead, to select an entire row or column, you need to click your mouse in a cell and then drag it across all the other cells in the row or column to select them.

# Tweaking the Table

Chances are that no matter how you initially configure the dimensions of your table, you'll probably need to tweak it once you start adding content. Perhaps you need to add more rows. Maybe a column needs adjusting. Or perhaps you want to merge two cells. It's always something. Not to worry, though. This section shows you how to adjust the table to fit your needs.

## Inserting a new row

You can insert a new row into a table either at the bottom of the table or above the currently selected row. You can do so by doing the following steps.

To append a row to the bottom of the table

1. **Click any table border to select the entire table.**

   Make sure you don't click in a cell (see Figure 8-5).

2. **Right-click and then choose Table⇨Insert Table Row from the contextual menu that appears.**

   A new row is added to the bottom of the table, as shown in Figure 8-6.

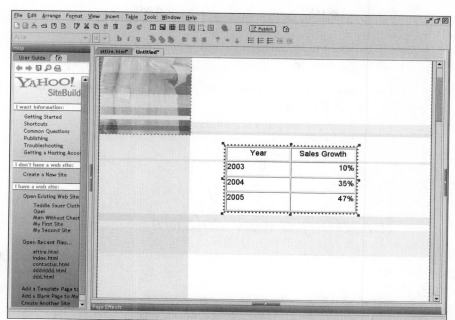

**Figure 8-5:**
Selecting
the table.

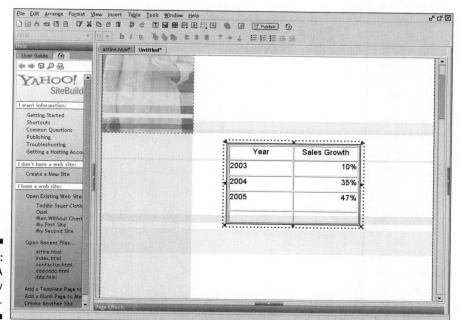

**Figure 8-6:**
Presto! A
new row
appears.

To add a new row above the currently selected row

1. **Click in a cell in the row you want to follow the new row.**

   Figure 8-7 shows a cell being selected for this process.

2. **Right-click and choose Table⇨Insert Table Row from the contextual menu that appears.**

   A new row is added above the row you're working on, as shown in Figure 8-8.

   If you have multiple rows selected, the new row is inserted above the topmost selected row.

## Inserting a new column

You can add new columns either at the end of your table or before the currently selected column.

To append a column to the right of the table

1. **Click any table border to select the entire table.**

   Make sure you don't click in a cell.

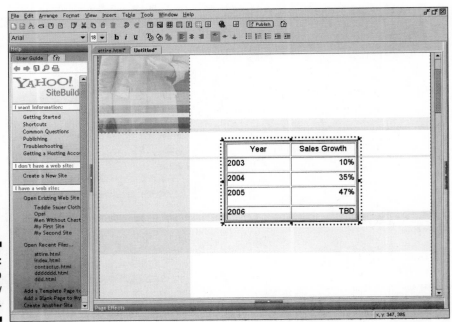

**Figure 8-7:**
Preparing to
add a new
row.

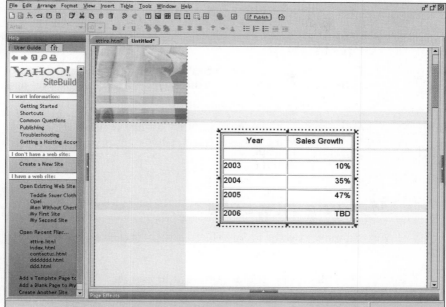

**Figure 8-8:**
A new row
is added
above the
previously
selected
one.

2. **Right-click and choose Table⇨Insert Table Column from the contextual menu that appears.**

   A new column is added to the right of the table.

To add a new column to the left of the currently selected row

1. **Click in a cell in the column you want to come after the new column.**

2. **Right-click and choose Table⇨Insert Table Column from the contextual menu that appears.**

   A new column is added before the column you're working on.

   If you have multiple columns selected, the new column comes to the left of the leftmost selected column.

## Deleting a row or column

If you've warned a row or column multiple times, and it's still acting up, you have only one choice left as a responsible Web site builder: Delete it.

To delete a column or row

1. **Click a cell in the column or row you want to remove from the digital face of the earth.**

2. **Right-click and choose either Table⊏>Delete Table Column or Table⊏>Delete Table Row from the contextual menu that appears.**

3. **Click Yes to confirm the deletion.**

   You won't see that row or column acting up again. However, if you feel bad and have a change of heart, you can always undo your action and restore the table piece.

## Merging two cells

You can merge two or more cells to form a single cell inside your table. To do so, follow these steps:

1. **Click the first cell that you want to merge.**

2. **Drag your mouse across the remaining cells to include in the merger.**

   Figure 8-9 shows two cells selected for merging.

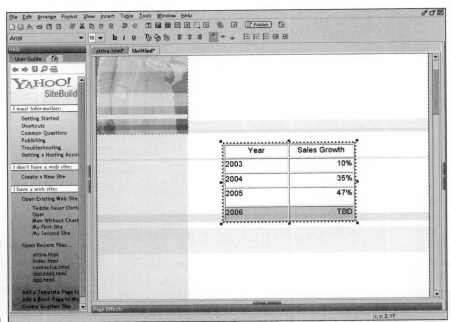

**Figure 8-9:** Selecting cells for a merger.

3. **Right-click and choose Table⇨Merge Cells from the contextual menu that appears.**

   The cells are now unified, solidified, and otherwise morphified into one (see Figure 8-10).

Any text in the cells now display inside of separate text elements. You need to combine them yourself by cutting the text from one text element and pasting it into the next.

## Splitting a cell

If you want to split a cell in your table, you don't need to go to a biochemistry lab at your local university. Instead, simply follow these steps:

1. **Click the cell(s) you want to split.**

2. **Right-click and choose Table⇨Split Table Cells from the contextual menu that appears.**

   The Split Table Cells dialog box appears, as shown in Figure 8-11.

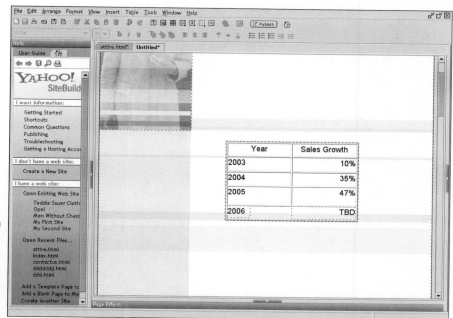

**Figure 8-10:** The two cells are now one big happy cell.

**Figure 8-11:**
It's gonna
be splitsville
for this
unlucky cell.

3. **Enter the number of Columns and Rows that you want to split the cell(s) into.**

   If you have multiple cells selected, each individual cell is split according to these settings.

4. **Click OK.**

   The table cell is split based on your settings.

# Chapter 9

# Making Columbus and Magellan Jealous: Adding Navigation Instantly

*T*he great explorers in history — such as Columbus and Magellan — had it rough. Back in the 1400s, they risked life and limb as they spent months, even years, navigating the globe. Yet had they been born 500 years later, they could have traversed the same distance in mere hours, riding in a climate-controlled airplane, even enjoying a snack pack of peanuts to boot.

In the same way, creating a stylish graphical navigation bar for a Web site used to be a task that took design skills and a lot of hard work. What's more, when the Web site layout changed — pages added or taken away — the Web site builder was forced to redo the whole navigation bar to account for the modifications. However, as you use SiteBuilder, you can think of yourself as being among the "jet set" crowd — hopping on board SiteBuilder and letting it do the hard work for you, designing and maintaining your navigation bar. Heck, in the time saved, you can even munch on a snack pack of peanuts!

In this chapter, you explore how site navigation works using SiteBuilder. Before diving into SiteBuilder itself, however, you begin by looking at some of the tricks of the trade on how you should design a navigation scheme for your Web site. After you lay that foundation, you look at how to add and modify navigation bars to your own piece of Internet real estate.

# Navigating Your Web Site

You can divide most books in your local bookstore or library into two categories — "read-through" books and "look up" reference books. A read-through book is anything that you read cover to cover, whether it is *Green Eggs and Ham,* a John Grisham novel, or a biography of Dwight Eisenhower. A reference book, on the other hand, is a work that you browse but often don't read from start to finish; usually, you use the index, table of contents, page header, or some other navigation aid to quickly look up a tidbit of information.

Web sites are much like reference books. A visitor comes to your site, usually for a specific purpose, and may browse for a few pages. But no one is going to read your whole site in a logical, sequential order. This "click in, browse around" nature of the Web means that your Web site needs a navigation aid, much like the ones used by that dictionary or encyclopedia sitting on your bookshelf. A visitor coming to your site should be able to quickly scan your home page, identify where to go and how to get there, and then "click in, browse around."

The graphical navigation bar has become the Web-standard way of handling the "click in, browse around" process. If you were to add this navigation scheme to your Web site manually, you would assemble button graphics you want to use, insert them into your pages, and then add links to them to create a navigation bar. However, by taking this route, not only do you have to create or obtain the graphics yourself, but you also are forced to update the graphics across each page of your site every time your Web site structure changes.

Fortunately, as I mention at the start of the chapter, SiteBuilder comes equipped with a smart navigation bar that does most of this work for you. You can easily create and drop a SiteBuilder navigation bar onto your pages — which means you can instantly take advantage of the following three major benefits:

- ✔ Twenty-eight built-in graphical button styles, so you don't have to do the design work yourself, including buttons that automatically provide a rollover or mouse-over effect. (A *rollover* is a Web technique in which the image changes its look when the mouse hovers on top of it.).

✔ A navigation bar style that is coordinated with the overall look of the template.

✔ Easily update navigation bars at any time as your site needs change. What's more, SiteBuilder manages the navigation bar updates across your entire Web site. As a result, you can make the change in one place, and SiteBuilder updates all instances of the navigation bar.

# Effective Navigation Bar Design

As you add navigation to your Web site, make sure you keep in mind these three design considerations: consistency, placement, and labeling, which I talk about in the following sections. A well-thought-out navigation bar makes your Web site much easier to navigate and helps ensure that visitors can easily find the information they're looking for.

## Consistency

More than anything else, your navigation should be consistent throughout your site. If you place a horizontal navigation bar on the top of your home page, you should stick with top-horizontal orientation throughout your site, even if you are using multiple navigation bars for different parts of your site. Otherwise, people can become confused and disoriented, and may simply leave.

## Navigation bar placement

"Western" people process information in a left-to-right, top-to-bottom manner. Given that, your navigation bar should be at the top and oriented horizontally or else on the left side and oriented vertically. A secondary text-only navigation bar at the bottom of the page is an optional feature you may want to add. (See the "Creating a text-based navigation bar" section, later in the chapter.)

## Crystal-clear labeling

When naming your labels on your navigation bar, be as clear and lucid as possible. For most sites, navigation bar labeling is no place to be creative, obtuse, and edgy. For example, if Gilligan Sportswear, Inc., has a page on its site that provides background information on the company, a good label is "About Us" or "About Gilligan Sportswear." Above all, avoid getting cute and coming up with your own vernacular and labeling it something like "Gilligan's Scoop" or "The Locker Room." Visitors will be clueless as to what the link sends them to.

## Short, descriptive labeling

The graphical buttons that make up a SiteBuilder navigation bar automatically expand in width based on the text length that you enter for the labels. While you have that flexibility, aim not to use it; stretched images never look as crisp as their original counterparts. Try to keep the labels as short as possible while still being descriptive. Also, while the labels inevitably have some variance in text length, work to keep them as close in length to one another as possible. Having their length range wildly makes for a messy looking navigation bar.

Figures 9-1 and 9-2 contrast the do's and don'ts of navigation bar design.

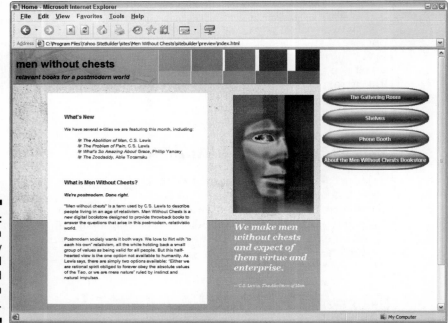

**Figure 9-1:**
The Don't: a poorly labeled and misplaced navigation bar.

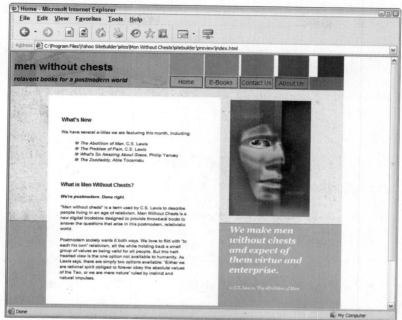

**Figure 9-2:**
The Do: a
well-
designed
navigation
bar.

# Adding a Basic Navigation Bar to Your Web Site

After you understand the basic tricks of effective navigation bars, you should be ready to add your own bar to your Web site in one of two ways:

- ✔ As part of the initial site creation process
- ✔ As you design your pages

## Adding a navigation bar when you create your site

When you create a new template-based Web site using the Site Creation Wizard (accessible through File➪New Site), you have the option of letting SiteBuilder build a navigation bar for you automatically, based on the starting pages of your Web site. (Chapter 4 walks you through the steps of creating a new site.) You don't need to do anything more. The navigation bar is waiting for you on each of your Web pages.

SiteBuilder templates use customized buttons for the navigation bar that are — luckily enough — available for you when you create a navigation bar on your own. You can find these buttons by browsing ypur way through the clipart. Just keep in mind that the buttons won't have the same name as their associated template. (Darn.)

When SiteBuilder creates a navigation bar through the Site Creation Wizard, it names the navigation bar as `navbar.nav`.

## Creating a navigation bar after your site is built

Whether you use a SiteBuilder template to create your Web site or work from a blank set of pages, you can easily add a graphical navigation bar to one or all pages of your site. If your site has at least two saved pages and if at least one of your site pages is open, then just do the following:

1. **Click the Insert Navigation Bar button on the toolbar.**

   If you already have navigation bars created for your site, they are displayed in a drop-down list under the button. The final entry is the Create Navigation Bar item.

2. **Choose Create Navigation Bar from the list.**

   The Create Navigation Bar dialog box appears, as shown in Figure 9-3.

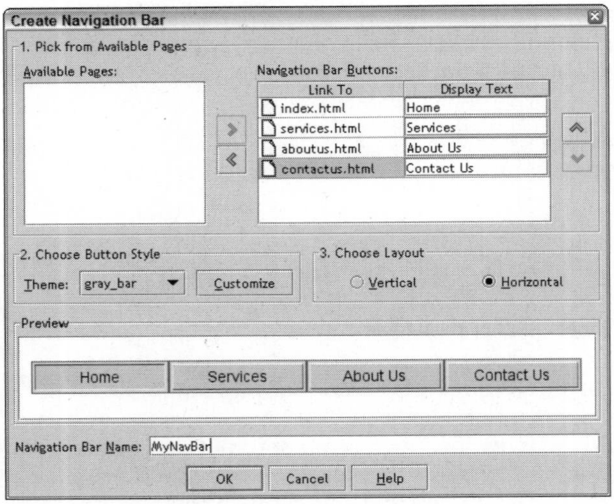

**Figure 9-3:** Laboratory for creating navigation bars.

| Create Navigation Bar |
|---|
| **1. Pick from Available Pages** |

Available Pages:

Navigation Bar Buttons:

| Link To | Display Text |
|---|---|
| index.html | Home |
| services.html | Services |
| aboutus.html | About Us |
| contactus.html | Contact Us |

**2. Choose Button Style** — Theme: gray_bar | Customize

**3. Choose Layout** — ○ Vertical  ● Horizontal

Preview

| Home | Services | About Us | Contact Us |

Navigation Bar Name: MyNavBar

OK  Cancel  Help

3. **In the Available Pages pane, select a page to include in the navigation bar and then click the right-arrow button next to the pane.**

   As you click the arrow button, the page moves over to the Navigation Bar Buttons list.

   SiteBuilder displays only Web pages that you have saved before. Therefore, if you have an untitled page that you added to your site but have not yet saved it, SiteBuilder doesn't display this file in the dialog box.

4. **Continue selecting and clicking until you place all the pages you want included as part of your navigation scheme in the Navigation Bar Buttons list.**

5. **For each page in your navigation bar, click in the Display Text field beside the page and enter the text that you wish to appear on the button.**

   See the "Effective Navigation Bar Design" section, earlier in the chapter, for tips on labeling your buttons.

6. **Set the order of the buttons on the navigation bar by selecting a page from the Navigation Bar Buttons list and clicking the up or down arrows to the right of the box.**

   The page moves up or down the navigation bar order one space each time you click.

7. **Select the desired style of the button from the Theme drop-down menu.**

   You can choose among approximately 30 built-in navigation bar styles. As you scroll through the list, the Preview area updates automatically, showing what the finished navigation bar will look like.

   If you'd like to create a customized button style different from the built-in styles, see the "Creating Customized Navigation Bars" section, later in this chapter.

8. **Choose the orientation (Vertical or Horizontal) of the navigation bar in the Choose Layout area.**

9. **Enter a descriptive name in the Navigation Bar Name text box.**

   This text doesn't appear on your Web site. It's only for use within SiteBuilder.

10. **Click OK.**

    The Add New Navigation Bar appears, as shown in Figure 9-4.

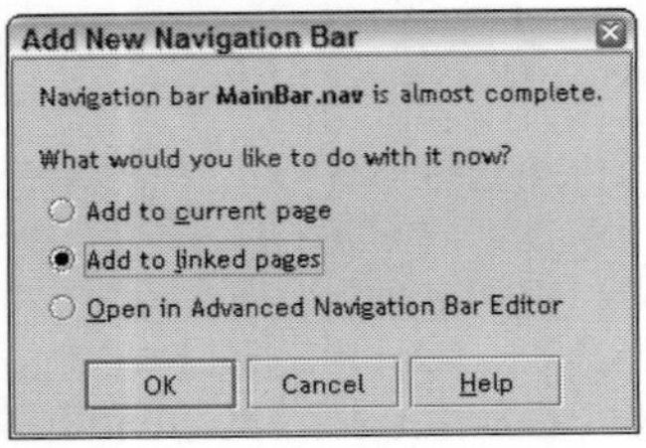

**Figure 9-4:**
Deciding
where to
add your
navigation
bar.

> **Add New Navigation Bar**
>
> Navigation bar **MainBar.nav** is almost complete.
>
> What would you like to do with it now?
>
> ○ Add to current page
> ● Add to linked pages
> ○ Open in Advanced Navigation Bar Editor
>
> OK    Cancel    Help

11. **Determine where to put the navigation bar: on just the current page or on all pages that are linked in the bar.**

    You can also open the navigation bar in the Advanced Navigation Bar Editor for more work — such as tweaking individual buttons to adjusting vertical and horizontal alignment of the label text. However, if you do so, you can't use the basic navigation bar editor later.

12. **Click OK.**

    As Figure 9-5 shows, SiteBuilder adds your newly created navigation bar to the current page or all linked pages. You can move this around on your page to the desired location (usually the top or left of your page).

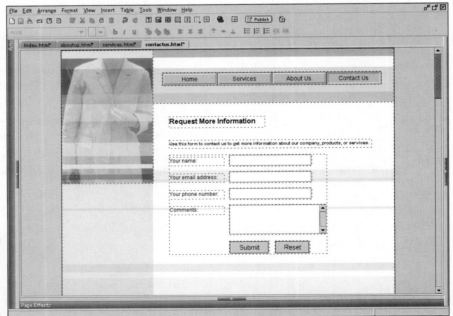

**Figure 9-5:**
Viewing the
finished
product.

# *Use It Again, Sam: Inserting Your Navigation Bar into Another Page*

After you create a navigation bar, SiteBuilder adds it to your site as an available resource. Having the navigation bar available as a resource comes in handy when you add a new page to your Web site. You can add a new instance of the navigation bar to this new pages by following these steps:

1. **Click the Insert Navigation Bar button on the toolbar.**

   A drop-down menu appears, displaying a list of existing navigation bars available for your site.

2. **Choose the navigation bar you want to insert from the list.**

   SiteBuilder adds the navigation bar to the top left-hand corner of your page.

3. **Click and drag to reposition the navigation bar in the desired location.**

# *Standardizing the Location of Your Navigation Bar*

Arguably the most important quality of any navigation scheme is consistency. Therefore, if you are adding a navigation bar to multiple pages of your site, you want to make sure that the navigation bar appears in the same location across all the pages. Even if the navigation bar is only a few pixels off, your Web site can look sloppy when a visitor ends up moving from page to page.

With that it mind, do the following to set the location of all instances of your navigation bar:

1. **In your current page, precisely position the navigation bar in the location that you want it to appear across your Web site.**

2. **Right-click the navigation bar, and select Set Location from the contextual menu that appears.**

   SiteBuilder asks you to confirm your action.

3. **Click Yes to continue.**

   SiteBuilder makes the needed updates to your site and then notifies you when the updates are done.

4. **Inspect each page of your site to ensure that the navigation bar fits correctly on the page and doesn't overlap any other page elements.**

   Make any tweaks as necessary to any overlapping page elements, but don't move the navigation bar itself.

# Tweaking Your Navigation Bar

After you create a navigation bar for your site, your needs may likely change over time, requiring you to adjust your navigation bar. Maybe you added a new page to your site and want to add it to your navigation bar. Perhaps you decide to change the label text. Or maybe you just want to tweak the look of the buttons. Regardless of what you wish to change, you can do so through the Edit Navigation Bar dialog box (see Figure 9-6), which is accessible two ways:

✔ Within your page, just double-click the navigation bar.

✔ From the Site Contents panel, expand the `navigation_bars` folder; then right-click the file for the navigation bar you're using and choose Modify from the contextual menu that appears.

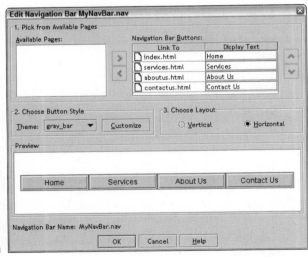

**Figure 9-6:**
Editing your navigation bar.

You can perform the following modifications using the Edit Navigation Bar dialog box:

✔ **Add a page:** Select the page from the Available Pages list and click the right-arrow button.

   A page needs to be saved before it shows up in the list.

✔ **Remove a page:** Select the page from the Navigation Bar Buttons list and click the left-arrow button.

✔ **Button order:** Select the page from the Navigation Bar Buttons·list and click the up or down arrow on the right to move the button one spot higher or lower on the list. Repeat as necessary.

✔ **Button text:** Click in the corresponding Display Text box for the page and modify as needed.

✔ **Graphical button theme:** Select one of the built-in themes from the Themes drop-down list.

✔ **Button font:** Click the Customize button. The Navigation Bar Properties dialog box appears (see Figure 9-7). Adjust the font style, size, and color as desired, and click OK.

The font that you choose for your navigation bar doesn't have the same limitations as the font for your pages. (For more on such limitations, see Chapter 6.) SiteBuilder "burns" the text into the buttons, so the text becomes part of the graphic itself. As a result, you can be assured that the font looks the same on every machine, even if the visitor's computer doesn't have the font installed.

✔ **Button and text spacing:** If you want to add more spacing between the text and the borders of the buttons or between the buttons themselves, click the Customize button. In the Navigation Bar Properties dialog box (refer to Figure 9-7), enter the number of pixels you'd like to space the text in the Left/Right Margin and Top/Bottom Margin boxes and the button spacing value in the Spacing box. Click OK.

✔ **Button orientation:** To switch between horizontal and vertical orientation, click the appropriate option in the Choose Layout box in the Edit Navigation Bar dialog box.

When you have made all the modifications to the navigation bar, then click the OK button to save your changes.

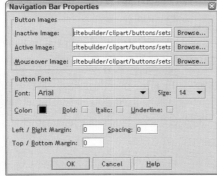

**Figure 9-7**
Even more navigation bar properties.

# Creating Customized Navigation Bars

In addition to the standard navigation bars that you can create using the built-in styles, you can add other types of navigation bars to your Web site, such as a template-based bar, text-based bar, or one that contains your own images.

## Adding a template-based navigation bar

When you use the Site Creation Wizard to create your Web site, SiteBuilder asks you whether you want to create a navigation bar at the time. If you do, a navigation bar is created using a customized style that coordinates with the template you selected. Well and fine, but suppose you do not select that option at the start and later decide to add one. To do so, simply create a new page in your site using the same template (see Chapter 3 for details). The new Web page will have a placeholder for the navigation bar that has the same template-based buttons. You can then customize the buttons as desired.

## Creating a text-based navigation bar

A common technique that many Web sites use is to provide a text-based navigation bar at the footer of each Web page. This feature enables people who scroll all the way to the bottom of your page an easy way to navigate around your site without being forced to scroll up to the top of the page. You have two options for creating a text-based navigation bar inside of SiteBuilder:

- **Text box approach:** Add a text box to your page and create a horizontal set of text links, spacing them evenly apart to simulate a navigation bar. (Chapter 6 discusses how to work with text and links.)

- **Navigation bar approach:** Create a custom navigation bar without specifying graphical buttons.

The navigation bar approach enables you to take advantage of SiteBuilder's built-in navigation bar management. However, this approach does mean that the labels are not actually text, but text displayed as graphics (though most visitors probably won't notice the difference). In contrast, the text box approach allows you to work with real text links, but because it's not really a navigation bar, you have to work with each link manually.

However, before you go ahead and click OK in the Create Navigation Bar dialog box, follow these steps:

1. **Follow Steps 1 through 6 in the "Creating a navigation bar after your site is built" section.**

2. **Click the Customize button in the Create Navigation Bar dialog box.**

   The Navigation Bar Properties dialog box appears. (Refer to Figure 9-7.)

3. **Clear all the contents of the Inactive Image, Active Image, and Mouseover Image text boxes.**

4. **Specify the font settings you want for the text.**

   You'll typically want the font to be the same typeface as your default font for your Web site, such as Arial or Verdana.

   The typical size for a footer navigation bar is 10 points.

5. **Enter a value of 5 in the Spacing box.**

6. **Click OK to close out the Navigation Bar Properties dialog box.**

7. **Click the Horizontal radio button in the Choose Layout section of the Create Navigation Bar dialog box.**

8. **Resume the steps in the "Creating a navigation bar after your site is built" section, starting at Step 9.**

Figure 9-8 shows a text-based navigation bar at the bottom of a page.

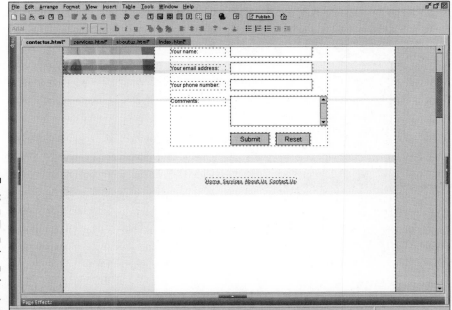

**Figure 9-8:**
Creating a text-based navigation scheme for the bottom of your pages.

REMEMBER

SiteBuilder doesn't exactly know how to handle your refusal to use graphics when creating a navigation bar, so if you edit your text-based navigation bar again, it automatically sets the style to be the first built-in graphical style. Therefore, each time you edit the text-based navigation bar, you need to click the Customize button and clear the image values from the Button Images section of the Navigation Bar Properties dialog box.

## Creating a navigation bar with your own images

If you have your own button images that you want to use instead of the built-in ones provided by SiteBuilder, you can incorporate them into your navigation bar design. To do so, follow these steps:

1. **Follow Steps 1 through 6 in the "Creating a navigation bar after your site is built" section.**

2. **Click the Customize button in the Create Navigation Bar dialog box.**

   The Navigation Bar Properties dialog box appears. (Refer to Figure 9-7.)

3. **Click the Browse button beside the Inactive Image box.**

   The Choose an Image dialog box appears, as shown in Figure 9-9.

REMEMBER

If the button image you choose already has text (see, for example, Figure 9-9), you should remove the title from the Display Text box in the Edit Navigation Bar dialog box.

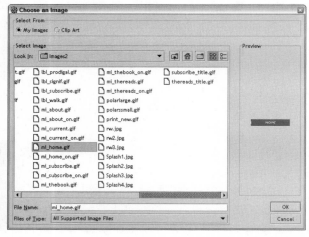

**Figure 9-9:**
Adding your
own button
images.

4. **Click the My Images radio button in the Select From box.**

5. **Navigate through the folders in the Look In pane to find the image you want to use.**

6. **After selecting your image, click OK to close the Choose an Image dialog box.**

   You return to the Create Navigation Bar dialog box.

7. **Repeat Steps 3 through 6 for the Active Image and Mouseover Image boxes.**

   The dimensions for the Active and Mouseover images should be the same as your Inactive image.

8. **Make any other settings changes in the Navigation Bar Properties dialog box, and click OK.**

9. **Resume the steps in the "Creating a navigation bar after your site is built" section, starting at Step 8.**

# Chapter 10

# Giving Your Site More Than Lip Service: Using Forms

. . . . . . . . . . . . . . . . . . . . . . . . . . . . . . . . . . . . . . . . . . . . . . . . . . . . . . . . .

*In This Chapter*

▶ Understanding how forms work

▶ Instantly adding pre-built forms to your Web site

▶ Creating your own custom form

▶ Understanding the different form elements

▶ Adding custom confirmation and error pages

. . . . . . . . . . . . . . . . . . . . . . . . . . . . . . . . . . . . . . . . . . . . . . . . . . . . . . . . .

*O*ne-sided conversations are almost always far more interesting for the person doing the talking. Once in a while, the person doing the listening would like to get a word or two in edgewise, if only to ask a question that spurs on another diatribe. Most Web sites are kinda like those one-sided conversations: They talk to the visitor but provide precious little opportunity for the visitor to respond back. Forms can then become an important outlet for your visitors to get in touch with you — to ask a question, submit a complaint, or request more information. Forms serve as the most common and user-friendly way in which your site visitors can communicate to you.

Forms can be complicated stuff when creating a Web site. But SiteBuilder makes working with forms amazingly easy. In fact, in many cases, you can just drop a pre-built form on your site, and it's ready to roll without any tweaks or configurations or confusing server settings.

This chapter explores how you can use pre-built and configuration forms inside of your Web site.

# How Forms Work: Discovering the "Form Factor"

A form on a Web page is part of a mini-system that is designed to take information a visitor submits, get that data to you, provide feedback to the visitor on the form's processing, and allow the visitor to easily get back to the rest of the Web site. Figure 10-1 shows each step in the process.

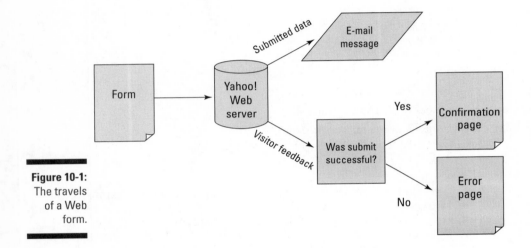

**Figure 10-1:**
The travels
of a Web
form.

In the Yahoo! world, when a visitor clicks the form's Submit button (see Figure 10-2), the form is submitted to the Yahoo! Web server for processing. Yahoo! handles all this processing, so you don't have to deal with what happens there. The server then sends all the data that was captured in the form to the e-mail address (see Figure 10-3) associated with your Yahoo! ID (or other e-mail address you specify). Finally, you can just leave your visitor at the Web form page, so the Yahoo! server sends him or her to a confirmation page (see Figure 10-4) or, in case something went awry in the process, to an error page (see Figure 10-5).

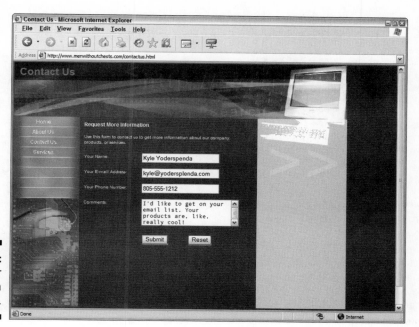

**Figure 10-2:**
A visitor
submits a
form.

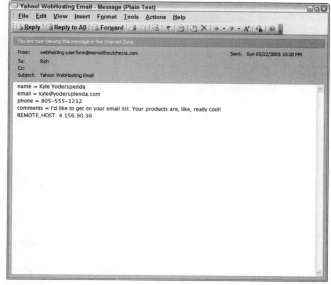

**Figure 10-3:**
The
captured
data arrives
in your
inbox.

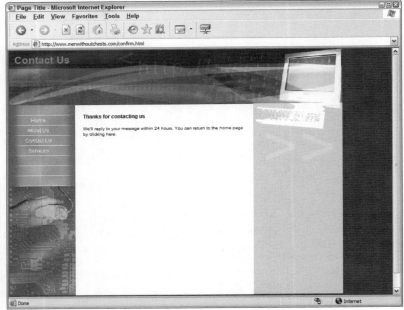

**Figure 10-4:**
Visitor
receives
confirmation
that the
form was
processed.

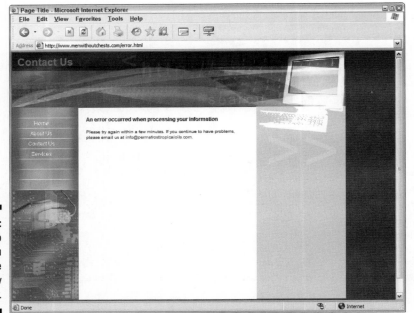

**Figure 10-5:**
If things go
awry, you
can let the
user know
of the error.

# Instant Forms: Adding Pre-Built Forms to Your Page

Forms are great additions to your site, but they can take a while to look just right — getting all the fields and labels arranged properly, for example — on your Web page. SiteBuilder comes to your rescue by allowing you to instantly add the two most popular forms out there — a Contact Us form and a Feedback form. What's more, SiteBuilder automatically sets up some basic validity checking (such as checking to ensure that the visitor filled in required fields) for the form text fields.

After you drop the forms into your page, they are completely ready to publish. You don't need to make any configurations to get them to work for you. However, while you can check out the layout anytime, you can't preview the form's functionality locally using File⇨Preview in Browser. You must publish them to the Yahoo! Web server in order for them to actually work.

For both of these pre-built forms, you can add them to your site and then customize them as desired. You can remove extra form elements you don't need. Or you can tweak the labels as well.

## The Contact Us form

A Contact Us form is an ideal way to allow visitors to contact you to submit questions, requests for call backs, or sign up for a newsletter. You can add a Contact Us form to your Web site in one of two ways:

- ✔ **To an existing page:** Choose Insert⇨Forms and Form Elements⇨Contact Us Form from the main menu. SiteBuilder adds the form to your current page in the Design pane. (See Figure 10-6.)

- ✔ **To your Web site:** Create a new template-based Web page by choosing File⇨New⇨With Template. In the Add New Page dialog box, choose the Contact Us Page option from the Select Page to Add drop-down menu and then click Add Page. SiteBuilder creates the new page and opens it in the Design pane.

The Contact Us form created using both of these commands is identical. The Contact Us page created using the template simply adds additional text above the form itself.

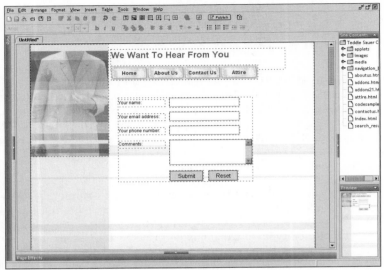

**Figure 10-6:**
The ever-
popular
Contact Us
form.

## The Feedback form

A Feedback form is quite similar to the Contact Us form but is targeted to get more information from the visitor. To add a Feedback form to an existing page, choose Insert⇨Forms and Form Elements⇨Feedback Form from the main menu. SiteBuilder adds the form to your current page in the Design pane. (See Figure 10-7.)

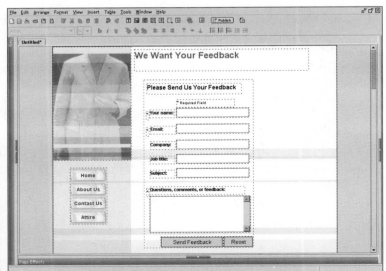

**Figure 10-7:**
The
question is:
Do you
really want
honest
feedback?

Unlike the Contact Us page, SiteBuilder doesn't have any template-based Feedback pages, so you need to create one by yourself.

# Made-to-Order Forms: Creating a Form from Scratch

The Contact Us and Feedback forms take care of many basic needs you have for interacting with your Web site visitors. However, forms have more to them than simply getting contact and feedback information. You can also use them to create online surveys and questionnaires or any other data gathering you need. For these cases, you need to create a blank form and add form elements and text labels on your own.

To add a custom form, follow these steps:

1. **Activate the page to which you want to add your form in the Design pane of SiteBuilder.**

2. **Choose Insert⇨Forms and Form Elements⇨Blank Form from the main menu.**

   An empty rectangular element is added to the middle of your page, as shown in Figure 10-8. The form looks rather lonely, so you better add something to it.

3. **Resize the form to a size that can hold all the elements you plan to add to it.**

   See Chapter 3 for the basics on resizing page elements in SiteBuilder.

4. **Add the desired form elements for data entry from the Insert⇨Forms and Form Elements menu.**

   See the "Working with Form Elements" section, later in the chapter, for instructions on how to add and work with each of the various kinds of form elements.

   Alternatively, you can also use the Insert palette, which I discuss in Chapter 17, to quickly add multiple elements to your form without needing to use the menus for each one.

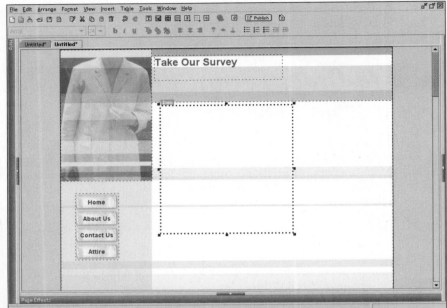

5. **Add a text element by clicking the Insert Text button on the toolbar to each form element.**

   You need to include an accompanying text element to serve as a description label.

   See Chapter 6 for more details on working with text elements.

6. **Add a Submit and Reset button to your form from the Insert⇨Forms and Form Elements menu.**

   The Submit button is the form element that provides the form's "power," telling the form to send the form data off to the Web server for processing.

As with the pre-built Contact Us and Feedback forms, you don't need to do anything else before they work. They just do. In the same way, you can't preview your custom form locally using File⇨Preview in Browser. You must publish it to your Yahoo! Web server in order for it to function.

Figure 10-9 shows a finished custom form in SiteBuilder.

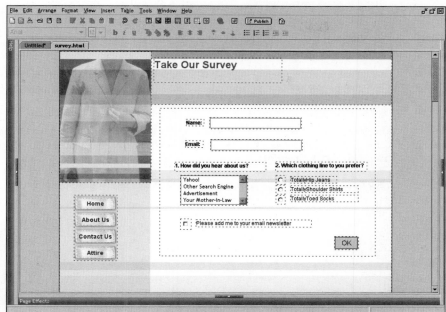

**Figure 10-9:**
An online
question-
naire.

# Working with Form Elements

Web forms provide a standard set of form elements that are designed to capture most every imaginable kind of data. These include the following:

- A **text field** is for basic text entry, such as name, address, and that sort
  of thing.

- A **text area** is for capturing data that may span multiple lines of text,
  such as comments, questions, essays, and dissertations.

- A **list box** provides a list of choices in which the visitor selects one (or
  more) of the items from the list.

- **Check boxes** capture yes/no or true/false values from the user.

- **Radio buttons** are used as another way to allow visitors to select one
  option from a series of options. Radio buttons are grouped, and a visitor
  can select only one radio button in a group at a time.

Two types of action buttons are associated with forms:

- ✔ **Submit button** triggers the submittal of the form to the Yahoo! Web server for processing.

- ✔ **Reset button** clears all the data entry fields in the form, so the user can start over with a clean slate, a fresh start, an empty canvas . . . well, you get the idea.

Figure 10-10 shows a form with each of these elements. If you've spent any time at all on the Web, you've almost certainly filled out forms containing these kinds of elements.

The following sections detail how to add each of these elements to your form.

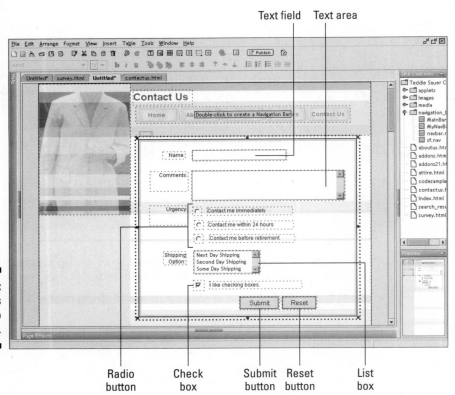

**Figure 10-10:**
Forms
are so
elemental.

# Adding a text field or text area

The Text Field and Text Area elements are the elements you want to use for fill-in-the-blank type information. If the data is one word or a group of words (such as name, e-mail, or address), then use a text field. If the data involves sentences or even paragraphs of information, then use a text area.

You can add either by following these steps:

1. **Click in the form to which you want to add the field.**

2. **Add a text field by choosing Insert⇨Forms and Form Elements⇨Text Field from the main menu. (If you want to add a text area, use Insert⇨Forms and Form Elements⇨Text Area.)**

   The Text Field Properties dialog box appears, as shown in Figure 10-11. (The Text Area Properties dialog box looks identical, except the Default Text box is multi-lined.)

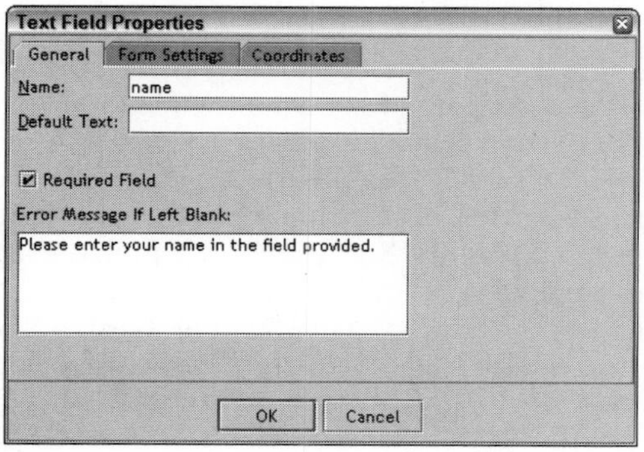

**Figure 10-11:** Setting up your text field.

3. **Enter a descriptive name for the field in the Name text box.**

   This value is never shown to the visitor but is included in the e-mail you receive as a way to identify the data that was captured.

4. **If you would like the field to start out with a default value, enter it in the Default Text box.**

5. **If you want to force visitors to add text in this field before they can submit, then click the Required Field check box.**

6. **If you checked the Required Field box, then add a customized error message in the space provided.**

   This text displays to the visitor as an error message in the event that the field is left blank when the Submit button is clicked.

7. **Click OK.**

   SiteBuilder adds the text field or text area to the middle of your form.

After you add your field, be sure to add a text element to your form as a label for the text field or text area.

## Adding a list box

The List Box element is ideal for allowing a visitor to select one or more items from a predefined list.

Each item in the list has two pieces of information associated with it:

- ✔ **Text:** The text that actually displays in the list box.
- ✔ **Value:** The text that is sent as part of the e-mail response when the visitor selects this item from the list.

The text and value are often identical. But by having these as two separate pieces of data, you have more flexibility. For example, suppose you have several free catalogs that a user can select from a list. You could have a list item presented to the visitor as `2005 Fall/Winter Sports Apparel`, while the data captured and sent to you shows up as `2005-FW-SP-GEN`, a catalog number more useful to you.

You can set up the list of items and the list box itself by following these steps:

1. **Click in the form to which you want to add the list box.**

2. **Choose Insert⇨Forms and Form Elements⇨List Box from the main menu.**

   The List Box Properties dialog box appears, as shown in Figure 10-12.

3. **Enter a descriptive name for the list box in the Name text box.**

4. **Click Add to enter your first item.**

   A row is added to the Contents table, and the text cursor is moved to the first cell in the Text column.

5. **Enter the text for the list item.**

   Be clear and descriptive in phrasing each item.

6. **Double-click the Value cell, and enter the text value you want returned as part of the e-mail response.**

7. **To have the item selected by default, check the Selected box in the table row.**

8. **Repeat Steps 4 through 7 for each item in your list box.**

   As you enter items into the list, note the Remove, Up, and Down buttons. After you select the item, you can do one of the following:

   - Click Remove to delete an entry from your list.
   - Click Up to move an item up in the list order.
   - Click Down to move an item down in the list order.

9. **You can optionally allow visitors to select multiple items in your list box. To allow this feature, click the Permit Multiple Selections check box.**

10. **Click OK.**

    SiteBuilder adds the list box to the middle of your form.

Be sure to add a text element to your form as a label for the list box.

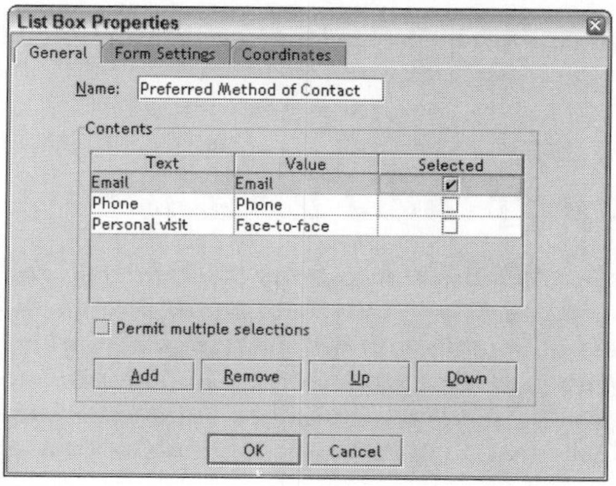

**Figure 10-12:**
Defining a
list of items
in the list
box.

## Adding a check box

A check box is the best way to capture information that has a yes/no or true/false format. You can a quickly add a check box to your form by doing the following:

1. **Click in the form to which you wish to add the check box.**

2. **Choose Insert⇨Forms and Form Elements⇨Checkbox from the main menu.**

The Checkbox Properties dialog box appears, as shown in Figure 10-13.

3. **Enter a descriptive name for the check box in the Name text box.**

4. **In the Initial State drop-down box, select the check box's default state: Unchecked or Checked.**

5. **Click OK.**

SiteBuilder adds the check box to the middle of your form.

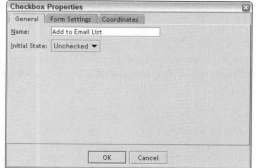

**Figure 10-13:**
There's no gray for a check box. It's a yes-or-no world.

A check box is pretty useless without a text label, so be sure to add a text element to accompany it.

## Adding a group of radio buttons

A set of radio buttons resembles those questions on standardized tests you probably used to take in school. You know what I am referring to — the ones that required a No.2 pencil and came with dire warnings of marking outside of the circle. Well, fortunately, with radio buttons, you no longer need to worry about the consequences of making smudges outside the circle. But the same principle still applies: You can choose one and only option among a set of options.

If you read the "Adding a list box" section, earlier in the chapter, you'll discover that each of the items in a list box is defined as part of that same list box. A group of radio buttons is defined in an opposite manner: Each radio button in a group is defined separately and then the buttons are linked with a common group name.

Because radio buttons are grouped based on a group name, you can have multiple groups of radio buttons within the same form. Simply give each set of buttons a unique group name.

To create a group of radio buttons, follow these steps:

1. **Click in the form to which you want to add the group of radio buttons.**

2. **Choose Insert⇨Forms and Form Elements⇨Radio Button from the main menu.**

   The Radio Button Properties dialog box appears, as shown in Figure 10-14.

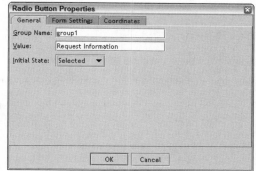

**Figure 10-14:**
Defining a
radio button.

3. **Enter a name for your button group.**

   You need to use the same name for each radio button so you can associate them.

4. **In the Value text box, enter the text to submit with the form for the radio button group when this button is selected.**

5. **In the Initial State drop-down box, select the Radio Button's default state: Unselected or Selected.**

   Only one radio button in your group can use the Selected state.

6. **Click OK.**

7. **Repeat Steps 2 through 6 for each radio button you wish to define in your group.**

   Be sure you use the same group name in order for the radio buttons to function correctly.

Don't forget to add text elements for each radio button in your group.

# *Adding Submit and Reset Buttons*

The Submit and Reset buttons don't capture data. Instead, they're responsible for triggering form-related actions. The Submit button sends the form data to the Yahoo! Web server for processing, while the Reset button clears any user data from the form.

Don't feel obligated to add a Reset button to your form. If you do use one, make sure you don't position it in a place where the visitor would naturally expect to find the Submit button. There's little more irritating than filling out a form only to accidentally click the Reset button by mistake and then have to start all over. (Okay, I can think of a few things in life that are even *more* irritating than that, but you get the picture.)

Follow these steps to add a Submit or Reset button:

1. **Click in the form to which you want to add the button.**

2. **Choose Insert⇨Forms and Form Elements⇨Submit Button (or Reset Button) from the main menu.**

   The Submit Button Properties dialog box makes an appearance, as shown in Figure 10-15. The Reset Button Properties dialog box looks identical except for the title of the dialog box.

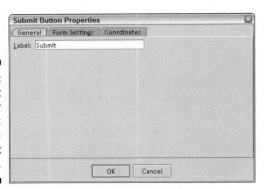

**Figure 10-15:**
Doesn't get any easier than this: adding a Submit button.

3. **If desired, modify the text for the button in the Label text box.**

   Don't get cute or creative with button labels for forms. If you change the text, make sure the action taken when the button is clicked is crystal clear to visitors. If they are unsure what happens, they probably will avoid processing the form.

4. **Click OK.**

   SiteBuilder adds the button to the middle of your form.

# What a Form Response Looks Like

When a form is processed, the data captured from the form is sent to you as an e-mail. By default, the form is sent to the e-mail address associated with your Yahoo! ID, although you can specify a different e-mail address. (See the "Sending the form responses to a different e-mail address" section, later in this chapter.)

The e-mail message you receive is based on the following conventions:

✔ The From address of the e-mail message is `webhosting-userform@` `yourdomainname.com` (where *yourdomainname.com* is your domain).

✔ The Subject of the e-mail message is `Yahoo! WebHosting Email`.

✔ The text of the e-mail message is structured as name-value pairs: *ElementName=VisitorData*. As shown in the "Working with Form Elements" section, earlier in the chapter, you supply a unique name for the element. This name is then placed before the value provided by the user. For example, the following is the e-mail text of a standard Contact Us form:

```
name = Kyle Yoderspenda
email = kyle@yoderspenda.com
phone = 805-555-1212
comments = I'd like to get on your e-mail list. Your products are, like,
           really cool!
REMOTE_HOST: 6.111.10.36
```

# After the Click: Tweaking the Form Settings

You can adjust what happens "after the click" from two different places within SiteBuilder:

✔ Right-click a form and choose Properties from the form's pop-up menu. The Form Properties dialog box, with the Form Settings tab, displays. (See Figure 10-16.)

Select a form either by clicking its rectangular border or any place inside of the form not taken up by another element.

✔ Right-click a form element and choose Properties from the form element's pop-up menu to display its Properties dialog box. The Form Settings tab of the dialog box shows the same information.

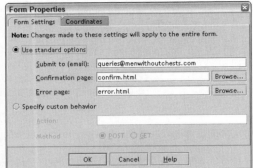

**Figure 10-16:**
The Form
Properties
dialog box.

For normal uses, you work with only the standard options, which I discuss in the following sections.

If you have advanced needs to connect with another Web service, you can use the Custom Behavior section of the Properties dialog box.

## Sending the form responses to a different e-mail address

If you would like to send form responses to a different e-mail than the one associated with your Yahoo! ID, enter it in the Submit To text box of the Form Settings dialog box (refer to Figure 10-16).

## Specifying your own confirmation and error page

By default, visitors who submit a form are taken to a Yahoo!-created confirmation or error page, such as the one shown in Figure 10-17. However, I recommend avoiding these standard pages for four reasons:

- ✔ The pages are text-only and look nothing like your Web site. So the visitor is visually removed from your Web site, which can be confusing for visitors and leave them wondering what happened.

- ✔ The pages can look geeky, which can confuse nontechnical visitors.

- ✔ The page has no links to your Web site. As a result, a visitor is forced to click the Back button to return to your site.

- ✔ The process doesn't look seamless to the visitor, making the interaction appear unprofessional.

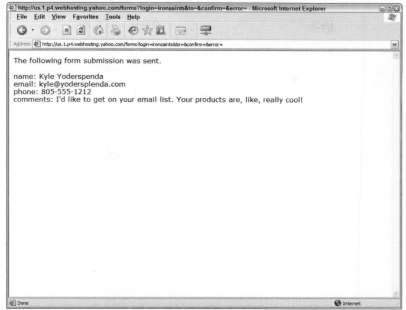

**Figure 10-17:**
A plain
vanilla
confirmation
page.

The following form submission was sent.

name: Kyle Yoderspenda
email: kyle@yodersplenda.com
phone: 805-555-1212
comments: I'd like to get on your email list. Your products are, like, really cool!

For these reasons, be sure to specify your own confirmation and error pages in the Form Settings dialog box.

To define custom confirmation and error pages

1. **Using the techniques from Chapter 3, create your own custom confirmation and error pages with the same look and feel as the rest of your site.**

   - For confirmation pages, you want to let the visitor know that the form was processed successfully and provide a link to return to your home page or other part of the Web site.

   - For error pages, inform visitors that something went wrong. Tell them to try again in a few minutes or to contact you via e-mail if the problem continues.

   The confirmation and error pages must be located in the same folder as the page containing the form.

2. **Right-click the form and choose Properties from the contextual menu that appears.**

   The Form Settings dialog box appears. (Refer to Figure 10-16.)

3. **Click the Browse button beside the Confirmation Page text box, and choose the custom confirmation page from your Web site. Click Open to confirm your choice.**

4. **Click the Browse button beside the Error Page text box, and choose the custom error page from your Web site. Click Open.**

5. **Click OK.**

Refer to Figures 10-4 and 10-5 for examples of custom confirmation and error pages.

# Part III

# Going Further: Developing "Wicked Cool" Web Pages

The 5th Wave          By Rich Tennant

"HONEY! OUR WEB BROWSER GOT OUT LAST NIGHT AND DUMPED THE TRASH ALL OVER MR. BELCHER'S HOME PAGE!"

## In this part . . .

*E*veryone wants to create a hip, jamming, and wicked cool Web site. But, in the quest for being innovative, many people throw gadgets on Web pages that they think are cool, but only end up looking tacky. In this part, you explore how to add great add-ons to your site, and still keep your Web site looking great, not cheesy.

# Chapter 11

# Yahoo! Add-Ons: Drag-and-Drop Productivity

*A*dd-ons. Talk up the add-ons. Back when I was in college, I worked part time as a waiter. One of the things that my manager drilled into the serving staff every night was "Talk up the add-ons." Appetizers, desserts, that sort of thing. Everyone dining in the restaurant would order a dinner already, so we waiters were supposed to entice them to order the extra add-ons to add zest and spice to their meal — as well as a few extra bucks to their total bill.

In SiteBuilder, you have the basic "meat and potatoes" of your Web site in text, image, and form elements. However, you also have add-ons that you can use to add instant interactivity and functionality to your Web site. Best of all, unlike those fried cheese sticks and brownie pies I used to flog, these add-ons don't cost extra; they are simply another part of your Yahoo! Web hosting plan. In this chapter, you explore how to work with add-ons inside of SiteBuilder.

# *Working with Add-Ons*

Add-ons are specialized page elements that you can add to your SiteBuilder Web site to provide increased functionality. Ordinary page elements, such as text, images, tables, or form elements, are generic in nature; they can be used for thousands of different purposes. In contrast, add-ons have a single purpose to them. When you need your Web site to perform that particular service, add-ons become invaluable timesavers for you. SiteBuilder comes with the following eight add-ons:

- ✔ **Counter:** Provides a visible counter that shows the number of people coming to your Web site.

- ✔ **Time and Date Stamp:** Provides the current time or date as text on your Web site.

- ✔ **Yahoo! Map:** Gives you a way to easily add a map to your business, organization, or other location.

- ✔ **Yahoo! Directions:** Provides a way to give your visitors an easy way to get instructions to your business or other location.

- ✔ **Yahoo! Search Box:** Provides a way for your visitors to do normal Web searches using the Yahoo! search engine.

- ✔ **Site Search:** Provides a search box for visitors to find specific content on your site.

- ✔ **Presence Indicator:** Lets visitors know whether you are online with Yahoo! Messenger at that moment or not.

- ✔ **Loan Calculator:** Enables people to calculate monthly payment amounts right on your Web page.

Adding this kind of functionality to your Web site without SiteBuilder's help usually means doing a lot of manual coding with HTML and JavaScript. With SiteBuilder, however, you get all these components put in nice neat packages, so you can work with them as easily as you can a text element or image.

I provide you a basic overview and instructions for inserting, previewing, and editing these add-on elements.

You can add some Yahoo! add-ons to your Web site — calendars and guestbooks, for example — that are not included inside of SiteBuilder itself. These special add-ons are accessible from the Yahoo! Web Hosting Control Panel (see Chapter 14) and then added to your SiteBuilder Web site as code. Chapter 12 provides full details on how to add these code-based add-ons to your site.

# Inserting an add-on

Choose Insert⇨Add-Ons from the menu and then select the desired add-on from the submenu that appears. You can also click the Insert Palette button on the toolbar to display the Insert palette, shown in Figure 11-1. In the palette, click Add-Ons from the left pane and then select the add-on of your choice. The add-on is added to your Web page.

**Figure 11-1:** Insert everything but the kitchen sink via the Insert palette.

For instructions on how to add each specific add-on to your page, see the sections that follow.

# Previewing your add-on

As you discover in Chapter 4, you can preview your Web site on your local computer before going live on the Web. To do so, click the Preview in Browser button on the toolbar (or press F12). The add-ons have different levels of support for local previews:

- ✔ **Preview with or without Internet connection.** Because they require no server connectivity, you can preview and test the Loan Calculator and Time and Date Stamp on your local computer before publishing, even if you don't have a live Internet connection.

- ✔ **Preview with Internet connection.** Other add-ons are fully functional during preview, so long as you have a live Internet connection. These include Presence Indicator, Yahoo! Map, Yahoo! Directions, and Yahoo! Search.

- ✔ **Publish only, no functional preview.** Not all the add-ons you insert into your Web pages can be previewed on your local computer. The Personal Site Search and Counter need to be published to your Yahoo! site to be fully functional. However, you can see how they look on your page when you preview the page.

## Accessing the properties of your add-on

Each add-on has properties you can modify. To do so, double-click the add-on on your page in the Design pane (or right-click and choose Properties from the contextual menu). The property dialog box that is displayed is the same as the dialog box that is shown when you first add the add-on to your page.

## Cutting, copying, and pasting add-ons

You can manipulate add-ons just like other elements on your page. You can cut, copy, paste, and duplicate them by using the toolbar, contextual menu, or menu commands. For more information on copying and pasting page elements, check out Chapter 4.

After you paste an add-on into the active page of the Design pane, you can move it around and place it where you want within it.

# Inserting a Counter

Time to move from all these generalities about add-ons to some real specifics. Case in point: the Counter. A Web page counter is perhaps the most ubiquitous add-on and one that you've probably seen all around the Web. The basic idea of a counter is that it keeps a running total of the visitors who view your Web page and displays the number as a graphical counter on your page.

A counter is a fun feature for personal and other sites in which you don't care who knows the total number of visitors who come to your site. However, for business sites, I don't recommend using the Counter add-on for two reasons:

- You may want to keep to yourself exactly how many people visit your site. If you really want to track this information, use the Site Activity module in the Yahoo! Web Hosting Control Panel instead. (See Chapter 14.) Not only is the information for your eyes only, but it also provides more descriptive information than just a raw number.

- Some people think visible counters look a tad nonprofessional. Once again, as Chapter 16 discusses, consider the "Big Boys" test: None of the major Web sites ever uses counters, so why should you?

If you're determined to forge ahead, here's how to add a Counter add-on to your Web site:

1. **Choose Insert⇨Add-Ons⇨Counter from the main menu.**

   The Counter Properties dialog box appears, as shown in Figure 11-2.

**Figure 11-2:**
Counting
your
blessings
with the
Counter
add-on.

2. **In the Style area, adjust the properties to set the desired look of the counter:**

   • Use the Font Color and Background properties in combination to determine the right coloring scheme. Keep in mind that the Transparent background option picks the color of the Web page itself.

   • The Counter Size property determines whether the counter is small, medium, or large.

   • The Counter Type property gives you 25 number styles to choose among.

   • The Number of Characters box enables you to specify the number of digits. You can specify 1 to 9 digits. *Hint:* If you need 9 digits, I think you need more than a standard counter for monitoring your traffic.

3. **In the Settings area, specify the settings associated with the tally.**

   • The Starting Value allows you to use the current setting (starting with 1) or else start at a number you specify.

   • Select your Time Zone from the list provided. This information is used only for your behind-the-scenes reporting and doesn't impact the visible counter.

4. **Click OK.**

   The Counter is added to your Web page, as shown in Figure 11-3.

In general, you want to move the Counter to the bottom center of your page.

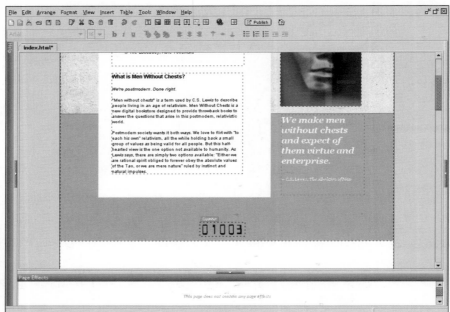

**Figure 11-3:**
Counter
add-on,
ready for
action.

# Displaying a Time and Date Stamp

The Time and Date Stamp add-on displays the current date and time on your Web page. This add-on comes in handy for occasions when you want your page to be continually "up to date" with the current date or time.

The Time and Date Stamp is the one SiteBuilder add-on that is a Java applet. While you generally don't need to concern yourself with such technical details, you should be aware that the visitor needs to enable Java applets to run inside the browser in order for the add-on to work as designed.

To add a Time and Date Stamp add-on to your Web site

1. **Choose Insert⇨Add-Ons⇨Time and Date Stamp from the menu.**

   The Time and Date Stamp Properties dialog box appears, as shown in Figure 11-4.

2. **Choose the Foreground Color and Background Color.**

3. **Select the Font name, style, and size.**

**Figure 11-4:**
The Time
and Date
Stamp takes
a licking but
keeps on
ticking.

| Time and Date Stamp Properties | ⊠ |
| --- |

General | Coordinates

Foreground Color: ■

Background Color: □

Font: Helvetica ▼ Bold ▼ 16 ▼

Date Format: Long (e.g. Sunday January 31 1999) ▼

☑ Show Time ☐ Military Time

OK | Cancel

4. **Choose the Date Format option you want to use: Long, Short, or Numeric.**

5. **Click the Show Time check box to display the time along with the date.**

6. **If you want to go military (24-hour clock), click the Military Time check box.**

7. **Click OK.**

Like magic, the Time and Date Stamp add-on is added to your Web page, as shown in Figure 11-5.

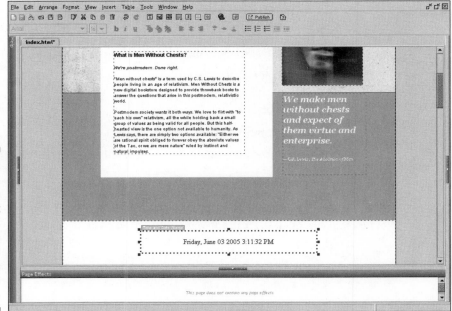

**Figure 11-5:**
Wrist-
watches are
"so last
century"
when you
can use a
Time and
Date Stamp
instead.

# *Providing a Yahoo! Map*

The Yahoo! Map add-on provides a way to easily link your Web site to a customized map from the Yahoo! Maps service. This feature is handy when you want to provide a way for customers or clients to easily locate your business location.

To add a Yahoo! Map add-on to your Web site

1. **Choose Insert➪Add-Ons➪Yahoo! Map from the main menu.**

   The Yahoo! Map Properties dialog box appears, as shown in Figure 11-6.

**Figure 11-6:**
Map-
making,
Yahoo!
style:
Gerard
Mercator
never had it
so easy.

2. **Enter your address information in the spaces provided.**

3. **Add a label in the Description box.**

   This text is used as the link text when the add-on uses the Large style (see next step).

4. **Specify either Small or Large style.**

   Figure 11-7 gives examples of both the small and large styles.

5. **Click OK.**

   The Yahoo! Map add-on is added to your Web page.

When visitors click the Yahoo! Maps add-on on your Web page, they're taken to a customized Yahoo! Maps map. The large style provides a text link for clicking. The small style add-on can be clicked anywhere inside of the graphic.

## Creating your own Yahoo! Map link

Suppose you want to offer the same functionality as the Map add-on but need to use your own text or image. If so, follow these instructions:

1. In your browser, go to Yahoo! Maps at `maps.yahoo.com`.

2. Enter your address information in the spaces provided to display the Yahoo! map.

3. Select the text in your browser's Address (URL) bar and press Ctrl+C.

   You are copying the URL for this customized map to the Clipboard.

4. In your SiteBuilder Web page, select the text or image you want to link to the Yahoo! map.

5. Click the Link button on the toolbar.

6. In the Link dialog box, choose Another Web Site in the Select the Type of Link box.

7. Paste the URL from the Clipboard into the Enter the Destination URL box.

8. Pick the target browser window you want to display the map in the When Clicked, the Link Will Open In list.

9. Click the Create Button link.

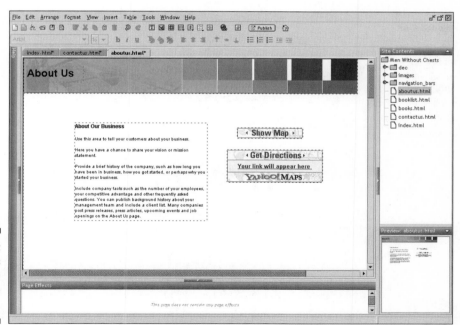

**Figure 11-7:** Two styles of Yahoo! Map add-ons.

When a visitor clicks the <u>Yahoo! Map</u> link, the browser leaves your site as it jumps to the Yahoo! Maps service. Visitors need to click the Back button in the browser to return to your site. The only way to have the map display in a new browser window is to use the technique I describe in the "Creating your own Yahoo! Map link" sidebar.

# Offering Yahoo! Directions

Like Yahoo! Map, the Yahoo! Directions add-on provides an easy way to link to Yahoo! Maps service. However, this add-on allows visitors to enter their address information and then receive customized driving directions to your location.

To add a Yahoo! Directions add-on to your Web site

1. **Choose Insert⇨Add-Ons⇨Yahoo! Directions from the main menu.**

   The Yahoo! Directions Properties dialog box appears, as shown in Figure 11-8.

**Figure 11-8:** Entering the destination information for Yahoo! Directions.

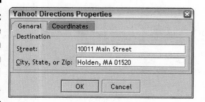

2. **Enter your address information in the spaces provided.**

3. **Click OK.**

   The Yahoo! Directions add-on is added to your Web page, as shown in Figure 11-9.

When visitors enter their address information and click the Show Me the Way button, they're taken to a customized page on the Yahoo! Maps Web site providing step-by-step instructions.

Like the <u>Yahoo! Map</u> link, the Yahoo! Directions add-on takes the visitor from your Web page. Visitors need to click the Back button in the browser to return to your site.

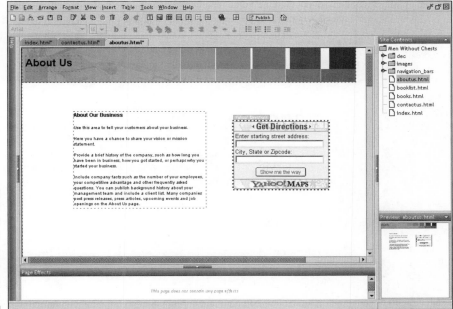

**Figure 11-9:**
Instant
directions
to your
business,
organization,
or pad.

# Searching the Web with a Yahoo! Search Box

While the Personal Site Search (covered later in this chapter) allows visitors to look for content on your Web site, the Yahoo! Search Box enables people to start a search of the Web from your site.

You don't actually have to do much to add a Yahoo! Search Box to your Web site; just do the following:

**1. Choose Insert➪Add-Ons➪Yahoo! Search Box from the main menu.**

Unlike most of the other add-ons, the Yahoo! Search Box doesn't have any position properties, so it is immediately added to your Web page without displaying a dialog box.

A search box like this looks good in the top-left or top-right corner of your Web page.

Figure 11-10 shows the Yahoo! Search Box added to a SiteBuilder Web page.

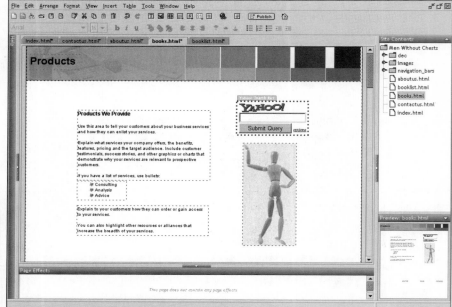

**Figure 11-10:**
Do you
wanna
Yahoo! from
your home
page?

Just because you can add a Yahoo! Search Box to your Web site doesn't mean you necessarily should. The advantage of having a Web search box on your page is that you can more easily get people to think of your Web site as a "home base," so to speak, on the Web. Your site becomes a good home page, not only because a visitor likes your site, but also because it provides Web searches. The disadvantage of having a Web search box on your page is that once the visitor begins a search, he or she is whisked away from your Web page, maybe never to return.

# Searching Your Site with a Site Search

Perhaps the most powerful of all the add-ons that come inside of SiteBuilder is the Site Search add-on. Once you add this search box to your Web page, visitors can use it to find content across your Web site as they search on a keyword or phrase.

## Understanding the two pieces of Site Search

The Site Search add-on consists of two parts:

- ✔ **The Site Search box:** Visitors enter search criteria.

- ✔ **The Site Search Results box:** Displays the results of the query. You can specify what kind of page to display the results:

  - **A plain page created on the fly.** This is the default option.

  - **An existing page in your site.** This page must be in the same folder as the page that has the Site Search box, which is typically the case with Yahoo! SiteBuilder sites unless you do something out of the ordinary.

  - **A copy of an existing page on your site.**

While the default plain page option is easiest — SiteBuilder handles all the details for you when you stick with the default — the resulting page appears quite vanilla and plain to your visitors. As a result, I recommend creating a special `results.html` page that matches the design and overall look of your Web site and then identifying that special page as the target for the search results. See Chapter 4 for more details on how to create a new SiteBuilder page.

## Inserting a Site Search add-on

You can add a Site Search add-on to your Web site by following these steps:

1. **Choose Insert➪Add-Ons➪Site Search from the main menu.**

   The Site Search Properties dialog box appears, as shown in Figure 11-11.

2. **Select the Results page option of your choice. (See the discussion earlier in this section for more details on these options.)**

   - Click the Use Default Results Page option for a blank search results page that SiteBuilder handles for you.

     As a result, this page doesn't show up inside of your SiteBuilder Web site, so you don't even have to think about it.

   - If you'd prefer to use a page you've already created, click the Use an Existing Page option and then select the page from the Results Page drop-down menu.

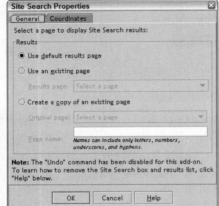

**Figure 11-11:**
Adding a
Site Search
to your
Web site.

SiteBuilder adds a Search Results box to this page.

- If you'd prefer to use a copy of an existing page, then choose the Create a Copy of an Existing Page option, select the page to be copied from the Original Page list, and then enter a new name for the page in the Page Name box.

  SiteBuilder makes a copy of the original, adds the new page to your Web site, and adds a Search Results box to it.

**3. Click OK.**

The Site Search box is added to the current page (see Figure 11-12), while the Search Results box is added to the page you specified.

As with a Web search box, you often want to place a Site Search box either in the top-right and top-left corner of your Web page. If you use a Yahoo! Search Box, just be sure visitors don't get confused between the two.

**4. If you didn't choose the default Results page, double-click the Results page in the Site Contents pane if you need to open it in the Design pane.**

You see the Site Search Results box added to the page, as shown in Figure 11-13.

**5. Size and position the Site Search Results box as needed.**

Figure 11-14 shows how the site search results display in the specified Results page.

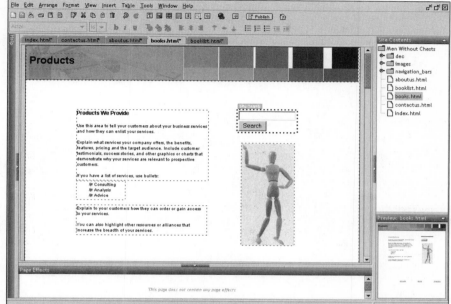

**Figure 11-12:**
Visitors can now become like Sherlock Holmes as they search through your site.

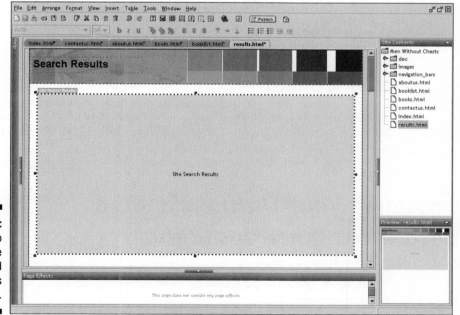

**Figure 11-13:**
Setting up the customized results page.

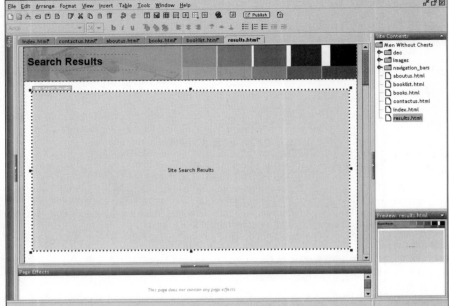

**Figure 11-14:**
Professional
results
using the
Site Search
add-on.

## *Removing the Site Search add-on from your site*

If you want to delete the Site Search add-on from your site, make sure you remove both the Site Search box and the Site Search Results box (if you have a customized Results page). If you delete just the Site Search Results box but keep the Site Search box, then your search results will be "all dressed up with no place to go."

# *Showing Your Online Persona with a Presence Indicator*

The Presence Indicator add-on enables visitors to see if you are available to chat live with them using Yahoo! Messenger. (See `messenger.yahoo.com` for more details on Yahoo! Messenger.) This feature can be extremely helpful for customers who have questions or problems about your products or services. When you are logged in, the add-on says "I'm Online"; when you are not signed in, it says "I'm Offline."

The Presence Indicator isn't indicative of your simply being connected to the Internet. Instead, the add-on tells if you are signed into Yahoo! Messenger using your Yahoo! ID and enables visitors to send you messages simply by clicking on it.

To add a Presence Indicator add-on to your Web site

1.  **Choose Insert➪Add-Ons➪Presence Indicator from the main menu.**

    The Presence Indicator Properties dialog box appears, as shown in Figure 11-15.

**Figure 11-15:**
Setting up
your
Presence
Indicator.

2.  **Enter your Yahoo! ID in the space provided.**

3.  **Select the style (size) of the indicator on your page: Small, Medium, or Large.**

    In general, I recommend using the Large style because it is the most descriptive. Avoid the Small style: If your visitors are not that familiar with Yahoo! Messenger, they probably won't understand what the smiley face signifies. Figure 11-16 displays all three styles.

4.  **Click OK.**

In order to receive chat messages from visitors, you need to be logged into Yahoo! Messenger. Go to `messnger.yahoo.com` for details.

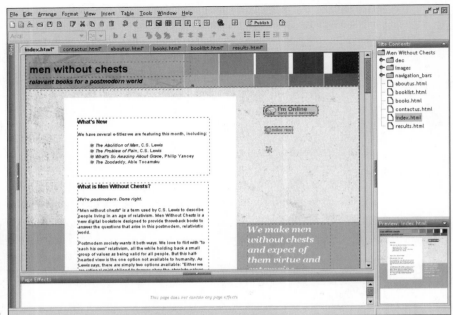

**Figure 11-16:**
Once, twice, three styles for an add-on.

# Keeping an Eye on the Bottom Dollar: Loan Calculator

The Loan Calculator add-on is one of those features that is either super-cool or super-boring, depending on your particular Web site needs. If you have a personal Web site or have a small business selling erasers, most visitors to your Web site won't be thinking about financing. However, if you are a real estate agent, the Loan Calculator is going to make you feel like a kid in a candy store.

Add a Loan Calculator add-on to your Web site by choosing Insert⇨ Add-Ons⇨Loan Calculator from the main menu. The Loan Calculator add-on is immediately placed on your Web page, as shown in Figure 11-17.

The Loan Calculator is not like the other add-ons in two distinct ways:

✔ **No real Properties dialog box.** You can't double-click the add-on to see its Properties dialog box. Oh, you can right-click and choose Properties from the menu. The dialog box that appears is called Loan Calculator

Properties, but none of the properties that appear is related to the functionality of the calculator. Instead, these properties are actually form element properties, which I discuss fully in Chapter 10. The reasoning is that the Loan Calculator uses a form element merely as a container for the add-on.

✔ **You can directly modify the labels inside of the add-on.** While the Loan Calculator has no Properties dialog box to work with, you can adjust the font style and labeling of the various pieces of the calculator. To do so, double-click the text to modify and then treat it as a standard text element. (See Chapter 6 for more on working with text.) However, you cannot modify the form text boxes themselves.

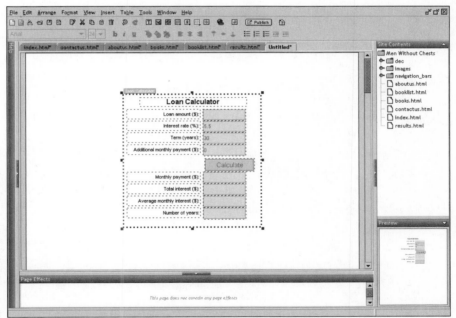

**Figure 11-17:** Becoming the next big "Loans R Us" or simply providing a finance tool for your visitors.

# Chapter 12

# The Wow Factor: Adding Multimedia and Page Effects

## In This Chapter

▶ Adding video and audio media to your site

▶ Adding flashy effects to your pages

▶ Knowing when to use multimedia and page effects and when to avoid them

*1t's a bird. It's a plane. No, it's a . . . SiteBuilder page effect.*

Whether in real life or the world of the Web, people love to be wowed. TV commercials aim to keep the clicker away by wowing their target audience. Filmmakers attempt to blast moviegoers with CGI effects that keep them "oooing and aahhing" for two hours. And Web site builders love to keep visitors at their sites by combining useful information with dynamic effects to make the Web site come alive.

In this chapter, you explore how to add multimedia and dynamic page effects to your Web site. However, as cool as they may be, they can backfire on you if you're not careful. So at the end of the chapter, you also examine the issues involved as you consider whether or not to use them in your Web site.

## Multimedia: Going Beyond Mere Pictures

Text and normal images are the "meat and potatoes" of any Web site. They are the primary means in which you communicate with your visitors. However, just as radio and TV proved in the last century, sometimes audio and video communication can be a better way to share certain messages with people. Responding to that reality, SiteBuilder enables you to add video and audio media to your Web pages.

As the "Knowing When and When Not to Use Them" section, later in this chapter, indicates, using video and audio clips come with a cost — they take time to download or stream. Therefore, be sure to consider all the factors I discuss in this chapter before you add multimedia to your page.

If you rely on video or audio files to communicate to your visitors, I recommend placing a link beside the media clip that takes visitors to the free download page of Windows Media Player (`www.microsoft.com/windows/windowsmedia/download`), RealPlayer (`www.realplayer.com`), or QuickTime Player (`www.apple.com/quicktime/download`).

## Working with video clips

SiteBuilder enables you to add several different types of video files to your Web site, including:

- ✔ Windows Media files (`.avi`, `.wmf`, `.asf`, `.mpa`, `.mpg`, `.mpeg`)
- ✔ RealVideo files (`.rm`, `.rmvb`, `.ra`, `.ram`)
- ✔ QuickTime video files (`.mov`)

When you add a video to your page, it becomes a part of the Web page in a rectangular container box on your page. The video file is uploaded to your Yahoo! Web hosting server when you publish your site. Then, when the video plays (automatically or when the user initiates the play), a media player on the visitor's browser — Windows Media Player, RealPlayer, or QuickTime Player — plays the video inside of a rectangular container.

Keep in mind that the visitor must have the appropriate player on his or her computer in order to watch the video. However, all three players are standard fare for nearly all computers today.

Add a video to your Web page with these steps:

1. **Choose Insert⇨Video from the main menu.**

   The Insert dialog box makes an appearance.

2. **Use the Look In pane to navigate to the media file of your choice in the dialog box.**

3. **Click the Insert button.**

   The video media element is added to your page in the Design pane of SiteBuilder. (See Figure 12-1.)

   You can also drag a video file from Windows Explorer and drop it onto your Web page.

After adding your video to your Web site, you can easily edit how it displays and plays; just do the following:

1. **Double-click the video media element on your page inside the Design pane.**

   You can also right-click the element and choose Properties from the contextual menu that appears.

   The Video Properties dialog box displays, as shown in Figure 12-2.

2. **Place a check in the Show Controls check box to display the player controls (play, rewind, fast forward) inside the Web page.**

   If you uncheck this option, the player hides these controls.

   Hiding the player controls creates a more seamless look for the video integrated into your Web page.

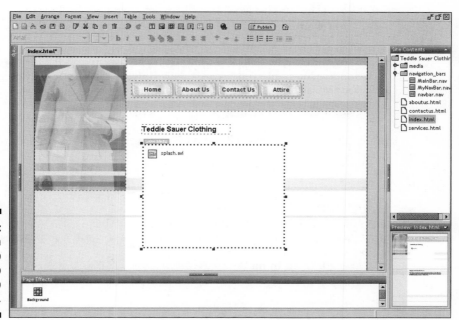

**Figure 12-1:** Adding a video element to your Web site.

**Figure 12-2:**
Changing
the way the
video shows
inside of the
Web page.

3. **Place a check in the Autostart check box to automatically kick off the video when the page loads.**

   Use this option when you want visitors to always view the video. However, if the media file is large, be careful about using this option. The visitor must first download the entire file before browsing your Web page.

   If Autostart is disabled, the visitor can play the video by clicking the video element on the Web page or by clicking Play if the player controls are visible.

4. **Place a check in the Loop check box if you want to play the video over and over and over again.**

5. **If you want to switch the media player that plays the file, then choose a different option in the Player area.**

   SiteBuilder determines the initial choice by looking at the video format. I don't recommend modifying this setting, because not all three players support all the various media formats.

6. **Click OK to save changes.**

Figure 12-3 shows a video clip playing inside of a browser without player controls visible.

## *Working with audio*

Much like video media, you can add audio files to your Web page. SiteBuilder supports the following audio media types:

- Windows Audio files (.mp3, .wav, .wma, .mid, .midi)
- RealAudio files (.rm, .ram)

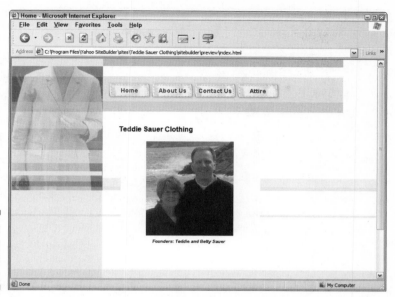

**Figure 12-3:**
Playing video media files.

These audio formats are standard stuff, but the visitor does need a media player installed that supports the format you're using.

Follow these steps to add an audio file to your Web page:

1. **Choose Insert⇨Audio from the main menu.**

   The Insert dialog box appears.

2. **Use the Look In pane to navigate to the audio file of your choice in the dialog box.**

3. **Click the Insert button.**

   The audio media element is added to your page in SiteBuilder's Design pane, as shown in Figure 12-4.

After adding your audio file to your Web page, you can modify how the visitor interacts with it.

Edit the properties of your audio file with these steps:

1. **Double-click the audio media element inside of the Design pane.**

   You can also right-click the element and choose Properties from the contextual menu that appears.

   The Audio Properties dialog box displays, as shown in Figure 12-5.

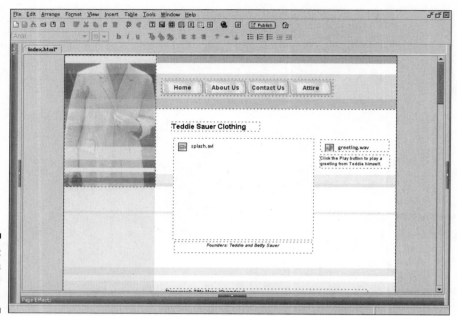

**Figure 12-4:**
Audio files
can do the
Web, too.

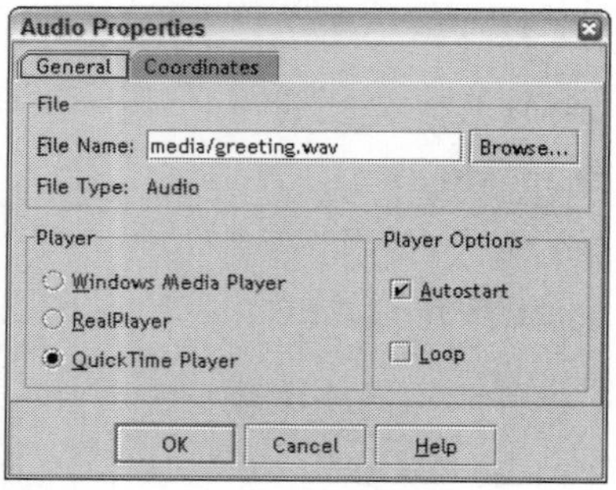

**Figure 12-5:**
Tweaking
the audio
properties.

2. **Place a check in the Autostart check box to automatically play the audio file when the page loads.**

   As with video media, if the file is at all large, be careful about using this option.

   If Autostart is disabled, the visitor can play the audio file using the Player button on the media player.

3. **Place a check in the Loop check box if you want to play the song or sound in a loop.**

4. **If you want to switch the audio player that plays the file, then choose a different option in the Player area.**

   SiteBuilder determines the initial choice by looking at the audio format. Therefore, in general, don't modify this setting unless you are certain that the player supports the file type you are using.

5. **Click OK to save changes.**

Figure 12-6 shows an embedded audio clip showing up inside of a browser.

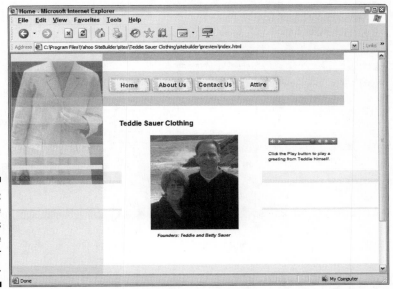

**Figure 12-6:**
A sound file always has visible player controls.

# Bringing Your Pages to Life with Page Effects

SiteBuilder comes packed with several built-in dynamic page effects that you can drop into your Web pages. For example, you can feature an image moving around your page border or flying in from the edge of the browser window. When used effectively, page effects can bring an otherwise dull page to life and bring a fun-loving aura to your Web site.

Page effects are different from normal elements you work with on your Web page. All the other elements drop onto the page of SiteBuilder's Design pane. You can then work with them inside the page itself — moving, resizing, and arranging them alongside the other elements. In contrast, page effects don't appear anywhere inside the Design pane. Visual effects are shown in the browser at *run time* — when the page is being viewed — but don't display at *design time* — when you're editing the page inside of SiteBuilder. Instead, the page effects show up as icons inside the Page Effects pane, as shown in Figure 12-7.

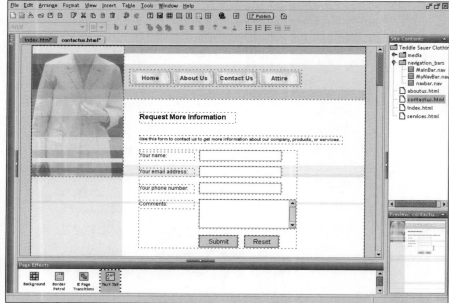

**Figure 12-7:**
The Page Effects pane is your home for the page effects icons.

# Viewing the Page Effects pane

If the Page Effects pane is not visible in SiteBuilder, you can perform one of two actions:

- ✔ Choose View⇨Show Page Effects Pane from the main menu.
- ✔ Click the up arrow in the blue region of the Page Effects pane to expand it to normal size.

# Accessing the Page Effects properties

After you add a page effect to your Web page, you can access its properties by double-clicking its icon in the Page Effects pane. You can also right-click the icon and choose Properties from the contextual menu that appears.

## *Cutting, copying, and pasting page effects*

Like all other elements inside of SiteBuilder, you can right-click the page effects icon to access several functions from its contextual menu, including Cut, Copy, Paste, and Duplicate. Using these commands, you can copy page effects between pages or inside the same page. If you need some help on copying and pasting inside of SiteBuilder, check out Chapter 4.

# *Adding SiteBuilder's Page Effects*

SiteBuilder comes with eight built-in page effects that are accessible from the Insert menu. Use this section to explore both what the page effects do and how you can add them to your Web page.

Before you go crazy and add page effects throughout your Web site, be sure to read the "Knowing When and When Not to Use Page Effects" section, later in this chapter. It contains several factors to consider before going live with them.

## *Dancing with the Border Patrol*

The Border Patrol creates an animation effect around the edge of your Web pages. You can specify an image or set of images to navigate around your page at various directions and speeds.

Follow these steps to add a Border Patrol effect to your Web page:

1. **Choose Insert⇨Page Effects⇨Border Patrol from the main menu.**

   You'll notice two things happen. First, a Border Patrol icon drops into the Page Effects pane. Second, the Border Patrol Properties dialog box appears, as shown in Figure 12-8.

**Figure 12-8:**
Setting up
the Border
Patrol.

2. **Choose an image to display for each of the four directions — North, West, East, and South.**

   You can use the Browse button to navigate to the file you need.

   You can use the same image in all four directions or else use different graphics on each side.

3. **In the Direction drop-down menu, choose the direction for the Border Patrol to travel: clockwise, counterclockwise, or random (periodically switches back and forth).**

4. **Determine the size of the margin between the Border Patrol and the edge of the Web page. Specify the size in the Margin drop-down menu.**

5. **Choose the speed at which you want your Border Patrol to move in the Movement Speed drop-down menu.**

6. **Click OK to save the effect.**

You won't notice any change to the Web page itself inside of SiteBuilder's Design pane — everything pretty much stays as is, including the Border Patrol icon you added to the Page Effects pane in Step 1.

 You can preview the Border Patrol by choosing File➪Preview in Browser (or simply by pressing F12). Figure 12-9 shows the sample Border Patrol.

**Figure 12-9:**
Border
Patrol,
ready to
take a run.

# Jumping with Bouncing Images

If your idea of being "edgy" goes beyond the perimeter walking behavior of the Border Patrol, you may want to spice things up with the Bouncing Images effect. The Bouncing Images effect animates one or more instances (actually, any number between 1 and 50) of an image, making them bounce all over your page.

You can add a Bouncing Images effect to your Web page with these steps:

1. **Choose Insert⇨Page Effects⇨Bouncing Images from the main menu.**

   A Bouncing Images icon drops into the Page Effects pane, and the Bouncing Images Properties dialog box appears, as shown in Figure 12-10.

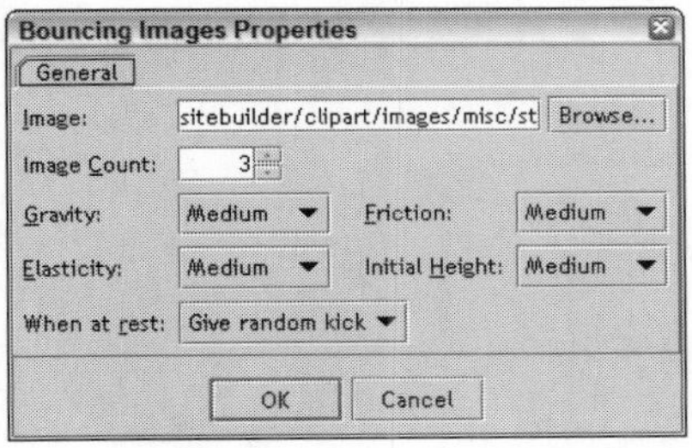

**Figure 12-10:** Bouncing your way through the Bouncing Images Properties dialog box.

2. **Choose an image that you want to bounce around all over your Web page.**

   You can use the Browse button to navigate to the image file you need.

3. **In the Image Count box, enter the desired number of jumping instances of your image.**

4. **Enter the desired jump settings for the image in the drop-down menus.**

   - *Gravity* indicates the amount of downward pull that the image has on its jumps. Making it low makes the jumps slower; increasing its value makes the jumps sharp.

   - *Friction* specifies the amount of resistance the image has on its upward jump.

   - *Elasticity* indicates the amount of bounce that the image has.

- *Initial Height* defines the image's starting point.

- *When at Rest* tells what to do with an image that has lost its bounce — drop from the sky, give it a kick, or let it just sit there.

**5. Click OK to save the effect.**

The Bouncing Images icon in the Page Effects pane stores your effect settings.

 You can preview the Border Patrol by choosing File⇨Preview in Browser (or simply by pressing F12). Figure 12-11 shows a sample Bouncing Images effect.

**Figure 12-11:**
Bouncin' and behavin' images.

# Hitchin' a ride with the Flyby

Call me crazy, but SiteBuilder's Flyby effect always reminds me of the climax of Hitchcock's *North by Northwest:* the classic crop-duster scene. If you recall the moment, Cary Grant's character is running and hiding from a plane bent on mowing him down. The crop-duster does several flybys as it attempts to encircle its victim but gets a little too carried away and ends up crashing and burning on the deserted road. Fortunately, when you use the Flyby, you don't need to worry about hiding in a cornfield or avoiding a fiery crash, but you do get an animated image that flies by your Web page — again and again and again.

To add a Flyby effect to your Web page

1. **Choose Insert⇨Page Effects⇨Flyby from the main menu.**

   A Flyby icon drops in the Page Effects pane, and the Flyby Properties dialog box appears, as shown in Figure 12-12.

**Figure 12-12:**
Ladies and gentlemen, you are now free to fly around your Web page.

2. **Choose an image that you want to fly by your Web page.**

   You can use the Browse button to navigate to the image you wish to use.

3. **Enter the desired flight motion settings for the image in the drop-down menus.**

   - *Speed* indicates the speed of the image as it performs its flyby.

   - *Direction* specifies whether you want the flyby to go right or left.

   - *Position* tells the vertical positioning of the flyby — top, middle, or bottom of page.

   - *Delay* indicates how long the image waits after it leaves the browser before starting the next flyby. You can specify no wait to a wait of up to 10 seconds.

   - The *Offset* value is the number of pixels to adjust the position the flyby relative to the Position value. This value is handy when you want to precisely position the flyby to a particular vertical location.

   - The *Offset Variation* indicates the range (in pixels) that the flyby can occur, relative to the Position value.

   The Offset Variation setting is particularly helpful when you want to use the Flyby effect but want a certain amount of randomness to the flybys.

4. **Click OK to save the effect.**

   The Flyby icon in the Page Effects pane stores your effect settings.

You can preview the Flyby choosing File⇨Preview in Browser (or simply by pressing F12). Figure 12-13 shows the sample Flyby effect.

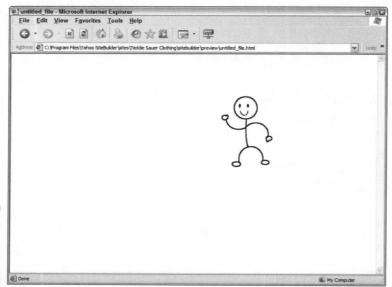

**Figure 12-13:**
Flying
around
the Web.

# Tagging along with the mouse: Text Tail and Image Tail effects

The Text Tail and Image Tail effects are reminiscent of my clunker of a car in high school, the one that was always trailing transmission fluid. The Text Tail effect adds a string of text that follows the mouse when you move it around on the Web page. The Image Tail effect has essentially the same behavior but uses an image.

The following sections show you how to add the Text Tail and Image Text effects to your site.

 Be prudent in using mouse tailing effects. You are probably going to enjoy these effects more than the visitor will.

To add a Text Tail effect

1. **Choose Insert⇨Page Effects⇨Text Tail from the main menu.**

   A Text Tail icon drops into the Page Effects pane, and the Text Tail Properties dialog box appears, as shown in Figure 12-14.

**Figure 12-14:**
Static cling,
text style.

2. **Enter the text you want to have as your text tail in the Message box.**

3. **Provide the desired settings for the text as it trails the mouse:**

   • *Speed* indicates how closely the text follows the mouse movements.

   • *Size* specifies the size of the text.

   • *Spacing* indicates the amount of space in between the text characters.

   • *Style* sets the text to be bold or normal.

   • *Color* indicates the text color.

4. **Click OK to save the effect.**

   The Text Tail icon in the Page Effects pane stores your effect settings.

Figure 12-15 shows the Text Tail effect when displayed in the browser.

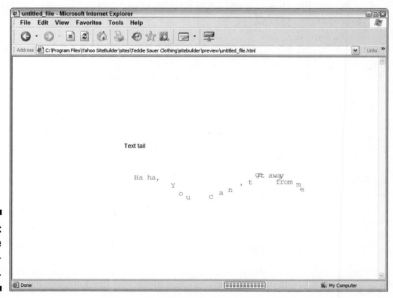

**Figure 12-15:**
The mouse
went that-
a-way.

To add an Image Tail effect

1. **Choose Insert⇨Page Effects⇨Image Tail from the main menu.**

   An Image Tail icon drops into the Page Effects pane, and the Image Tail Properties dialog box appears, as shown in Figure 12-16.

**Figure 12-16:** Catching a mouse by his tail.

2. **In the Tail Image box, enter the image filename that you want to use as the tailing image, the one displayed when following the mouse.**

   You can use the Browse button to navigate to the image you wish to use.

3. **In the Resting Image box, specify the image that you want to display when the mouse stops.**

   Once again, you can use the Browse button beside the Resting Image box to navigate to the image you wish to use.

4. **Choose the desired settings for the image as it tags along behind the mouse:**

   • *Position* indicates the starting position of the Tail Image when the effect begins.

   • *Tail Length* specifies the number of image instances that are shown as the animated tail.

   • *Speed* indicates how closely the image follows the mouse.

5. **Click OK to save the effect.**

   The Image Tail icon in the Page Effects pane stores your effect settings.

Figure 12-17 shows the Image Tail effect when displayed in the browser.

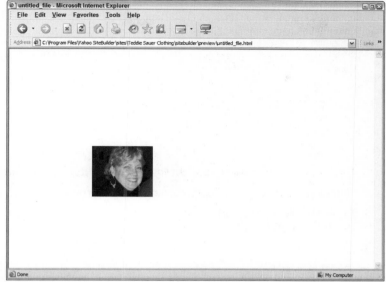

**Figure 12-17:**
Image Tail effect: a relentless pursuit of a mouse.

# Adding random acts of effects with Random Apparitions

In naming the Random Apparitions effect, I wonder if Yahoo! somehow teamed up with some word-of-the-day dictionary site to include a word in SiteBuilder that many people may not be familiar with. Well, in case you are in that boat and don't know exactly what "apparition" means, let me give you the definition: An apparition is the appearance of something unexpected or ghostly. Therefore, the Random Apparitions effect displays images on the Web page at random locations at random times. It's all so unexpected!

Follow these steps to add a Random Apparitions effect to your Web page:

1. **Choose Insert⇨Page Effects⇨Random Apparitions from the main menu.**

   A Random Apparitions icon drops into the Page Effects pane, and the Random Apparitions Properties dialog box appears, as shown in Figure 12-18.

**Figure 12-18:**
Ghostly and
unexpected.
What else
could
you expect
from an
apparition?

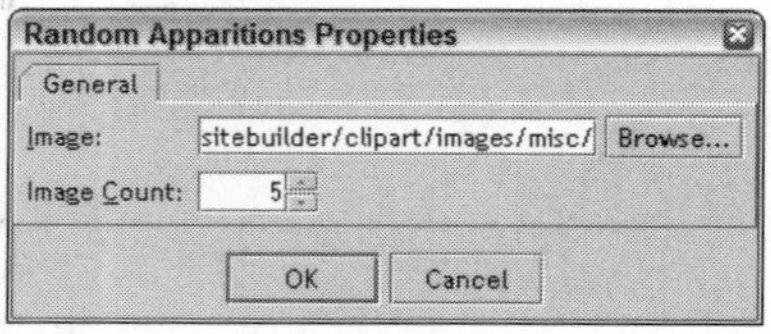

2. **Choose an image that you want to appear randomly on your Web page.**

   You can use the Browse button to navigate to the image you wish to use.

3. **Enter the desired number of instances that you want to appear randomly at a given time.**

4. **Click OK to save the effect.**

   The Random Apparitions icon in the Page Effects pane stores your effect settings.

You can preview the Random Apparitions by choosing File⇨Preview in Browser from the main menu (or simply by pressing F12).

## Staying put with an Edge-Locked Picture

Most of the SiteBuilder page effects are designed to animate an image or string of text and have it move around on the page. In contrast, the Edge-Locked Picture effect does just the opposite: It places an image on the edge of your browser window and then locks up the image and throws away the key, so to speak. Therefore, even when the visitor scrolls down the page, the image remains stationed at the exact position in the browser window.

The Edge-Locked Picture effect is perhaps the most useful of the page effects, because it can be employed for practical purposes, even on business sites. However, you must use it carefully and appropriately so that it does not become a nuisance to site visitors.

To add an Edge-Locked Picture effect to your Web page:

1. **Choose Insert⇨Page Effects⇨Edge-Locked Picture from the main menu.**

   An Edge-Locked Picture icon drops into the Page Effects pane, and the Edge-Locked Picture Properties dialog box appears, as shown in Figure 12-19.

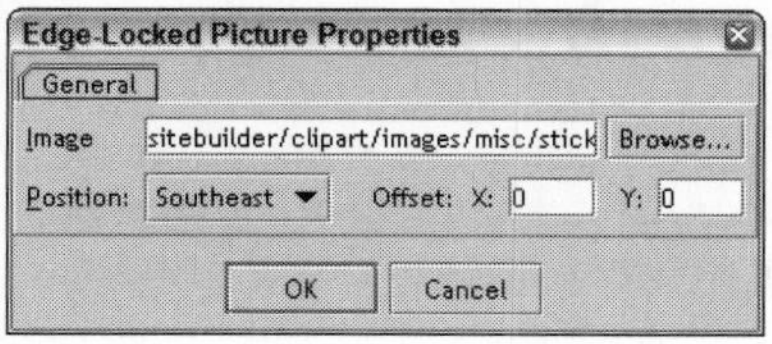

**Figure 12-19:**
Anchoring a
picture to
the edge of
the browser.

**Edge-Locked Picture Properties** ⊠

General

Image   sitebuilder/clipart/images/misc/stick   Browse...

Position:   Southeast ▾      Offset:   X: 0      Y: 0

OK          Cancel

2. **Choose an image that you want to set as the edge-locked picture on your Web page.**

   You can use the Browse button to navigate to the image you wish to use.

3. **Use the Position drop-down menu to specify the directional position that you want the picture to display in the browser window.**

4. **Use the Offset X and Y boxes to tweak the exact positioning of the text.**

   The X and Y coordinates are always relative to the Position value.

5. **Click OK to save the effect.**

   The Edge-Locked Picture icon in the Page Effects pane stores your effect settings.

When you display the edge-locked picture in the browser, the picture stays put even when the page is scrolled. (See Figure 12-20.)

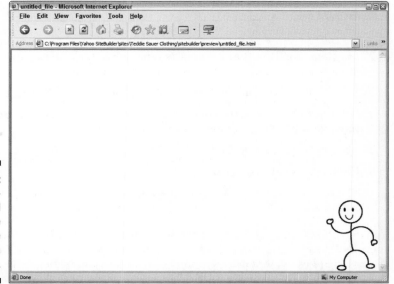

**Figure 12-20:**
The Edge-
Locked
Picture
effect at the
bottom of a
Web page.

# *Adding IE Page Transitions*

The IE Page Transitions effect provides animated transitions when you enter or leave a Web page. If you've ever seen transitions used in a PowerPoint slide presentation, then you have an idea what IE Page Transitions do.

The caveat, however, is the "IE" you see at the front of the name. IE stands for *Internet Explorer,* which means that these effects work only in IE browsers. Because IE has the vast majority of browser market share, most of your visitors will be able to see them, but you can't count on it, especially with the recent surge in popularity of the Mozilla Firefox browser.

To add an IE Page Transitions effect to your Web page, follow these steps:

1. **Choose Insert⇨Page Effects⇨ IE Page Transitions from the main menu.**

   An IE Page Transitions icon drops into the Page Effects pane, and the IE Page Transitions Properties dialog box appears, as shown in Figure 12-21.

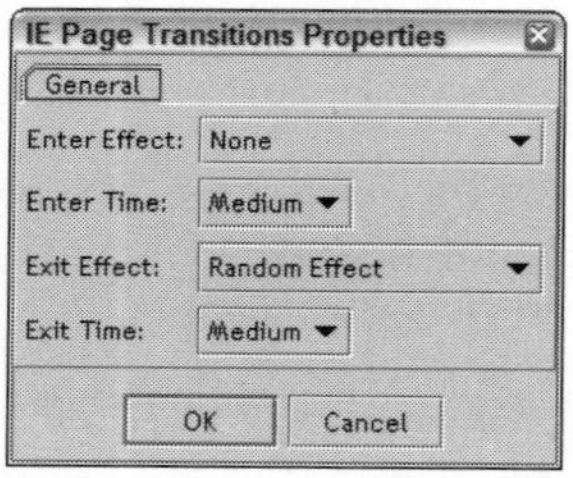

**Figure 12-21:**
Adding a
transition to
your page.

2. **For the transition that kicks in when the visitor enters your page, choose a transition effect from the Enter Effect list.**

3. **Specify the speed of the Page Enter transition in the Enter Time list.**

4. **Use the Exit Effect drop-down menu to declare the effect you want to have kick in when the page is exited.**

5. **Specify the speed of the Page Exit transition in the Exit Time list.**

6. **Click OK to save the effect.**

   The IE Page Transitions icon in the Page Effects pane stores your effect settings.

You can choose among over 25 page transitions. In trying to decide which ones look best, experiment. To do so, double-click an icon in the Page Effects pane to display the IE Page Transitions Properties dialog box. Choose a different transition effect, and click OK. Then preview the page by pressing F12. Repeat for as many of these transitions as you wish.

# Knowing When and When Not to Use Page Effects

Multimedia elements and page effects are a great way to add life to your Web site and can be a breath of fresh air to an otherwise dull and lifeless Web presence. However, exactly how much you should use the "Wow Factor" on your public Web site depends largely on the site's purposes.

If you have a personal or family site, go for it. In general, you can be as creative and artistic as you like for your friends and family who frequent it. If they become annoyed by anything, they probably know you personally and can complain about it. However, if you're designing a Web site for a business or other organization, you have many more factors to consider.

## Multimedia issues

A video or audio file can be an effective way to communicate with visitors on your site. However, multimedia files always are expensive in terms of their size, so be careful in how you use them. This reality is not always easy to realize when you test your site on your local machine (where transmission speed is a nonissue) or if you personally have a high-speed connection to the Internet. However, always consider the dialup visitor to your site, and be sensitive to the exponentially longer times downloading any kind of multimedia data takes. Given that reality, always allow a site visitor to initiate the playing of a large multimedia file. Frankly, in most situations, unless the file is under 100K, I recommend not enabling Autostart.

In addition, you'll want to avoid automatically playing an audio clip when the visitor comes to your Web page. Just say no. Cheesy background music cheapens the impact of the site and probably chases more people away from sites than any other single annoyance.

## Page effects issues

If you are designing a Web site for your company or organization, you'll usually want to steer away from using page effects. Yes, they are fun and can add pizzazz to your Web site, but they're almost always inappropriate for normal business usage. As nifty as they may be, many visitors coming to your site will find them distracting, annoying, and unprofessional — the online equivalent of plastic gnomes in the middle of your front lawn. And, just as you won't find any cute little gnomes in front of the corporate headquarters of Microsoft or Toyota, you're not going to find a flyby or page transition at their Web sites.

Above all, don't add Text Tail or Image Tail effects to any site that you wouldn't also be willing to put a "we want to annoy you just for the heck of it" banner on your home page.

However, some of the effects could be perfectly acceptable for business Web sites in certain occasions. Suppose, for example, a section of your Web site is used as a slide-like presentation showing off your products or services — much like a PowerPoint presentation might look. In this scenario, SiteBuilder page effects can be an effective, creative way of presenting the information to the visitor and transitioning between "slides."

# Chapter 13

# For Geeks Only?
# Adding HTML and JavaScript
# Code to Your Pages

*"P*ixie dust" refers to a trail of sparkly, magical material that follows pixies and fairies. Ancient myth has it that Web geeks have a similar mysterious trail that follows them, called "geeky dust." According to the legend, however, once you get the substance on your hands, you're done for: you slowly begin to turn into a geek yourself. Your previous normal life is transformed into one filled with late-night Web programming, chat rooms about the latest code optimization techniques, and a closet full of *Star Wars* t-shirts and comic books.

In this chapter, you enter geek territory, the "subterranean world" lurking beneath the surface of your Web site. This techie world is filled with such terms as *HTML, JavaScript,* and *code* — words that can initially seem intimidating. But before you run for cover, allow me to reassure you; I explain only what you really need to know about this stuff to improve your Web site. If you follow my steps, you can discover how to add HTML and JavaScript to your SiteBuilder Web site and get through the process unscathed — emerging at the end of the chapter 100 percent free from any geeky dust residue.

# Looking Behind the Curtain: HTML and JavaScript

I've not often spoken of it, but as you work with various aspects of SiteBuilder to create your Web site, you are actually adding and editing HTML markup code and occasionally even JavaScript scripts to create your Web pages. As Chapter 1 discusses, HTML is the "language of the Web" — the coded instructions that tell the browser what to display and how to display it. JavaScript is a script programming language that allows you to add interactivity to your pages.

## Letting SiteBuilder get its hands dirty, not yours

The great thing about SiteBuilder is that it allows you to create and work with Web pages using the handy Design pane rather than being forced to code the pages manually. In this regard, SiteBuilder acts much like a translator, taking the design that you create inside the visual domains of SiteBuilder and turning it into code that the browser can display. For example, consider the Web page shown in Figure 13-1, created using SiteBuilder. Listing 13-1 shows portions of the actual HTML and JavaScript code that displays this page. (Please note that major portions of the code are actually missing, because the complete file listing ran for over 13 pages. Aren't you glad you don't have to type all this stuff in??!!)

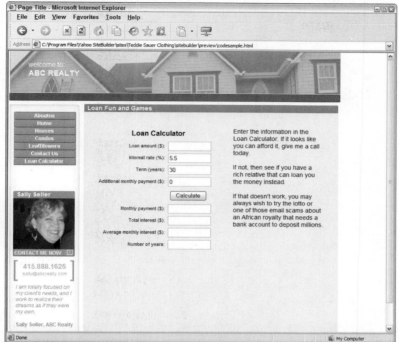

**Figure 13-1:**
Beauty
really is
skin deep.
Behind this
nice-looking
Web page
is some
ugly code.

## Listing 13-1: Sampling of HTML Markup Instructions

```
<!--$templateKey Real Estate Agent|Urban - Green|2.0$-->
<html>
  <head>
    <title>Page Title</title>
    <meta name="generator" content="Yahoo! SiteBuilder/2.2 ">
    <style type="text/css"><!--
      BODY {font-family:"Arial"; font-size:14;}
      P {font-family:"Arial"; font-size:14;}
    --></style>
  </head>
<body bgcolor="#FFFFFF" text="#000000" link="#0000FF" vlink="#800080"
            onLoad="init()" onResize="if (ns4) history.go(0);"
            marginheight="0" marginwidth="1" topmargin="0" leftmargin="1"
            hspace="1" vspace="0">
```

*(continued)*

## Listing 13-1 *(continued)*

```html
<form name="Form0" method="POST" action="" onSubmit="return checkForm0()">
<!--$name Loan Calculator$--><!--$table$--><table style="table-
               layout:fixed;border:0px none #000000" width=312 height=311
               border=0 cellspacing=0 cellpadding=0><col width="312"><tr>

<td style="border:0px none #DCDCDC" width="312" height="311" valign="top">
               <table border="0" cellspacing="0" cellpadding="0" width="312"
               height="311">
    <tr>
      <td width="312" height="7" colspan="9"></td>
    </tr>
    <tr>
      <td width="37" height="20" colspan="2"></td>
      <td nowrap height="20" colspan="5" align="center" valign="top"><!--
               $begin locked [xAxis, yAxis]$--><!--$name Loan
               Calculator$--><!--$name Loan Calculator$--><span
               class="text"><b><font size="3"><span style="font-size:16px;line-
               height:19px;">Loan Calculator<br
               soft></span></font></b></span><!--$end name$--><!--$end locked$--
               ></td>
      <td width="32" height="20" colspan="2"></td>

    </tr>
<!--$begin locked [contents, xAxis, yAxis]$--><!--$begin htmlBefore$--><SCRIPT
               LANGUAGE="JavaScript1.2"><!--

function computeLoan(f) {
  var errorMessage = "";
  var principal = stringToNumber(f.amount.value);
  var rate      = stringToNumber(f.rate.value);
  var years     = stringToNumber(f.term.value);
  var addition  = stringToNumber(f.additional.value);

  if (principal == null || isNaN(principal) || principal <= 0) { errorMessage +=
               "Please enter a positive number for the loan amount.\n"; }
  if (rate == null      || isNaN(rate)      || rate <= 0)      { errorMessage +=
               "Please enter a positive number for the interest rate.\n"; }
  if (years == null     || isNaN(years)     || years <= 0)     { errorMessage +=
               "Please enter a positive number for the term.\n"; }
  if (addition == null  || isNaN(addition)  || addition < 0)   { errorMessage +=
               "Please enter 0 or a positive number for the additional monthly
               payment.\n"; }

  if (errorMessage != "") {
    alert(errorMessage);
    setLoanCalcResults(f,"","","","");
  }
  else {
    var period   = 12;
    var interest = rate / (period * 100);
```

```
      var periods  = years * period;
      var periodPayment = addition + ( principal * ( interest / ( 1 - Math.pow( (1
              + interest) , (0 - periods) ) ) ) );
      periods = 0 - ( Math.log( 1 - (interest * principal / periodPayment) ) /
              Math.log(1 + interest) );
      var interest_total = (periodPayment * periods) - principal;
      setLoanCalcResults( f, periodPayment, interest_total, (interest_total /
              periods), (periods / period) );
  }
}

<!--$end htmlBefore$--><input type="button" value="Calculate"
            onClick="computeLoan(this.form);"><!--$end locked$--></td>
        <td width="14" height="30"></td>
      </tr>
      <tr>
        <td width="312" height="2" colspan="9"></td>

      </tr>
      <tr>
        <td width="7" height="22"></td>
        <td nowrap height="22" colspan="2" align="right"><!--$begin locked
            [xAxis, yAxis]$--><!--$name actual_term$--><!--$name actual_term$-
            -><span class="text"><font size="1"><span
            style="font-size:11px;line-height:14px;">Number of years:<br
            soft></span></font></span><!--$end name$--><!--$end locked$--
            ></td>
        <td width="7" height="22"></td>
        <td height="26" colspan="2" rowspan="2" valign="top"><!--$begin locked
            [contents, xAxis, yAxis]$--><input name="num_of_years" value=""
            size="12"><!--$end locked$--></td>
        <td width="34" height="22" colspan="3"></td>
      </tr>

      <tr>
        <td width="181" height="4" colspan="4"></td>
        <td width="34" height="4" colspan="3"></td>
      </tr>
      <tr>
        <td width="312" height="17" colspan="9"></td>
      </tr>
    </table>
</td>
</tr>
</table>
</form>
</div>
    <div id="e1"
            style="position:absolute;left:13;top:145;width:141;height:126;"><!
            --$navbar
name=sf.nav
assetID=%NavbarAsset:/navigation_bars/sf.nav
```

*(continued)*

**Listing 13-1** *(continued)*

```
$--><!--$begin exclude$--><table border="0" cellspacing="0"
        cellpadding="0"><tr><td><a href="sitebuilder/preview/aboutus.html"
        onMouseOver="document.images['i1'].src='sitebuilder/images/sf-0-
        mouseOver-04000.png'"
        onMouseOut="document.images['i1'].src='sitebuilder/images/sf-0-
        inactive-03906.png'"><img name="i1"
        src="sitebuilder/images/sf-0-inactive-03906.png" border="0"
        width="141" height="18" alt=""/></a></td></tr><tr><td><a
        href="sitebuilder/preview/addons21.html"
        onMouseOver="document.images['i2'].src='sitebuilder/images/sf-1-
        mouseOver-04171.png'"
        onMouseOut="document.images['i2'].src='sitebuilder/images/sf-1-
        inactive-04062.png'"><img name="i2"
        src="sitebuilder/images/sf-1-inactive-04062.png" border="0"
        width="141" height="18" alt=""/></a></td></tr><tr><td><a
        href="sitebuilder/preview/index.html"
        onMouseOver="document.images['i3'].src='sitebuilder/images/sf-2-
        mouseOver-04312.png'"
        onMouseOut="document.images['i3'].src='sitebuilder/images/sf-2-
        inactive-04218.png'"><img name="i3"
        src="sitebuilder/images/sf-2-inactive-04218.png" border="0"
        width="141" height="18" alt=""/></a></td></tr><tr><td><a
        href="sitebuilder/preview/contactus.html"
        onMouseOver="document.images['i4'].src='sitebuilder/images/sf-3-
        mouseOver-04500.png'"
        onMouseOut="document.images['i4'].src='sitebuilder/images/sf-3-
        inactive-04359.png'"><img name="i4"
        src="sitebuilder/images/sf-3-inactive-04359.png" border="0"
        width="141" height="18" alt=""/></a></td></tr><tr><td><a
        href="sitebuilder/preview/search_results.html"
        onMouseOver="document.images['i5'].src='sitebuilder/images/sf-4-
        mouseOver-04656.png'"
        onMouseOut="document.images['i5'].src='sitebuilder/images/sf-4-
        inactive-04546.png'"><img name="i5"
        src="sitebuilder/images/sf-4-inactive-04546.png" border="0"
        width="141" height="18" alt=""/></a></td></tr><tr><td><a
        href="sitebuilder/preview/addons.html"
        onMouseOver="document.images['i6'].src='sitebuilder/images/sf-5-
        mouseOver-04812.png'"
        onMouseOut="document.images['i6'].src='sitebuilder/images/sf-5-
        inactive-04718.png'"><img name="i6"
        src="sitebuilder/images/sf-5-inactive-04718.png" border="0"
        width="141" height="18" alt=""/></a></td></tr><tr><td><a
        href="sitebuilder/preview/services.html"
        onMouseOver="document.images['i7'].src='sitebuilder/images/sf-6-
        mouseOver-04984.png'"
        onMouseOut="document.images['i7'].src='sitebuilder/images/sf-6-
        inactive-04875.png'"><img name="i7"
        src="sitebuilder/images/sf-6-inactive-04875.png" border="0"
        width="141" height="18" alt=""/></a></td></tr></table><!--$end
        exclude$--></div>
```

```
    <div id="e0"
            style="position:absolute;left:512;top:180;width:205;height:265;"><
            span class="text"><span style="font-size:14px;line-
            height:17px;">Enter the information in the <br soft>Loan
            Calculator. If it looks like <br soft>you can afford it, give me a
            call <br soft>today.<br><br>If not, then see if you have a <br
            soft>rich relative that can loan you <br soft>the money
            instead.<br><br>If that doesn't work, you may <br soft>always wish
            to try the lotto or <br soft>one of those email scams about <br
            soft>an African royalty that needs a <br soft>bank account to
            deposit millions.<br soft><br soft></span></span></div>

    </body>
</html>
```

Okay, now that you are probably feeling itchy all over for fear of geeky dust contamination, don't fear. You never need to look at your document like this using SiteBuilder. Instead, when you need to dip inside of HTML, you can do it through a much simpler manner, which I discuss in the "Peeking into the HTML Behind Your Web Page" section, later in the chapter.

## Yup, you can "do code," but why?

For nearly all page-building tasks, SiteBuilder allows you to ignore, bypass, and simply forget all about that yucky code lurking underneath the surface. In this way, you can create, design, and edit in peace without fear of being exposed to geeky dust. However, you may wish to incorporate some advanced features and functionality into your Web site — features that aren't directly supported inside of SiteBuilder itself, including

✔ Yahoo! add-ons that are available from within the Web Hosting Control Panel.

✔ JavaScript scripts that provide additional functionality, such as image effects.

✔ Any HTML markup that you want to add to your site, such as special meta information and code for integrating with a third-party Web service.

## Peeking into the HTML Behind Your Web Page

Any HTML file is divided into two main parts: head and body. The *head* contains behind-the-scenes information about the Web page, and none of the contents of the head actually display inside the browser. You can place the page's title, search engine keywords, and author information in the head (though SiteBuilder does this automatically for you via the Page Properties dialog box). The head is also a common catchall place to enter JavaScript scripts. The *body* contains all the text and markup instructions that tell the browser what to display and how to display it.

The Head section is enclosed in a `<head>` and `</head>` tag pair, while the Body section is surrounded by a `<body>` and `</body>` tag pair.

SiteBuilder gives you three separate ways to access this world of HTML:

- The HTML element
- The HTML item on the right-click contextual menu of the page (see Figure 13-2)
- The HTML item on the right-click contextual menu of several page elements, such as Text or Image

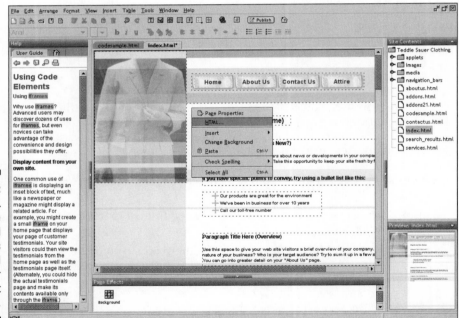

**Figure 13-2:** The HTML item on the contextual menu allows you to add HTML or JavaScript code.

In each of these ways, SiteBuilder opens a dialog box that enables you to add HTML or JavaScript code. SiteBuilder doesn't provide a page editor for working with the entire HTML code of your Web page, such as what you see in Listing 13-1. That'd be full-fledged geeky dust territory!

Instead, SiteBuilder opens up "portals" into specific parts of the Web page. Exactly where you add HTML and JavaScript code is critical to its correct display and operation. Therefore, before you add code to your Web pages, be sure you understand the differences in these locations — an understanding that will magically come to you if you read the next sections.

## HTML element

SiteBuilder has an HTML element that you can add to your Web page. This element serves as a container for HTML code that you wish to add to your page. Follow these steps to add an HTML element:

1. **Choose Insert⇨Code Elements⇨HTML from the main menu.**

   The HTML Code dialog box appears, as shown in Figure 13-3.

**Figure 13-3:** The home base for geek wannabes in SiteBuilder.

2. **Paste any HTML code you may have received from elsewhere, or type your own code into the box provided.**

3. **Click OK.**

   The HTML element is added to your Web page, as shown in Figure 13-4.

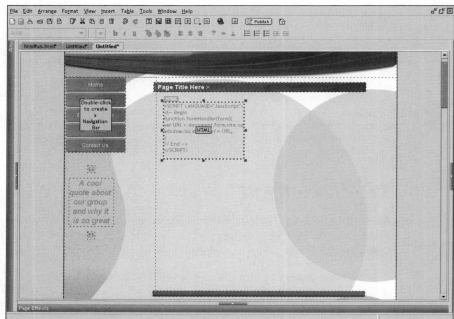

**Figure 13-4:**
The HTML element, a "home sweet home" for your code.

Keep in mind the following in terms of size and positioning on the page:

- ✔ The underlying HTML code uses the top-left corner of the HTML element as the starting point for its display. You can move the HTML element around on your page like any other page element in SiteBuilder to position it appropriately.

- ✔ The dimensions of the HTML element have no bearing on the amount of space that the HTML code inside of the element uses for displaying itself. Therefore, I recommend resizing the HTML element in SiteBuilder's Design pane after you preview the page in a browser. Doing so enables you to approximate the real estate being used by the HTML inside of your SiteBuilder page.

You can also edit the HTML code inside of an HTML element by double-clicking it.

# Page level HTML

If you right-click the page itself and choose HTML from its contextual menu, the page-level HTML Properties dialog box, shown in Figure 13-5, makes an appearance.

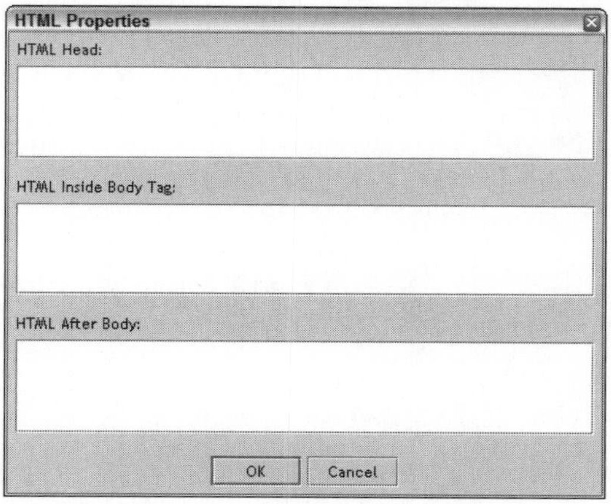

**HTML Properties**

HTML Head:

HTML Inside Body Tag:

HTML After Body:

OK    Cancel

**Figure 13-5:**
Page-level
HTML
properties.

As Figure 13-5 makes abundantly clear, the HTML Properties dialog box has three locations where you can add code:

✔ **HTML Head:** Any markup code that you add here goes inside of the Head section.

Place any JavaScript scripts that impact the whole page here.

✔ **HTML Inside Body Tag:** Code you insert here is added inside the `<body>` tag.

Given that, the code must be in the form of a name-value pair, such as `marginheight="0"` or `bgcolor="#ffffff"`.

✔ **HTML After Body:** Any code you add here is placed at the end of the Body section, just inside the `</body>` tag.

## Page element HTML

The HTML element and the page-level locations for adding code can generally handle nearly all your needs. However, on occasion, you may need to add HTML code either before or after another on-screen element that you have. For these situations, right-click the page element itself and then select HTML from the contextual menu that appears in order to access a slightly different dialog box. (See Figure 13-6.)

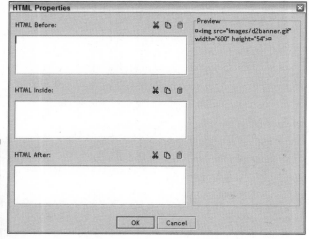

**Figure 13-6:**
HTML
properties
for an image
element.

In the HTML Properties dialog box for the element, you can add code in any of the following three places:

- **HTML Before:** Code added inside this box is placed *before* the element you're modifying.

- **HTML Inside:** For code added inside this box, SiteBuilder adds it into the tag itself. As a result, format the code as a name-value pair, such as `font="Arial"`.

- **HTML After:** The code that you add in this box is placed just *after* the element you're modifying.

# Adding Yahoo! HTML Add-Ons to Your Web Site

As Chapter 11 discusses, SiteBuilder has several Yahoo! add-ons — the Yahoo! Map and Counter, for example — built right into the product itself. However, Yahoo! also has several more add-ons that aren't inside SiteBuilder. You can access these by going to your Yahoo! Web Hosting Control Panel (accessible from Tools⇨Web Hosting Control Panel from the menu). Once there, click the Create & Update tab and then click the <u>Add-Ons</u> link. The Add-Ons page displays, as shown in Figure 13-7.

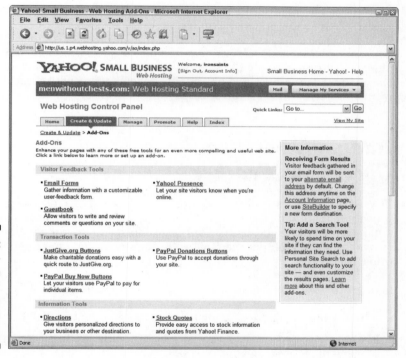

**Figure 13-7:** The Add-Ons page in the Yahoo! Web Hosting Control Panel.

On this Web page, you can choose among several add-ons, but some of the most noteworthy include

- ✔ **News Headlines:** Incorporates news or sports headlines into your Web page.
- ✔ **Stock Quotes:** Displays the latest stock quotes.
- ✔ **Weather:** Lists the weather forecast from one or more cities around the world.
- ✔ **Pull-Down Menu:** Adds a drop-down menu to your site as an alternative navigation tool to a navigation bar.
- ✔ **Guestbook:** Allows visitors to leave you messages.

All you need to incorporate these add-ons to your Web site are a few simple steps, which I show you in the following sections.

You'll notice that some add-ons featured on this page (Counter, Yahoo! Map, and Site Search) are the same as the ones provided already inside of SiteBuilder. Ignore these add-ons on this page: Working with these add-ons within SiteBuilder itself is much easier.

## Adding News Headlines, Stock Quotes, or Weather

The News Headlines, Stock Quotes, and Weather add-ons follow a similar procedure for adding them to your site. Use the following instructions for adding any of these add-ons to your page. I focus on the process for the News Headlines add-on, but you can follow these same general instructions for the other two as well.

In order to use these add-ons, you need to go through a three-step process:

1. Configure your add-on using the Web Hosting Control Panel.
2. Activate the add-on as a way of telling the Yahoo! Web server that you're using the add-on on your Web site.
3. Copy the add-on HTML code from the Web Hosting Control Panel and paste it into an HTML element on your Web page.

To add news, stock quotes, or weather to your Web site, follow these steps:

1. **Choose Tools⇨Web Hosting Control Panel from the menu.**

   SiteBuilder opens your default Web browser and takes you to your Yahoo! Web Hosting Control Panel.

**2. In the Quick Links list located on the top-right of the page, choose Add-ons and then click the Go button.**

The Add-On page displays.

**3. From your Web Hosting Control Panel's Add-On page, click the <u>News Headlines</u>, <u>Stock Quotes</u>, or <u>Weather</u> link on the Add-Ons page.**

**4. Navigate through the configuration process specific for the add-on that you selected.**

Each service has various options that you need to configure. The News and Weather add-ons take you through a few pages to select the information you want to display. The Stock Quotes add-on provides everything in a single page.

**5. When you configure all your options, click the Generate Code button.**

The HTML code for the add-on displays in a text box in your browser. Figure 13-8 shows the HTML code provided for the News Headlines add-on. The Weather add-on provides a similar-looking page.

*Note:* The Stock Quotes add-on generates the code and displays it in Step 6.

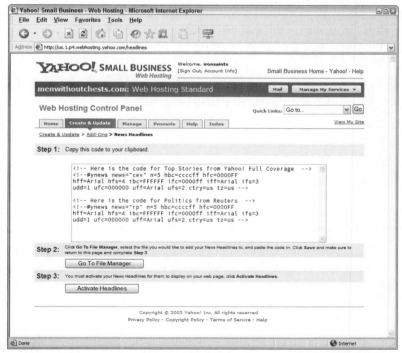

**Figure 13-8:**
HTML code
for an
add-on.

6. **Select all the HTML code provided in the text box and choose Edit⇨Copy from the browser menu.**

   For each of these services, the next step shown is a Go To File Manager button. Ignore this step! Because you are using SiteBuilder, you don't need to use the File Manager.

7. **Click the Activate Headlines, Activate Weather, or Activate Stock Quotes button.**

8. **Return to SiteBuilder.**

9. **Choose Insert⇨Code Elements⇨HTML from the menu.**

   The HTML Code dialog box appears. (Refer to Figure 13-3.)

10. **Click the Paste button or right-click and choose Paste from the contextual menu that appears.**

    The add-on code from the Web Hosting Control Panel is pasted into the dialog box.

11. **Click OK.**

    The HTML element is added to your Web page.

12. **Click and drag to position the HTML element in the desired location on your Web page.**

These add-ons do not function when you perform a local preview. Therefore, you need to publish your Web page in order to see how the add-on displays. Figure 13-9 shows the News Headlines add-on included on a Web page.

What's more, when you activate a new add-on service, you may need to wait a few minutes for the service to become active for your Web site. Therefore, if the add-on does not work correctly immediately after activating it, wait a few minutes and try again.

## Incorporating a pull-down menu

A pull-down menu — also known as a *drop-down* menu — is a space-saving alternative to a navigation bar to enable people to quickly go from one part of your site to the next. Or, if you have a large Web site, you could use it in combination with a navigation bar: The navigation bar could provide access to the major sections of the site, while the pull-down menu provides a list of the most frequently requested pages of your site. (However, for smaller Web sites, I don't recommend using both.)

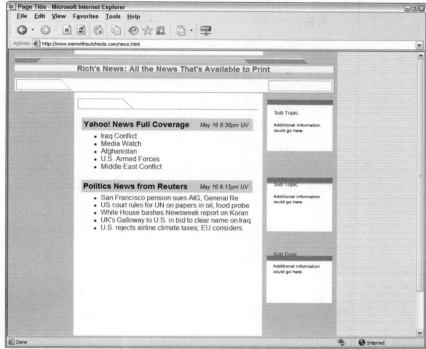

**Figure 13-9:**
Your Web
site, the
go-to place
for news-
hounds.

To add a pull-down menu add-on to your page, do the following:

1. **Choose Tools⇨Web Hosting Control Panel from the menu.**

   SiteBuilder opens your default Web browser and takes you to your
   Yahoo! Web Hosting Control Panel.

2. **In the Quick Links list located on the top-right of the page, choose
   Add-Ons and then click the Go button.**

   The Add-On page is displayed.

3. **From your Web Hosting Control Panel's Add-On page, click the
   <u>Pull-down Menu</u> link.**

   The Pull-down Menu page appears, as shown in Figure 13-10, with a
   sample pull-down menu displayed. The Step 1 box contains the HTML
   code to display this particular menu.

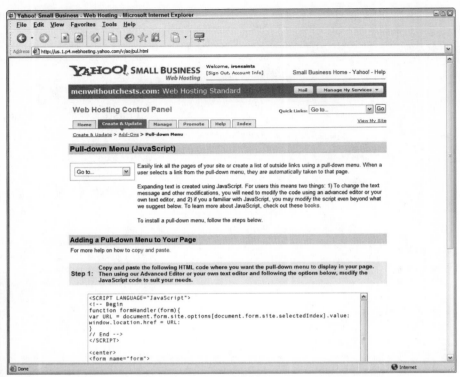

**Figure 13-10:**
Setting up
your own
pull-down
menu.

4. **Scroll down in the text box and locate the menu item code.**

   Look for this code:

   ```
   <option value="http://www.yahoo.com">Yahoo
   <option value="http://webhosting.yahoo.com/">Yahoo! Web Hosting
   <option value="http://shopping.yahoo.com/">Yahoo! Shopping
   <option value="http://travel.yahoo.com/">Yahoo! Travel
   ```

   Each of these items contains two pieces of information: (a) the URL that is navigated to when the item is selected and (b) the text that displays inside the menu drop-down list.

5. **Edit the first line of menu item code to point to a Web page on your site:**

   • Change the URL inside the quotation marks to point to a page on your site. Make sure that your URL remains enclosed in quotation marks.

   • Change the text after the > mark to create a label for the list item.

If you don't know the URL for a Web page of your site you want to link to, publish your site and then navigate to the page in your browser. Copy the URL from the browser's Address box and then paste the URL into the Edit box.

6. **Repeat as necessary for each item you want to include in your pull-down menu:**

   • To add more items, use Copy and Paste from the right-click menu.

   • To remove items, simply select the item line text and press Delete.

7. **Select the entire contents of the Step 1 text box and choose Edit⇨Copy from your browser menu.**

8. **Return to SiteBuilder.**

9. **Choose Insert⇨Code Elements⇨HTML from the main menu.**

   The HTML Code dialog box appears. (Refer to Figure 13-3.)

10. **Click the Paste button or right-click and choose Paste from the contextual menu that appears.**

    The add-on code from the Web Hosting Control Panel is pasted into the HTML Code dialog box.

11. **Click OK.**

    The HTML element is added to your Web page.

12. **Click and drag to position the HTML element in the desired location on your page.**

You can preview the pull-down menu locally by clicking the Preview in Browser button or pressing F12. Figure 13-11 shows a pull-down menu inside of a Web page.

If your pull-down menu doesn't display properly, double-click the HTML element in the SiteBuilder Design pane, and check for mistakes in the menu item HTML code — a mistyped URL, for example. If you feel like you screwed up the code and can't figure out how to fix it, simply start the process over and try again.

## Opening a Guestbook

A Guestbook is a powerful add-on you can add to your Web page to increase interaction between visitors and yourself. Visitors can send you a message using the Guestbook. You can decide whether you want to have the message simply e-mailed to you or whether you want to also display the response either publicly or privately.

Pull-down menu

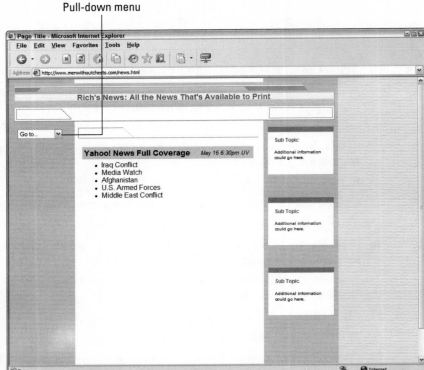

**Figure 13-11:**
Navigation,
pull-down
style.

Unlike the other Yahoo! add-ons included as part of your Web page, the Guestbook displays in separate pages from your Web site and is only integrated into your Web site through standard Web links. An integrated Guestbook consists of three parts:

- ✔ A **Sign Guestbook page** that enables visitors to submit information through your customizable Guestbook form.

- ✔ A **View Guestbook page** that displays the information that people have submitted to you. This information can be public or private, depending on how you set up the Guestbook.

- ✔ **Links** from your Web site to the Sign Guestbook and View Guestbook pages, as well as links from the Guestbook pages back to your Web site.

Guestbooks are designed for a particular purpose and are not the same as general-use Web forms. Check out Chapter 10 for full details on Web forms.

Use these instructions for adding a Guestbook to your Web site:

1. **Choose Tools⇨Web Hosting Control Panel from the menu.**

   SiteBuilder opens your default Web browser and takes you to your Yahoo! Web Hosting Control Panel.

2. **In the Quick Links list located on the top-right of the page, choose Add-ons and then click the Go button.**

   The Add-On page is displayed.

3. **From your Web Hosting Control Panel's Add-On page, click the <u>Guestbook</u> link.**

4. **On the Guestbook page, click the <u>Guestbook Setup</u> link to configure the add-on.**

   The Guestbook Setup page appears, as shown in Figure 13-12.

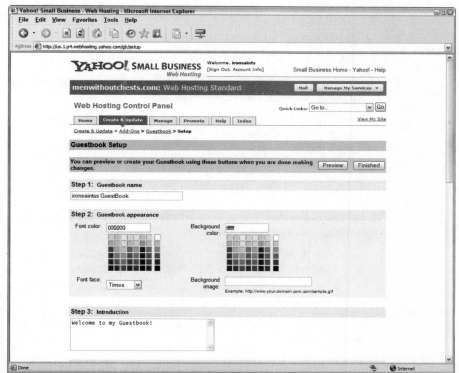

**Figure 13-12:**
Setting up your Guestbook.

5. **Enter a name of the Guestbook in Step 1.**

6. **Customize the font and background in Step 2.**

   Keep in mind that the Guestbook pages are separate from your Web site pages and not embedded in them. Therefore, you need to try to customize the look of these pages to get as close as possible to your SiteBuilder Web site look.

7. **In the Step 3 box, enter any opening instructions or text that you want to provide.**

   Because the Sign Guestbook is on its own page, you want to be sure that people understand where they are and what they are signing.

8. **In Step 4, enter the type of information you wish to gather from the visitor:**

   - In the Question column, enter the Field Name or question text for each type of information you're collecting from the visitor.

   - In the Entry style column, select Text Entry for one-line text entries or Comment Box for multi-line text entries.

   You can enter up to eight questions.

9. **In Step 5, edit the label for the Submit button.**

10. **In Step 6, select 5, 10, or 15 for the number of entries that you want to display on your View Entries page.**

11. **Also in Step 6, choose a separator to insert between each of the Guestbook entries.**

   You can choose from a few graphical lines, a gray horizontal line, or you can specify your own (by clicking the Browse button and navigating to a image of your choice). Whatever you choose, make sure that it's consistent with your overall SiteBuilder Web site design.

12. **In Step 7, determine where you want the visitor to return to after submitting a Guestbook entry.**

   - Click the Return Page button and enter a URL to specify a specific page on your site, such as your home page.

   - Click the Link to Refer Page button to return to the Sign Guestbook page.

13. **In Step 8, choose the desired options for handling Guestbook submissions.**

   If you only want Guestbook submissions viewable by you, make sure you click the Private (Only You Can View) option.

**14. Click the Preview or Finished button to continue.**

The Preview button takes you to a preview screen. This option is particularly helpful when tweaking the look of the Guestbook and getting it to look consistent with your overall Web site design.

When, after finishing the configuration and preview process, you dutifully click the Finished Editing button, a page that provides the HTML code for linking to the Guestbook appears, as shown in Figure 13-13.

The URL for viewing your Guestbook is provided at the top of the page. Bookmark that page so you can refer to it later.

**15. Select the HTML code in the Step 1 box and choose Edit⇨Paste from your browser menu.**

**16. Return to SiteBuilder.**

**17. Choose Insert⇨Code Elements⇨HTML from the main menu.**

The HTML Code dialog box appears. (Refer to Figure 13-3.)

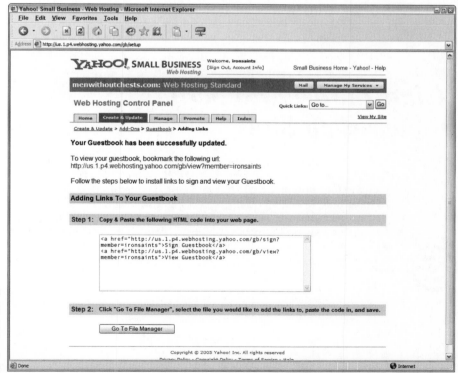

**Figure 13-13:**
Setting up your Guestbook.

18. **Click the Paste button or right-click and choose Paste from the contextual menu that appears.**

    The add-on code from the Web Hosting Control Panel is pasted into the HTML Code dialog box.

19. **Click OK.**

    The HTML element is added to your Web page.

20. **Click and drag to position the HTML element in the desired location on your page.**

    The HTML code displays the links for your Guestbook.

Rather than set these Guestbook links as HTML code, you can re-create these links as normal Web links inside of your Web page. But if you do so, you do risk getting some geeky dust on your hands.

To do so, open up the HTML element dialog box by double-clicking it. Select the URL that is provided inside of the first `href=""` attribute and copy it to the Clipboard. Press Esc to exit the dialog box and then create a link (based on instructions in Chapter 6). Paste the URL into the Destination URL in the Link dialog box. Repeat this process for the second link. After you've done that for both, you can delete the HTML element.

# Using Third-Party Scripts in Your Web Site

Many third-party and community-based sites on the Web provide free downloadable JavaScript and Dynamic HTML *(DHTML)* scripts. These scripts can provide functionality that isn't available inside SiteBuilder. Each script is going to have unique instructions concerning how and where to add the code to your Web page. However, keep in mind that you usually place these scripts either in your page-level Head section or inside of an HTML element on your page.

Two recommended sites I've used in the past include

- ✔ www.dynamicdrive.com
- ✔ www.javascript-fx.com

# Adding Iframes to Your Web Page

An *iframe* (short for *inline frame*) is something like a Web page within a Web page. It is a region of your Web page whose content is filled from another URL. Iframes have several practical uses, although perhaps the two most noteworthy include

✔ **The ability to display scrollable content within a confined area of your page.** For example, suppose you have a Latest News area on your home page that may contain a variable amount of text. However, you don't want to always redesign your page based on the number of news blurbs. You can use an iframe and define a standard rectangular area for the news. If the news needs more space, then a visitor can simply scroll down using scroll bars.

The iframe is particularly helpful when you're using some of the SiteBuilder templates that have fixed regions for displaying context. Using an iframe, you can be sure that your content always fits inside of these areas.

✔ **The ability to update content on your page without updating the entire Web page.** Imagine, for example, that you get your home page design perfected and would rather not even mess around with updating content on it. Using an iframe, you could update a separate text-only page that contains the updatable content (weekly sales, latest news). Then, when you publish the iframe page, the results display within the unchanged home page.

Iframes are particularly helpful if multiple people update your Web site: The design-challenged individual can update the iframe page without the resident designer freaking out about changes.

You can add an iframe to your Web page by following these steps:

**1. Choose Insert⇨Code Elements⇨iframe from the main menu.**

The Iframe Properties dialog box appears, as shown in Figure 13-14.

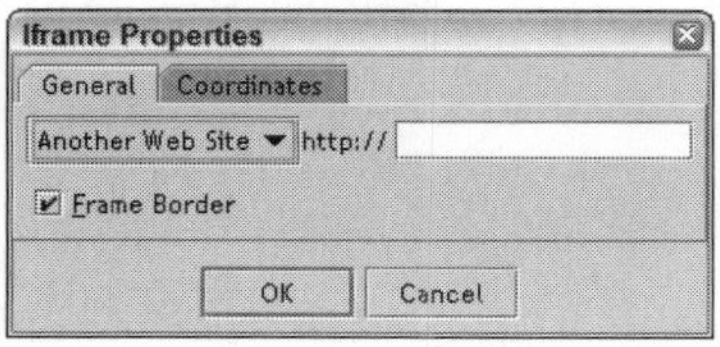

**Figure 13-14:**
Setting up
the iframe.

Iframe Properties

General | Coordinates

Another Web Site ▾ http://

☑ Frame Border

OK | Cancel

2. **In the drop-down list, select the source of the iframe Web page: Another Web Site or A Page in My Site.**

3. **In the http:// text box, enter the source URL or filename.**

   • If the source is from another Web site, then enter the URL.

   • If the source is from your site, then click the Browse button, select the filename from the list, and then click Open.

4. **Check the Frame Border box if you want to visually separate the iframe content from the "parent" Web page with a boxed frame. Uncheck if you want the separation to be seamless.**

5. **Click OK.**

6. **Size and position the iframe as desired.**

   Figure 13-15 shows the iframe element inside of the Design pane.

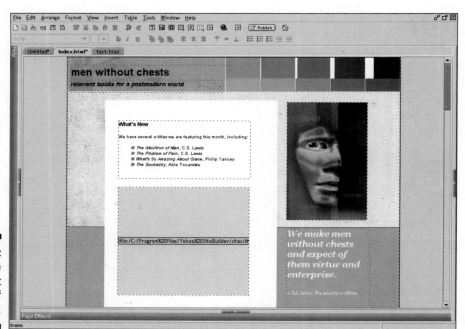

**Figure 13-15:**
An iframe element inside of SiteBuilder.

When you preview the page inside your browser, the source Web page for the iframe displays in the iframe box inside of your Web page, as shown in Figure 13-16.

The iframe automatically adds scroll bars if its content is not fully viewable within the display area.

Source Web page in iframe

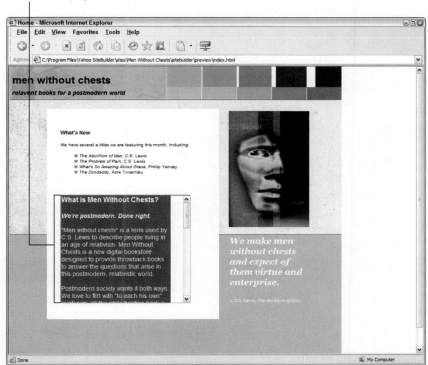

**Figure 13-16:** An iframe shown inside of the browser.

# Part IV

# Managing Your Web Site

The 5th Wave    By Rich Tennant

"Children- it is not necessary to whisper while we're visiting the Vatican Library Web site."

# In this part . . .

*Q. How many managers does it take to change a light bulb?*

*A. Three. Two to determine whether the bulb needs chang-ing, and one to tell an employee to change it.*

The sheer number of manager jokes tells you that, in our increasingly bureaucratic business world, a manager has about as bad a reputation as does a lawyer. But, in this book, whether you're a manager by trade or some-one who works for one doesn't matter: Everyone becomes a hands-on manager of their Web site. Karl Marx would be proud!

Part IV helps you explore how to manage your Web site as you work with the Yahoo! Web Hosting Control Panel. Finally, you round out the tour with a very un-Marxian discussion on how to add a capitalist shopping cart to your site.

# Chapter 14

# Becoming a Webmaster: Administering Your Site Online

*W*hen you consider your Yahoo! SiteBuilder Web site, you can think of it much like a small-town doughnut shop. The owner makes the doughnuts in a back room kitchen, puts them on trays for display, and then sells them at the front counter. You may not be creating jelly-filled Web pages, but how you work with the Web site is much the same way — and far better for a low-carb diet! Using SiteBuilder, you create your Web site in a back room, office, or really anywhere you can put a computer. When you're ready, you publish your files to a Yahoo! Web server. Your visitors then come to your "front counter" — the home page — and browse away.

In addition, not all tasks performed by the owner in his doughnut shop are done so in the kitchen. He creates the doughnuts in the back, but then deals with other matters — such as cash receipts, doughnut displays, and menus — in the front. Similarly, you create and design your Web site in SiteBuilder. But the actual maintenance and administration of your site are done online via the Yahoo! Web Hosting Control Panel.

In this chapter, you explore the basics of administering your Yahoo! SiteBuilder Web site. So wipe those doughnut crumbs off your keyboard and discover what becoming a Webmaster is all about.

# Connecting Major Tom to Ground Control

You use Yahoo! SiteBuilder for creating, designing, and editing your Web site, but it hands off the responsibilities of administering the Web site to its online cousin, the Yahoo! Web Hosting Control Panel.

The Yahoo! Web Hosting Control Panel is your online command and control center. You can use it to access any administrative task you want to perform, such as viewing the number of visitors you're getting, adding or removing site files, and promoting your Web site.

If you ever get confused on whether to make a change in SiteBuilder or on the Yahoo! Web Hosting Control Panel, follow these rules:

- ✔ Use SiteBuilder if the change relates to the look or content of the site and how it's organized.

- ✔ Use the Yahoo! Web Hosting Control Panel for finding information about the site's usage, managing the Web server files, and working with other online services, such as those dealing with e-commerce or promoting your site.

When you want to access the Control Panel, make sure you're online and then follow these steps:

1. **Within SiteBuilder, choose Tools⇨Web Hosting Control Panel from the main menu.**

2. **If needed, enter your Yahoo! ID and password in the Sign In to Yahoo! dialog box, as shown in Figure 14-1.**

**Figure 14-1:**
Signing in to
Yahoo! to
begin your
session.

Sign in to Yahoo!

Please sign in to your Yahoo! Web Hosting or Yahoo!
Merchant Solutions account.

Yahoo ID: Ironsaints

Password:

Don't have a Yahoo! Web Hosting or Yahoo! Merchant
Solutions account? Learn more about our services.

OK    Cancel    Help

If this is the first time you've accessed the Control Panel this session, then you need to supply this information. Otherwise, SiteBuilder skips this step.

SiteBuilder then launches your default Web browser and takes you to the Web Hosting Control Panel, shown in Figure 14-2.

**Figure 14-2:**
Houston,
looks like
we have no
problems!

You can also access the Control Panel outside of SiteBuilder by going to `smallbusiness.yahoo.com/services`.

From this Web page, you can access anything related to your Web site. However, most of your needs focus on the following features:

- **Site Activity module:** Your site activity — how many people are visiting your site — displays on the main page, though you may need to scroll past the Getting Started box to see it.

- **Site Status module:** Your site status (including information like the amount of bandwidth or disk space you are using) is shown in the bottom box on the page. You can also find service announcements.

- **Manage tab:** The Manage tab takes you to the main area for managing your files and other resources.

- **Promote tab:** The Promote tab displays a list of optional promotional services that are designed to drive Web traffic to your site.

The modules in the Web Hosting Control Panel are collapsible and expandable. For example, if you no longer need to view the Getting Started module, click the down arrow beside the Getting Started text to collapse the whole box. This technique enables you to see the Site Activity module without needing to scroll down on the page. (See Figure 14-3.) You can click the arrow again to expand the module to its original size. Yahoo! saves the state of your panels for future visits.

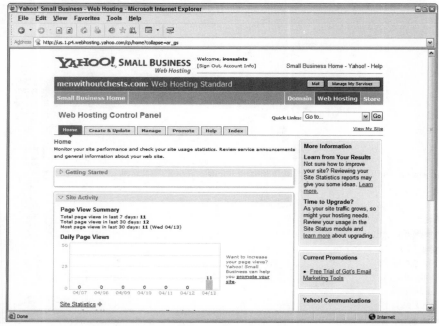

**Figure 14-3:**
Customizing
the look of
your Control
Panel.

In addition, to get rid of the Getting Started module permanently, click the Delete Module button inside of the module area.

You can return to this main page of the Control Panel anytime by clicking the Home tab.

# Viewing Site Activity

Perhaps the most fascinating feature of the Control Panel is the Site Activity Statistics section. You can know exactly how many people are coming to your site and when they are coming, as well as discrete pieces of information about your visitors.

The Site Activity module on the main page of the Control Panel (refer to Figure 14-3) provides a summary view of recent page views at your site. (*Page views* are the number of times visitors have looked at your Web pages.)

You can drill down and get more detailed information by clicking the Site Statistics link in the Site Activity module. When you click this link, the Site Statistics feature appears, as shown in Figure 14-4.

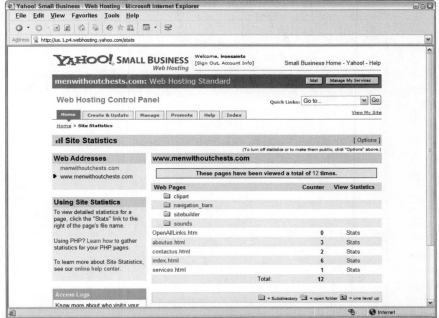

**Figure 14-4:**
"Big
Brother"
watching
your site
activity and
taking lots
of notes
for you.

The Site Statistics page displays a directory view of your Web pages. You can use this interface to find a specific page you are interested in viewing information for.

To view the statistics for a given page, click the <u>Stats</u> link to the right of the filename. To view your home page statistics, for example, you want to view the details for the `index.html` page. The Summary Report page displays for the requested page, as shown in Figure 14-5.

For each given page, you can click the links in the Page Reports box and get more detailed reports, including

- **Page views:** Explore the total page views and unique page views (duplicate sessions by a visitor aren't counted) in hourly, daily, weekly, and monthly views.

- **Visitor profile:** Discover the kind of software and other equipment your visitors are using to view your site. You can view the type of browser, operating system, screen resolution, color depth, and support for JavaScript and Java.

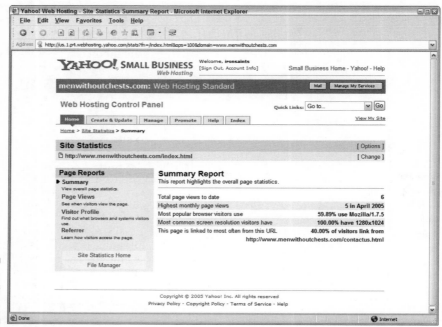

**Figure 14-5:**
Activities of
a page.

This information is extremely helpful to help you make certain design decisions. For example, if you know that 95 percent of your visitors view your site with an 1024 x 768 monitor, then you can feel comfortable that you can make your page size up to 1024 pixels in width and it's still viewable by the vast majority of your visitors without needing to scroll.

Alternatively, if for some crazy reason your Web site attracts a majority of visitors who are using computers from the Stone Age and who have monitors that view just 256 colors, then you want to redesign your site with that information in mind, rather than assume that everyone is viewing your site with the photo-realism you expected.

✔ **Referrer:** The Referrer Report displays how your visitors come to your site — from a search engine, from another Web page, or by a user typing in your Web address directly into the browser.

The Referrer Report is an excellent way to determine if people are discovering your site from search engines or ads or links you placed on other Web sites.

If you set your Web site's home page as the home page for your browser, your visits will be counted in the Yahoo! Site Statistics.

# *Checking Your Site's Status*

I recommend keeping an eye on the Site Status module on the main page of the Control Panel from time to time, just to make sure your Web site is within the disk space and data transfer allowance that Yahoo! allows on a monthly basis.

> ✔ **Disk Space Usage** is the amount of storage capacity that your Web site takes up on the Web server. If your Web site contains just Web pages and normal-size images, the total amount of space probably is fairly small. The size grows rapidly, however, if you're putting up multimedia or other application files for people to download.
>
> ✔ **The Data Transfer Usage** is the total amount of bandwidth, or information downloaded from your Web site by visitors. If you have a normal amount of visitors viewing a normal Web site (one that doesn't have lots of really large files people are downloading), then this statistic is a nonissue. However, if you have a huge amount of traffic or large files that many people are downloading, then this usage figure can climb.

If you exceed your limit, you may want to purchase more disk space or bandwidth from Yahoo!.

# *Working with the File Manager*

If you know your way around Microsoft Windows at all, you probably are used to working with Windows Explorer or the My Computer window. These are views of the files on your hard drive organized into various folders, such as Program Files or My Documents.

In the Control Panel, your Web site is similarly arranged into folder views and is displayed in the File Manager.

Follow these steps to access the File Manager:

1. **From any Web Hosting Control Panel page, click the Manage button in the top tab bar.**

2. **Click the <u>File Manager</u> link inside of the Tools for Managing Your Site module.**

   The File Manager page displays, as shown in Figure 14-6.

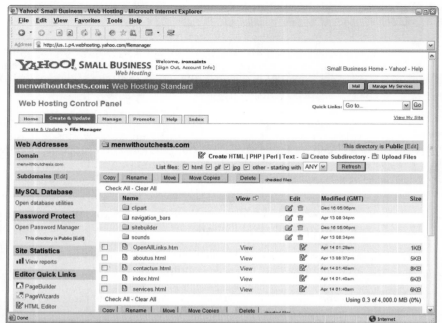

**Figure 14-6:**
Viewing
your
Web site
resources.

Alternatively, you can save a step and go directly to the File Manager by choosing File Manager from the Quick Links box in the top-right corner of the Web page.

One of the advantages to using SiteBuilder is that it takes care of the behind-the-scenes stuff for you. You don't have to get your hands dirty worrying about the names of your Web page files, copying your files to the server using FTP, or creating subdirectories to place your files. Therefore, you may never need to even visit the File Manager section of the Control Panel, because you can handle much of this functionality inside SiteBuilder. Having said that, you need to know how to perform a couple of tasks using the File Manager, including uploading a file and deleting a file.

## Uploading a file

Normally, you'll upload files associated with your Web site inside of SiteBuilder itself (see Chapter 6). However, if you have a need to manually copy the file to your Web site online, you can do that as well.

Follow these steps to upload a file:

1. **From the File Manager page, click the <u>Upload Files</u> link.**

   The Easy Upload page appears, as shown in Figure 14-7.

   You can also use the Quick Links drop-down box and go directly to the Easy Upload page.

2. **On the Easy Upload page, click the Browse button beside the top file-name box and select the file to upload.**

   As the site warns, make sure you don't have spaces in the filenames (such as `Rich Favorite Document.doc`). Rename your file if necessary (`Richfav.doc`).

3. **If you have more than one file to upload, continue adding your files using the boxes.**

4. **Click the Upload Files button.**

   Your files upload to the root folder on your Web site located on the Yahoo! Web server.

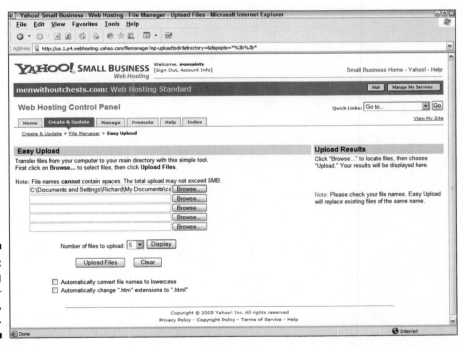

**Figure 14-7:**
The Big Easy —
uploading,
that is.

# Deleting a file

You may need to manually delete a file from your Web site on a couple of common occasions:

- ✔ Suppose you delete a page from your Web site inside of SiteBuilder. It's removed from within the Site Contents pane of SiteBuilder, and you never see it again. But the HTML file that was published to your Web site stays there, forever orphaned. Now, a file or two won't hurt anything, but once you start getting a bunch of orphaned files, then you're needlessly taking up space on your Web site.

- ✔ Suppose you upload one or more MP3 files, multimedia videos, PowerPoint presentations, or other large files on your Web site. After you no longer need them, deleting them is a good idea to make sure you don't fill your Web site storage with large, unused files.

When you need to delete a file, follow these instructions:

1. **From the File Manager page, click the check box beside the file or files you want to delete.**

   If the file you want to get rid of is in a folder, then click the folder to view it.

   Figure 14-8 shows the check box checked beside a Word document that is no longer needed on the Web site.

**Figure 14-8:** Selecting the file to delete from your Web site.

2. **Click the Delete Files button to confirm that you want to get rid of the file(s)**

   The Delete Files confirmation page displays, as shown in Figure 14-9.

   You're taken to the File Manager, with a message indicating that the files were deleted.

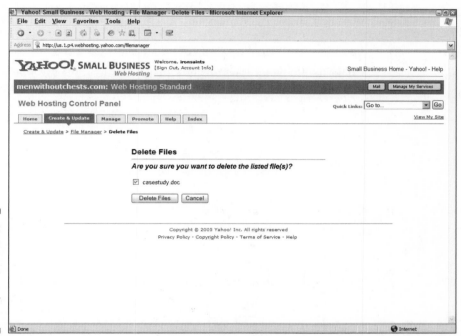

**Figure 14-9:** Confirming that you are serious about this dastardly deed.

# Have a Snafu? Recover an Earlier Version of Your Web Site

I promise it's gonna happen at some point or another. Everything is going along fine with your Web site, and then you mess it up. Perhaps you get a great idea on how to reorganize the site or are inspired to redo the home page. Or maybe you simply make a mistake and type the wrong prices on your sale page. But a day later, you visit your site and realize that your reorganization is confusing, your home page design looks awful, or your sale prices are all marked down to $.05. What's a person to do? Your first step is usually simply restoring one or more files to the way they were before you made changes. When (notice I say *when*, not *if*) this happens, you have two options:

✔ Keep backup versions of your SiteBuilder sites on your hard drive so you can simply open up a backed-up site and then republish it.

✔ Use the Snapshot Backups feature in the Control Panel.

To restore a Web site using the Snapshot Backup

1. **From any Web Hosting Control Panel page, click the Manage tab.**

2. **Click the <u>Snapshot Backups</u> link inside of the Tools for Managing Your Site module.**

   The Snapshot Backups page displays, as shown in Figure 14-10.

3. **Click the snapshot you want to retrieve.**

   The view for that particular snapshot appears, as shown in Figure 14-11.

   You can restore one or more files within a given folder.

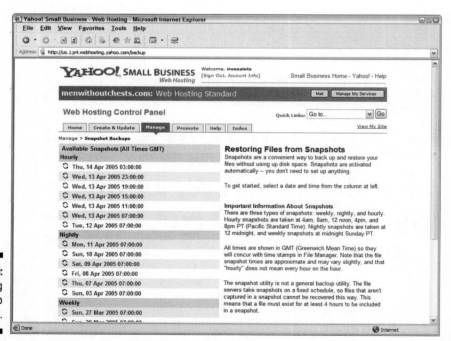

**Figure 14-10:** Restoring your Web site.

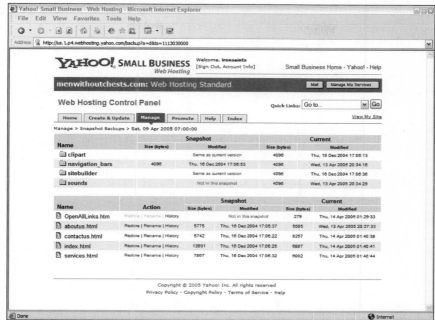

**Figure 14-11:**
Deciding
which files
to restore.

4. **Click the <u>Restore</u> link beside each file.**

Each page you choose is restored from this snapshot.

Keep in mind that the version you are reverting to is on the published Web site only. When you reopen the site inside of SiteBuilder, your recent changes are still there. If you wish to use the snapshot copy inside of SiteBuilder, then import the Web site (see Chapter 4 for details on importing) and use this version as your new working Web site.

# Chapter 15

# From Rags to Riches: Selling Products on Your Site

**A**s the other chapters in this book have explored, your Web site can revolutionize the way in which you communicate and interact with people. If you own a business, you can use your Web site to better serve your existing customers or reach new ones. If you have a nonprofit organization, you can better communicate your mission and programs to potential sponsors and donors. Or, if you have a family or hobby site, you can correspond with friends, relatives, or fellow enthusiasts.

However, if you have a business that sells products, you may wish to go to the next step beyond mere communication and actually transact business from your Web site. If you decide to take this next step, SiteBuilder can lead you through the often confusing world of e-commerce.

In this chapter, you explore how you can enable your SiteBuilder Web site to sell products on it. You explore the simplest way — through PayPal buttons — as well as the more involved Online-Store-and-Shopping-Cart route using Yahoo! Merchant Solutions.

You can use the PayPal buttons with any Yahoo! Web hosting plan. However, in order to use the online store and Catalog Manager, you need to upgrade your hosting plan to a Yahoo! Merchant Solutions plan.

# *Working with PayPal Buttons*

The easiest way into the world of e-commerce is through PayPal. PayPal is an online payment service that acts as a middleman between the purchaser and seller of a product. PayPal is a popular option for online transactions on Web sites such as eBay where the seller doesn't have the need for a full-scale e-commerce solution. PayPal charges a small fee to the seller for each transaction made using its service.

For complete details on paying fees, receiving payments, and establishing an account, go to www.paypal.com. (Note that PayPal is neither owned by nor affiliated with Yahoo!.)

SiteBuilder provides support for PayPal through Buy Now and Donations buttons:

- ✔ **Buy Now:** Visitors can purchase an individual item using PayPal.
- ✔ **Donations:** Visitors can send donations to your nonprofit organization, charity, church, or fundraising campaign using PayPal.

When a visitor clicks a Buy Now or Donations button, he or she goes to a secure PayPal Web site to enter order information and complete the transaction. After PayPal processes the order or donation, the visitor is sent to a confirmation page you specify. Or, if the visitor cancels out before completing the transaction, then he or she is sent to a cancellation page supplied by PayPal or yourself.

Keep in mind the following capabilities of the PayPal buttons:

- ✔ Each Buy Now button is linked to a specific product, and each Donations button is associated with a specific fundraising campaign. Therefore, if you have five different types of chili you wish to sell on your Web site, you would need five different Buy Now buttons, each linked to a particular item. In the same way, if you operated a Web site for a world hunger program and allowed visitors to choose between giving for an African famine campaign or Asian Tsunami relief campaign, you would need two different Donations buttons.

- ✔ While each button is linked to a single item or campaign, you can have multiple buttons on your Web site that point to the same product or campaign.

- ✔ For Buy Now e-commerce, there is no PayPal "shopping cart" per se, in which you gather various products into a single order. But you can optionally allow customers to purchase more than one of the same product in a single order.

# *Adding a PayPal Buy Now button*

You can add a PayPal Buy Now button by following these steps:

1. **Choose Insert⇨PayPal Buttons⇨Buy Now from the main menu.**

   The Buy Now Properties dialog box appears, as shown in Figure 15-1.

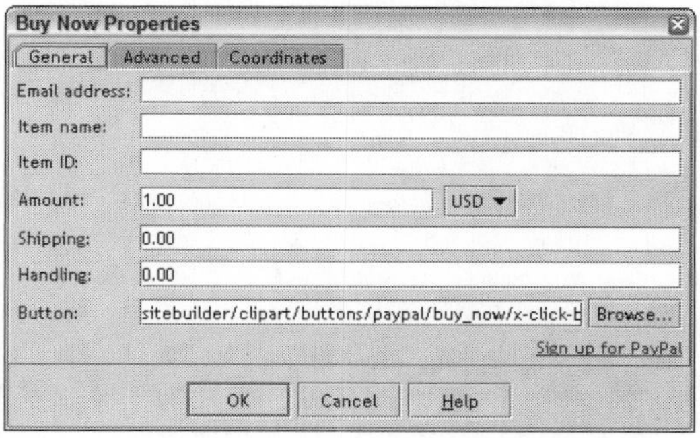

**Figure 15-1:**
The Buy
Now
Properties
dialog box.

2. **Enter the e-mail address that is associated with your PayPal account in the Email Address text box.**

3. **Enter the product name in the Item Name text box.**

   PayPal uses this information in the transaction details of the purchase.

4. **If your products have a unique ID associated with them, enter this value into the Item ID text box.**

5. **Enter the price for the product in the Amount text box and specify the unit of currency in the adjoining drop-down menu.**

6. **Enter the shipping charge per item in the Shipping text box.**

   This per item cost is added to the order for each item purchased. If customers can purchase more than one of this item in a single order, this cost is charged for each item.

7. **Enter the handling charges for the order in the Handling text box.**

   This cost is added to the order. Unlike the shipping charges, which are per item, this handling charge is a flat rate regardless of the number of items in the order.

8. **Click the Browse button beside the Button text box and select the desired button image from the Choose an Image dialog box.**

9. **Click the Advanced tab to continue.**

   The Buy Now Properties dialog box updates, as shown in Figure 15-2.

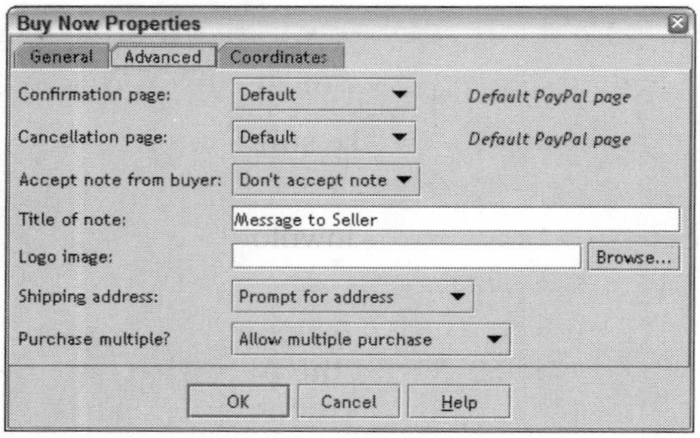

**Figure 15-2:**
Additional settings for the Buy Now button.

10. **Specify the page you would like the customer to go to after a purchase: Default (a page created and provided by PayPal showing transaction details), A Page in My Site, or Another Web Site.**

    The default PayPal page provides details of the transactions but doesn't have the look and feel of your Web site. In contrast, if you specify your own confirmation page, you need to provide a generic "we're processing your order" message. You can't provide specific details about the current order in your Web page.

11. **Specify the page you would like the customer to go to if he or she cancels out from the ordering process: Default (a page created and provided by PayPal), A Page in My Site, or Another Web Site.**

12. **If you'd optionally like a Note field to be provided on the PayPal order form, choose Accept Note from the Accept Note from Buyer drop-down menu.**

    The Note field could be a place in which customers provide special requests.

13. **If you chose the Accept Note option, enter the title of the note in the Title of Note text box.**

    Make sure this text fully explains the Note field to the customer.

14. **If you have a product logo or picture that you want to display on the PayPal payment page, enter the image name in the Logo Image text box.**

    Click the Browse button to select an image from your local computer or from SiteBuilder clip art.

The image must be 150 pixels wide and 50 pixels in height or smaller.

If you plan on using a logo image, make sure you place it inside an SSL-protected folder in your Web site. See the "Adding your logo image to an SSL-protected folder" sidebar for details.

15. **Set the Shipping Address field to one of the following values: Prompt for Address, Don't Prompt for Address, or Requires Address.**

    If have a physical product you ship, make sure the shipping address is required.

    If you have a digital product that is for downloads only, choose Don't Prompt for Address.

16. **If you want the customer to be able to order multiple copies of the same item within a single order, select the Allow Multiple Purchase from the Purchase Multiple drop-down menu (the default).**

17. **Click OK.**

    The Buy Now button is added to your Web page. Reposition the button to the appropriate position.

TIP

# Adding your logo image to an SSL-protected folder

If you use a logo image, you need to add a special Secure Sockets Layer (SSL)-protected folder to your Web site and then place your image file inside it. If you don't, customers or donors receive a message indicating that some parts of the PayPal payment page are not secure, a warning that can frighten some customers from completing the process. To provide a secure PayPal logo, do the following steps:

1. Specify your logo image in the Buy Now Properties or Donations Properties dialog box. (See the "Adding a PayPal Buy Now button" and "Adding a PayPal Donations button" sections in this chapter.)

   The image is automatically added to the images folder of your Web site.

2. In the Site Contents pane, right-click the root node and choose Create New Folder from the contextual menu.

   A new folder is added to your Web site.

3. Name the folder ssl. (Make sure you use all lowercase characters.)

4. Expand the images folder and select your logo image.

5. Drag the logo to the ssl folder.

   Yahoo! treats the ssl folder as an SSL-protected folder.

# *Adding a PayPal Donations button*

You can add a PayPal Donations button to your Web page to help your charity or nonprofit organization in fundraising. To do so, follow these steps.

1. **Choose Insert⇨PayPal Buttons⇨Donations from the main menu.**

   The Donations Properties dialog box appears, as shown in Figure 15-3.

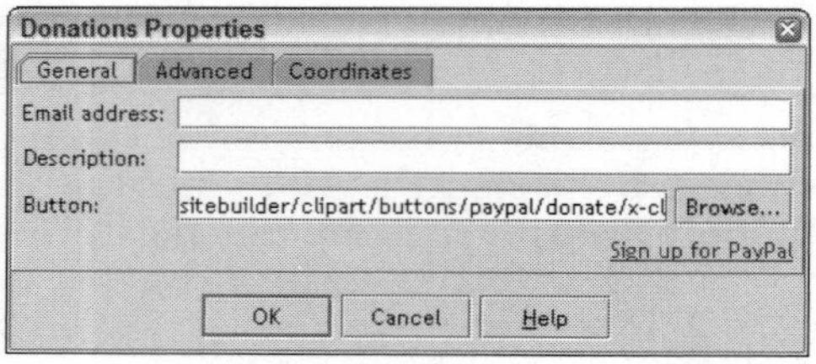

*(Donations Properties dialog box showing tabs: General, Advanced, Coordinates; Email address, Description, Button fields with value sitebuilder/clipart/buttons/paypal/donate/x-cl and Browse... button; Sign up for PayPal link; OK, Cancel, Help buttons.)*

2. **Enter the e-mail address that is associated with your PayPal account in the Email Address text box.**

3. **Enter a description of the campaign or organization in the Description text box.**

   PayPal uses this information in the transaction details of the donation.

4. **Click the Browse button beside the Button text box and select the desired button image from the Choose an Image dialog box.**

5. **Click the Advanced tab to continue.**

   The Donations Properties dialog box updates, as shown in Figure 15-4.

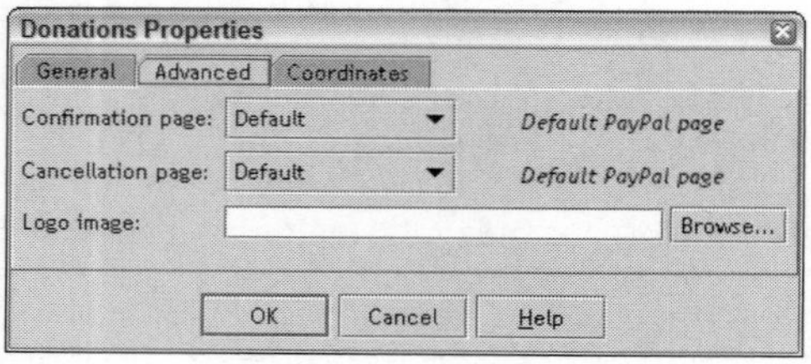

*(Donations Properties dialog box showing tabs: General, Advanced, Coordinates; Confirmation page: Default, Default PayPal page; Cancellation page: Default, Default PayPal page; Logo image with Browse... button; OK, Cancel, Help buttons.)*

6. **Specify the page you would like the donor to go to after a donation: Default (a page created and provided by PayPal showing transaction details), A Page in My Site, or Another Web Site.**

As with the Buy Now process, the default PayPal page provides details of the transactions but doesn't have the look and feel of your Web site. In contrast, if you specify your own confirmation page, you need to provide a generic "Thanks for the donation. We're processing it now." message. You can't provide specific details about the current donation in your Web page.

7. **Specify the page you would like the donor to go to if he or she cancels the donation process: Default (a page created and provided by PayPal), A Page in My Site, or Another Web Site.**

8. **If you have an organization or campaign logo that you want to display on the PayPal payment page, enter the image name in the Logo Image text box.**

    Click the Browse button to select an image from a local computer or from SiteBuilder clip art.

    The image must be 150 pixels wide and 50 pixels in height or smaller.

    If you plan on using a logo image, make sure you place it inside an SSL-protected folder in your Web site. See the "Adding your logo image to an SSL-protected folder" sidebar for details.

9. **Click OK.**

    The Donations button is added to your Web page. Move the button to the desired location.

# Building an Online Store with Yahoo! Merchant Solutions

If you have a Yahoo! Merchant Solutions hosting plan, you can create a full-scale online store, complete with shopping cart and credit card transactions. Who knows, maybe you'll have eBay and Amazon squirming in their shoes in no time!

The process of creating an online store is relatively straightforward when you use SiteBuilder in combination with the Yahoo! Merchant Solutions Catalog Manager. Here are the nine steps:

1. Add a new field to the online product catalog for handling your SiteBuilder store.

2. Enter product information in the Catalog Manager, part of the online Yahoo! Store Manager.

3. Publish your catalog.

4. Enable your product catalog to be accessible by SiteBuilder.

5. Import your catalog into SiteBuilder.

6. Add a store page to your Web site.

7. Add a View Cart button to your page.

8. Complete the final steps online.

9. Publish your site and go live.

You must be enrolled in the Yahoo! Merchant Solutions plan if you want to create an online store. If you have a normal Web Hosting plan, you can't utilize the services. However, if you want to upgrade to a Merchant Solutions account, go to `smallbusiness.yahoo.com/services` and click the Change or Cancel Plan link.

## Adding a new field to the product catalog

In order to use SiteBuilder with your online product catalog, you first need to add a new field called Product-url to the catalog. The Product-url links a Web page on your site to the product record in your Catalog Manager. (It's also used in the shopping cart after the product has been added.) In addition, if you plan to list your products on Yahoo! Shopping, you must have this field for integration into it. You can add this field by following these steps:

1. **Choose Tools⇨Web Hosting Control Panel from the main menu.**

   You may be asked for your Yahoo! ID if you've not established a Yahoo! session yet.

   SiteBuilder opens your default Web browser and displays the Yahoo! Web Hosting Control Panel.

2. **Click the <u>Store</u> link in the top-right-hand corner of the Web page.**

   You're taken to your online Store Manager (see Figure 15-5), the home base for all things e-commerce.

3. **Click the <u>Catalog Manager</u> link in the Edit section.**

   The main Catalog Manager page displays, as shown in Figure 15-6.

4. **Click the <u>Manage Your Tables</u> link.**

   The Tables page displays (see Figure 15-7).

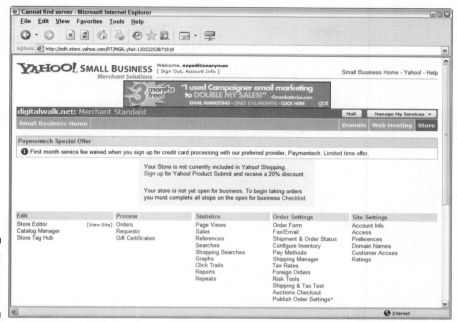

**Figure 15-5:**
The Yahoo!
Store
Manager.

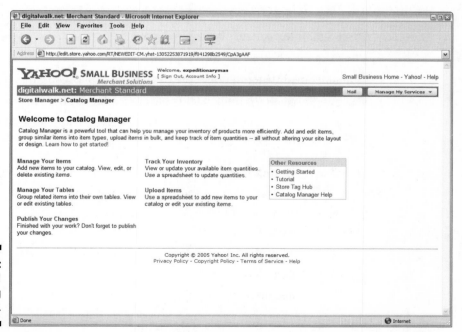

**Figure 15-6:**
The Yahoo!
Catalog
Manager.

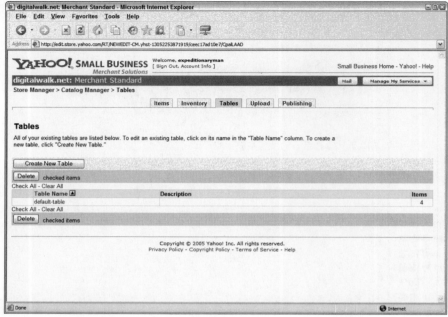

**Figure 15-7:**
The Tables
page shows
the table
entries in
your product
catalog.

5. **Click the <u>default-table</u> link.**

   The Edit Table page displays (see Figure 15-8).

6. **Click the Edit button in the Shopping Fields section.**

   You may need to scroll down the page to find this section.

   The Edit Table — Shopping Fields page now displays.

7. **From the Select Field drop-down menu, select Product-url from the list and click Add Field.**

   The Product-url is added to the Shopping Fields list, as shown in Figure 15-9.

8. **Enter your domain name in the Default Value box.**

   This step makes your data entry process easier, especially if you have many products to enter in your catalog. The text you enter here is automatically entered in the Product-url field when you enter a new item in the Catalog Manager.

9. **Click Update.**

   You return to the Edit Table — default-table page.

10. **Click the Save button to make your changes permanent.**

    Yahoo! returns you to the main Tables page (refer to Figure 15-7).

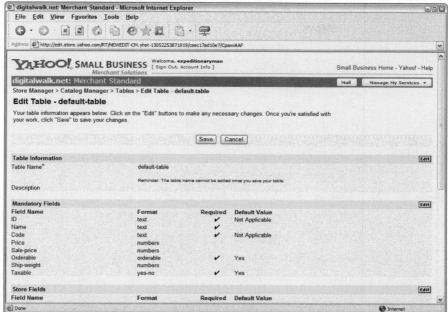

**Figure 15-8:**
Editing the default-table of your catalog.

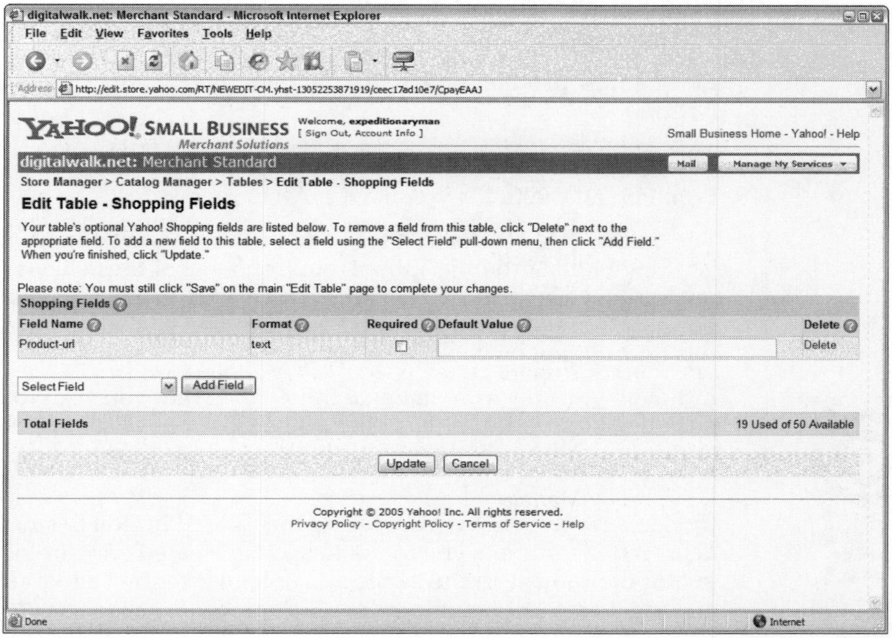

**Figure 15-9:**
Adding the Product-url field.

# *Adding products to your product catalog*

Your next step in preparing your product catalog is to enter your product information into the online Catalog Manager. You can do so by following these steps:

1. **Choose Tools⇨Web Hosting Control Panel from the main menu.**

   You may be asked for your Yahoo! ID if you've not established a Yahoo! session yet.

   SiteBuilder opens your default Web browser and displays the Yahoo! Web Hosting Control Panel.

2. **Click the <u>Store</u> link in the top-right-hand corner of the Web page.**

   You're taken to your online Store Manager (refer to Figure 15-5).

3. **Click the <u>Catalog Manager</u> link in the Edit section.**

   The main Catalog Manager page displays (refer to Figure 15-6).

   Yahoo! provides you with a default table for entering basic product information. I focus on using this table. If your needs are more advanced, click the <u>Manage Your Tables</u> link and modify the fields of the default table or else create your own new table.

4. **Click the <u>Manage Your Items</u> link.**

   The Items page displays (see Figure 15-10).

5. **Enter a new product entry into the table by clicking the Add Item button.**

   The Add Item page displays, as shown in Figure 15-11.

6. **Populate all the fields you need for this record.**

   The default-table contains a set of fields that captures information about your individual product. Yahoo! requires some of these fields to be filled out for its usage (these fields are marked with an asterisk beside them), but others are optional and need only be used if you plan on displaying this information on your Web page.

   Although you may have many of these fields that you wish to include as part of your product listings, the basic fields you will almost always want to display on your SiteBuilder Web page include Name, Price, Image, and Caption.

   Upload a product image by clicking the Upload button beside the Image field. Yahoo! prompts you for an image file located on your local computer. After you send the image and upload it to the Yahoo! server, you can use it as part of your product listing.

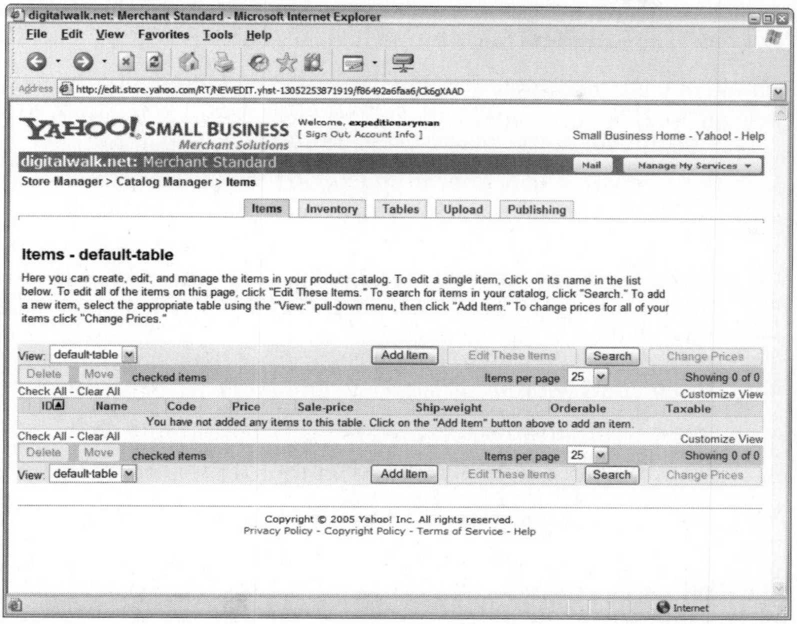

**Figure 15-10:**
The Items
page.

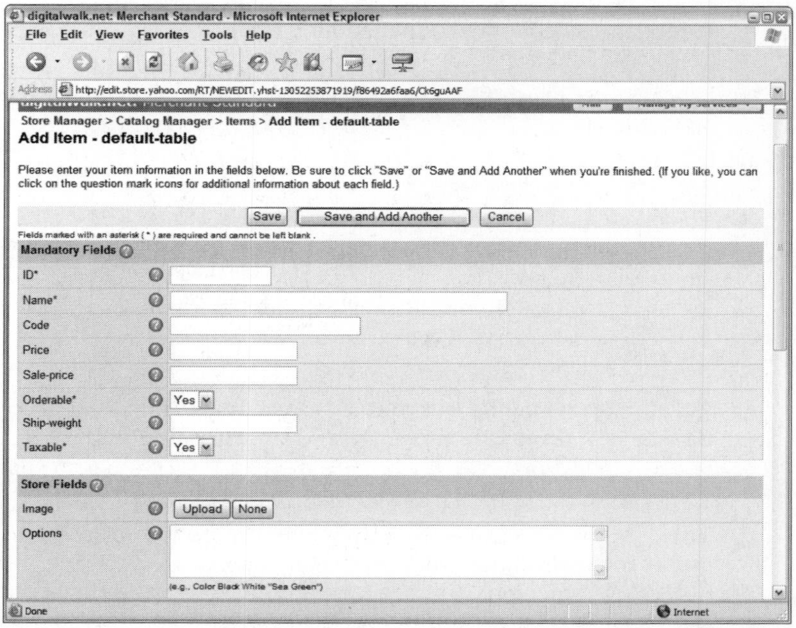

**Figure 15-11:**
Adding a
new product
record.

If you have questions about the purpose of a field, click the blue question mark button beside it to display Help.

For each product entry, enter a value in the Product-url field. (You may need to scroll down the page to see this field.) You'll want to use your domain name and a page name for the product.

If you display all of your products on the same page, such as `products. html`, then you can use the same Product-url value for each entry in your table.

If you use a separate Web page for each product you sell, I recommend incorporating the product ID in its filename. For example, suppose I have a domain named `www.mmlean.com` and have a sweater that I am going to sell with an ID of D3003. I'd enter the following value into the Product-url field:

```
www.mmlean.com/D3003.html
```

If you have several products, you may wish to place all your product pages in a separate products subfolder. See Chapter 4 for more on creating subfolders on your Web site.

7. **Click the Save and Add Another button to save the current record and fill out the next.**

8. **Repeat Steps 6 and 7 for each product in your catalog. When you have entered the last product entry, click the Save button.**

Figure 15-12 shows a product catalog table.

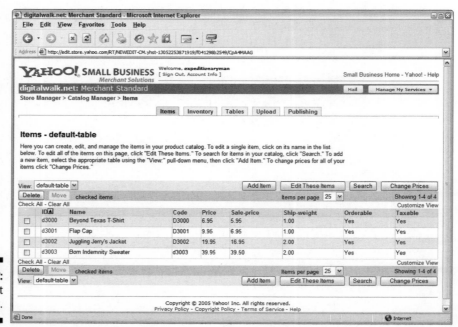

**Figure 15-12:** A product catalog.

## *Publishing your product catalog*

After you add data to your product catalog, you need to publish the changes in order for them to take effect. To do so, follow these steps:

1. **Choose Tools⇨Web Hosting Control Panel from the main menu.**

   You may be asked for your Yahoo! ID if you've not established a Yahoo! session yet.

   SiteBuilder opens your default Web browser and displays the Yahoo! Web Hosting Control Panel.

2. **Click the <u>Store</u> link in the top-right-hand corner of the Web page.**

   You're taken to your online Store Manager (refer to Figure 15-5), the home base for all things e-commerce.

3. **Click the <u>Catalog Manager</u> link in the Edit section.**

   The main Catalog Manager page displays (refer to Figure 15-6).

4. **Click the <u>Publish Your Changes</u> link.**

   The Publishing page displays.

5. **Click the Publish Catalog button to make your changes take effect.**

## *Enabling your product catalog for use with SiteBuilder*

While your product catalog is available from your Yahoo! Catalog Manager, you need to enable it so that SiteBuilder can retrieve this information and use it inside your Web site. You can do so by performing the following steps:

1. **Choose Tools⇨Web Hosting Control Panel from the main menu.**

   You may be asked for your Yahoo! ID if you've not established a Yahoo! session yet.

   SiteBuilder opens your default Web browser and displays the Yahoo! Web Hosting Control Panel.

2. **Click the <u>Store</u> link in the top-right-hand corner of the Web page.**

   You are taken to your online Store Manager (refer to Figure 15-5).

3. **Click the <u>Search Engines</u> link in the Promote section.**

   You may need to scroll down to see this link.

   The Promote Your Site on Search Engines page displays, as shown in Figure 15-13.

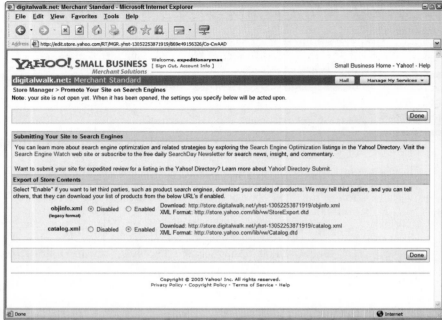

**Figure 15-13:**
Enabling
your product
catalog
for use in
SiteBuilder.

4. **Click the Enabled radio button beside the catalog.xml line.**

5. **Click the Done button.**

   Your product catalog is now ready for importing into SiteBuilder.
   Continue to the next section for details on how to import.

## *Importing your online catalog*

After you create, publish, and enable your online catalog, you're ready to import
it into SiteBuilder. The import process retrieves a catalog file (`catalog.xml`)
from the Yahoo! server and adds it as part of your Web site. Follow these steps
to import your product catalog:

1. **Choose Tools⇨Store Catalog⇨Import from the main menu.**

   The Import Store Catalog dialog box displays, as shown in Figure 15-14.
   It displays your domain in the Domain box.

2. **Click OK to import.**

   SiteBuilder connects to the Yahoo! server and retrieves the file. When
   finished, SiteBuilder lets you know the import process was completed.

**Figure 15-14:**
Preparing
to import
a product
catalog from
the Yahoo!
server into
SiteBuilder.

**Figure 15-14:**
Preparing
to import
a product
catalog from
the Yahoo!
server into
SiteBuilder.

## Creating a store page

When you've added the catalog data into your SiteBuilder Web site, you're ready to begin the process of displaying your products on a Web page in your site. The easiest way to do this is by using the Store Products Wizard:

1. **Click the New Page with Template button from the toolbar.**

   The Add New Page dialog box displays, as shown in Figure 15-15.

2. **Keep the default template setting in the Select a Category and Template pane.**

   In almost every case, you want to keep the same template as your Web site. However, if for some reason you wish to choose another, then use the Categories list and Templates box to navigate to the desired template.

3. **Select the Store Products Wizard from the Select Page to Add drop-down menu.**

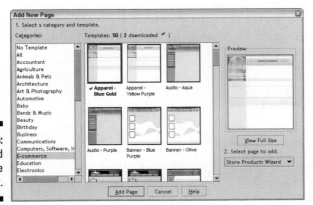

**Figure 15-15:**
The Add
New Page
dialog box.

4. **Click the Add Page button.**

   The Store Products Page dialog box displays with the General pane showing, as shown in Figure 15-16.

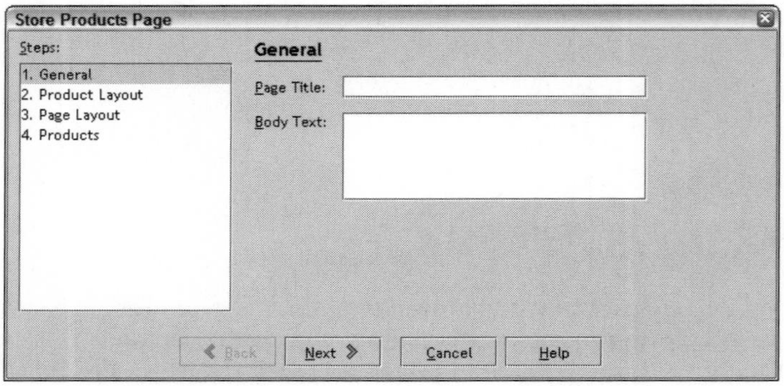

**Figure 15-16:** Adding general information about the Store Products page.

5. **Enter a page title along with the body text that you wish to have on the top of the page.**

6. **Click Next.**

   The Product Layout pane displays (see Figure 15-17).

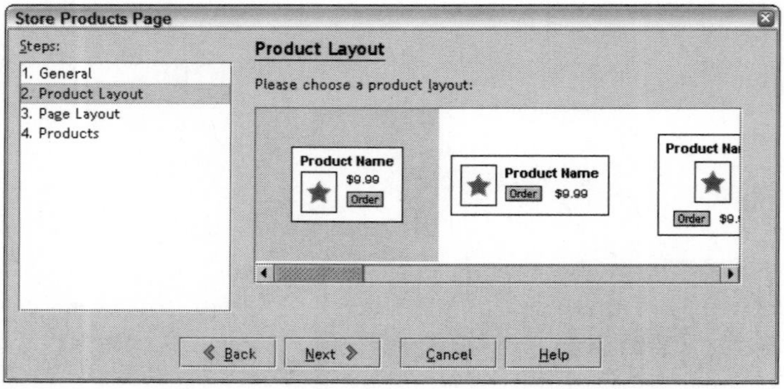

**Figure 15-17:** Selecting a product layout.

7. **Choose a product layout from the scrolling list.**

   The product layout determines the format and presentation of each product listing in your catalog.

8. **Click Next.**

   The Page Layout pane displays, as shown in Figure 15-18.

9. **Select the number of columns and rows in the products grid.**

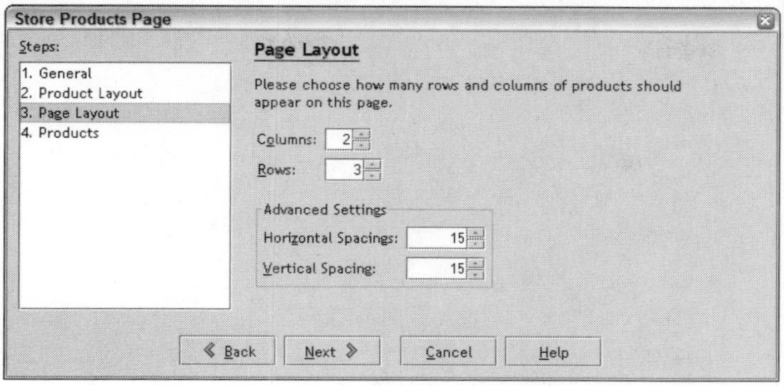

**Figure 15-18:**
Setting the page design for the products page.

10. **In the Advanced Settings section, adjust the amount of horizontal and vertical spacing between product listings.**

11. **Click the Next button.**

    The Products pane displays; see Figure 15-19.

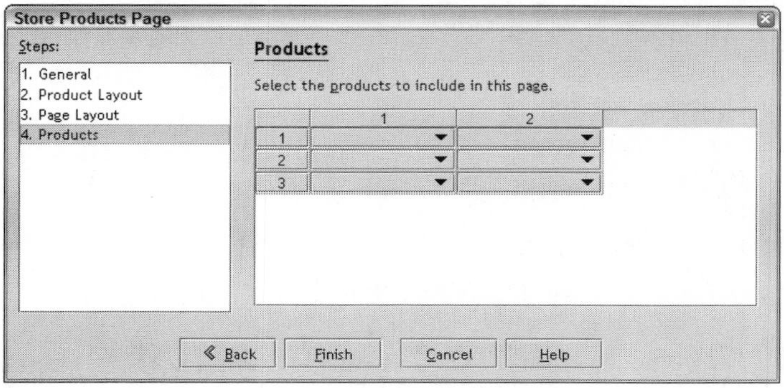

**Figure 15-19:**
Identify the products to include on the page.

12. **For each entry in the Products grid, select the products you want to include from the cell's drop-down menu and place them in the desired order.**

    The cell's drop-down menu is populated with the product items from your store catalog.

13. **Click the Finish button.**

    SiteBuilder creates a new products page for you (see Figure 15-20) and displays the products from your catalog.

    Each product is contained in a *product module,* a SiteBuilder page element that is used for housing your store data. Each module contains store tags, which you can move around and tweak. A *store tag* is a placeholder for a field from your product catalog, such as description, price, and image.

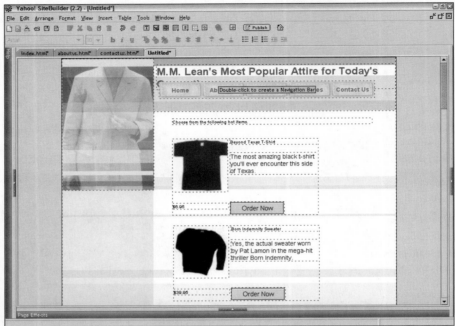

**Figure 15-20:**
The new
product
page in the
Design
pane.

**14. Click the Save button.**

The Save As dialog box displays.

**15. Save the file as** products.html **or another filename.**

## Adding a Shopping Cart button

After you create your Store Products page and add product modules to the
page, your final step is to add a Shopping Cart button to your page. A Shopping
Cart button enables visitors to view the products that they've added to their
Shopping Cart when they click the order button for a product.

The shopping cart displays in a page managed and created by Yahoo! and is
not one that you specify as a page in your SiteBuilder Web site. To adjust the
look and feel of your e-commerce shopping cart, visit the Store Editor, which
is available from the Store Manager (refer to Figure 15-5).

To add a shopping cart button to your page, perform the following steps:

1. **Click the Insert Store Tags button from the toolbar.**

   The button displays a drop-down menu.

2. **Choose View Cart from the drop-down menu.**

   The View Cart Properties dialog box is shown (see Figure 15-21).

**Figure 15-21:**
Selecting a
Shopping
Cart graphic.

3. **If you wish to change the default shopping cart button, click the Browse button and navigate to the desired button.**

4. **Click OK in the View Cart Properties dialog box.**

   The shopping cart button is added to your products page.

5. **Reposition the button to the desired location for visitors.**

## Completing the final merchant requirements

Before your store is ready to accept orders from customers, you need to set up a merchant account with a bank (which enables you to perform credit card transitions from your Web site) and complete an Open for Business order form. See help.yahoo.com/help/us/store/store-08.html#step6 for full walkthrough details.

## *Publishing your site*

After you complete all the necessary requirements established by Yahoo!, you're finally ready to open your Web site for business. At that time, you can publish your Web site, adding your online store pages during the update. See Chapter 4 for full details on how to publish your Web site.

# Additional Store Catalog Tasks

After you have your store up and running, you can perform several additional store catalog tasks, such as adding another product, deleting a product, and refreshing your catalog. I discuss how to do such maintenance chores in this section.

## *Adding a product module*

A product module is the page element you add to your Web page that contains your store's product items. In addition to using the Store Products Wizard (see the "Creating a store page" section, earlier in the chapter), you can add individual product modules to your Web page by performing the following steps:

1. **Click the Insert Store Tags button from the toolbar.**

   The button displays a drop-down menu.

2. **Choose Product Module from the drop-down menu.**

   The Insert Store Product dialog box appears (see Figure 15-22).

**Figure 15-22:** Inserting a product module into a Web page.

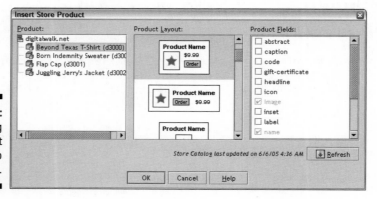

3. **Click the Refresh button if you've made changes to the catalog.**

    SiteBuilder downloads the latest version of the catalog available on the Yahoo! server.

4. **Select the product you want to add from the Product section.**

5. **Choose the desired layout design from the Product Layout section.**

6. **Check the fields that you want to include in the module from the list of available fields shown in the Product Fields section.**

7. **Click OK.**

    The new product module is added to your Web page.

## Adding store tags

Store tags are placeholders that you add to a product module to display data from your product catalog. You can add individual store tags to product modules by following these steps:

1. **Click the product module to which you'd like to add a store tag.**

2. **Click the Insert Store Tags button from the toolbar.**

    The button displays a drop-down menu.

3. **Choose the desired store tag from the menu.**

    The store tag is added to the selected product module.

4. **Reposition the store tag to the desired location.**

## Viewing product module properties

You may have instances where you'd like to switch which product from your catalog that a product module is pointing to, such as in the case of reorganizing your products into a different order. You make this switch through its Properties dialog box.

Like all other page elements in SiteBuilder, you can right-click a product module to display its contextual menu. Choose Properties, and the Product dialog box displays (see Figure 15-23).

If you'd like to switch the product to which the module points to, select another product from the Product pane.

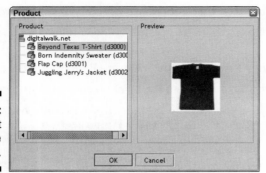

**Figure 15-23:**
Product
module
properties.

## Refreshing your catalog information

The product catalog that is imported as part of your SiteBuilder Web site on your local computer is a "point in time" image of your catalog. Therefore, when you make changes to the online catalog, you need to refresh your products catalog inside SiteBuilder to ensure your Web site is up to date. You can do so by performing the following steps:

1. **Choose Tools⇨Store Catalog⇨Refresh from the main menu.**

   The Import Store Catalog dialog box (refer to Figure 15-14) displays.

2. **Click OK to perform the update.**

   SiteBuilder retrieves a fresh version of the product catalog from the Yahoo! server and copies it to your local computer. Your pages update to reflect any changes.

## Deleting your catalog

If you would like to remove your product catalog from your Web site, you can do so by following these steps:

1. **Choose Tools⇨Store Catalog⇨Delete from the main menu.**

   A Warning message box displays, asking whether you really want to delete your catalog.

2. **Click Yes to delete the catalog.**

   Your product modules and store tags no longer work.

# Part V
# The Part of Tens

The 5th Wave — By Rich Tennant

"What do you mean you're updating our Web page?"

# In this part . . .

The number ten is certainly the most commonly used number in the world. It's everywhere! Think of its many instances: the number of days in a week, the number of items in a dozen, the number of wheels on the average car. . . . Oops, maybe I was too hasty . . . maybe it's not used everywhere just yet, but the number ten is still the official number for *For Dummies* books with its Part of Tens section.

In this part, you get a dose of "10" as you explore ten real-world design tips and ten mega-useful tips to help you when you use Yahoo! SiteBuilder.

Don't let the TENsion build, read on. . . .

# Chapter 16

# Ten Design Tips to Rival the "Big Boys"

*I*n the world of "bricks and mortar," the only way a small business can put up a storefront that rivals the "Big Boys" is to sink millions of dollars into the effort. Okay, I suppose technically you could also move in on a holiday to the headquarters of a major corporation, place your own company logo on top of theirs, and become a squatter. However, I wouldn't recommend that option.

Yet as Chapter 3 details, the Web is the great equalizer. No squatting is even needed! You can run a business out of your basement and create an economical, do-it-yourself Web site that, for all intents and purposes, is as attractive and effective as a Fortune 500 company's Web site.

If your goal for your Web site is to look as professional and impressive as the large companies, consider the following ten tips.

# Don't Reinvent the Wheel

When you are looking to design your Web site, make sure you have a list of trend-setting corporate Web sites that you can turn to for ideas. For example, suppose you're trying to determine the best font to use for your navigation bar. Check out what Honda, IBM, or Microsoft are using (and what they're not using) on their sites. You can bet they've probably spent a lot of bucks researching that very issue.

Don't get me wrong: I am not recommending that you steal ideas from another Web site and directly duplicate them on your site. In fact, I've seen others that provide mirror replicas of Amazon, Microsoft, or Apple. Instead of looking impressive, these sites look just like a bunch of copycats!

Without stealing, you can get many ideas from the "Big Boys:"

- ✔ Look at how "crisp and clean" their Web sites are.
- ✔ Notice the unity and amount of colors that they use.
- ✔ Notice how often white is used as a background color. This color choice is not by accident: White generally looks crisper and more professional. In fact, very few commercial-quality Web sites use dark background colors, and none uses "loud" or distracting background graphics.

Finally, check out a variety of larger sites — car makers, computer and software makers, media outlets, e-commerce centers, trendy design Web sites, and companies related to your business. These can give you a variety of perspectives and ideas of how to construct your Web site.

# Eliminate Counters, Clichés, and All Things Cute

*Because I can.* That's the response I get when I ask most people why they added a cute little gadget, such as a counter or stock ticker, to a Web site. With SiteBuilder, you can easily add a lot of neat stuff to your Web pages, but that doesn't mean you always should

Visit, for example, the Web sites of Toyota, CNN, or Macromedia. They may have a Flash or ActiveX multimedia controls, but probably only one, and the actual size is quite small. But you won't see much else "cute" on their sites.

Before adding something to your Web page, always ask yourself: Would I see this on one of the "Big Boys" Web sites? If so, consider it. If not, you better have a much better reason to add it than "because I can."

With that in mind

- ✔ Most animated GIFs and scrolling messages look cheesy. Avoid them unless they're really professional looking.

- ✔ Avoid those cute construction signs if part of your site is not completed. Instead, add some descriptive text.

- ✔ I know, SiteBuilder enables you to easily add these, but for your business site, avoid page fade-in or fade-out effects anyway. There's absolutely no reason for it other than "because you can." In fact, if you can find a "Big Boy" site that uses fade-in effects, I'll treat you to a Tuscan holiday.

- ✔ Avoid using a visible page counter. The number of visitors should be like a James Bond case: *For Your Eyes Only*. Do you, for example, really want to tell the world that you've only had 50 people come to your site since last year? Instead, if you really want to capture this info, do so with a behind-the-scenes solution, which I discuss in Chapter 15.

- ✔ Not a gadget, but it is a cliché: Don't say anywhere on your site "Web site of," "Home of," "Online home of," or any derivation thereof. A visitor *already* knows it's your Web site. What else could it be?

- ✔ Using Flash or Java is normal, but beware of using nonstandard plug-ins. Unless it is a plug-in, such as Flash, that 99.9 percent of your visitors probably already have, you almost never want a visitor to be forced to download a plug-in to view content on your Web site.

# Don't Let Your Site Grow Mold

You don't have to act like a CNN.com or Amazon.com and update your site hourly or daily, but you should regularly provide new information on your site to keep visitors coming back. For example:

- ✔ Consider having a What's New or Latest News box or page so that people can check out any new stuff you may have added.

- ✔ Make sure your Web site doesn't date itself:

    - • Don't keep up old news. For example, if you're announcing a Christmas sale, don't keep that information up there through St. Valentine's Day in February.

- Check your copyright date. If you have a copyright notice in the footer of your Web pages, make sure it is updated to the current year. Nothing looks more dated than a Web site with copyright notices from two years ago.

- Only have a Last Updated date on your Web site if you update the site at least once a month. Otherwise, let visitors think you *may* have actually updated it, rather than knowing that you've not touched the thing in six months.

✔ Consider revising your overall site design at least once a year to keep things looking fresh.

# Hobbit-Size Your Pages

The "Big Boys" are fanatics on keeping the size of each page to a bare minimum, particularly the home page. You need to be, too. With that in mind

✔ No matter how much it hurts, keep your home page at around 50K in total size. On a sublevel page, you have slightly more leniency, but you should aim for 80K or less on nearly every page.

✔ Pictures are critical to a well-designed site, but avoid using too many.

✔ If you are using JPG files, see how much you can squeeze out of the compression before the quality of the image degrades too much. (See Chapter 7 for more details.)

I have a site that I like to frequent occasionally that has a navigation bar built using Flash. Bless their hearts, but the silly thing takes so long to load for each page that I've only seen it load fully on one occasion. All other times, I go to the site, check out the info I need, only to leave before the Flash presentation loads.

# Hey, They're Free: Test with Multiple Browsers

While today's generation of browsers are mature and show 95 percent of Web pages identically, the browsers have differences that you simply have to be aware of and test for. Therefore, make sure that your Web site has an identical look and functionality on all the major browsers, including

- ✔ **Microsoft Internet Explorer:** If you use Windows, having Internet Explorer is a given. Even if you use another browser, you'll have this one on your system for testing.

- ✔ **Mozilla Firefox:** Firefox is an up-and-coming browser that is gaining a lot of interest and a growing community of enthusiastic users. Make sure your site works well with it. Visit www.mozilla.org to download.

- ✔ **Netscape:** Also built with the Mozilla browser engine like Firefox, Netscape still maintains a Web browser that you should test with. Go to www.netscape.com for a free download.

- ✔ **Opera:** The Opera browser has a very small market share, but it is a good idea to test with it. Visit www.opera.com for a free download.

# Don't Forget About the Text

I've been talking all along about the look and design of your Web site, but don't forget another key component of your overall presentation: the text! Many people spend all their time and energy on their Web site design and end up throwing up text that wouldn't pass a tenth-grade writing assignment. Keep in mind the following tips:

- ✔ Separate text writing from your Web design process. Consider writing the text in your word processor first and then copying and pasting the text into your SiteBuilder page. When you write text inside of SiteBuilder, you can easily become distracted with how the text is going to look on your page rather than the text itself.

- ✔ Check your spelling and grammar. The "Big Boys" do.

- ✔ Communicate in a friendly but professional tone. Don't chit-chat. Save your "personal touch" for the phone or in person.

See also Chapter 3 for more on writing content for your Web site.

# Take the Ten-Second Test-Drive

When you're designing a Web site to which you want to attract more and more visitors, do your best to check it out as a first-time visitor would. Within 5 to 10 seconds, the home page should communicate the gist of what your company or organization does, what kind of products you're selling, or perhaps the hobby you're showing off. If not, your visitor may get itchy and go on. Above all, never force the user to click to another page to understand who you are or what you're trying to communicate.

If you are selling a product or service, having a catchy slogan or a picture that communicates through metaphor is fine. But somewhere on your home page, plainly state what you are or what you do.

Your goal: Make your message brain-dead easy.

# Design for Technology Laggards, but Leave Behind the Stone Age

If you have a brand-new computer and broadband Internet connection, it is easy to assume that everyone else in the world can view your Web site using the same technology as you do. Big mistake. Many of your visitors will lag behind in technology; this reality must impact how you design your Web site. This is particularly important in three areas:

- ✔ **Screen resolution:** Design for 800 x 600 screen resolution, though most people by now are at 1024 x 768.
- ✔ **Browser version:** Design for Internet Explorer 5.0 and higher and Netscape 6.0 and higher.
- ✔ **Internet connection speed:** Design for the dialup user.

At the same time, don't feel obligated to account for the 5 percent of people who are still in the Stone Age, using really old equipment or software. If someone is using Netscape Navigator 2.0, every site on the Web will give him fits.

# Publishing Your Text as an Image

If you have access to graphics software, such as Adobe Photoshop or Paint Shop Pro, use it for some of your text. Most graphics software worthy of the name enables you to anti-alias your text, which gives it a much crisper and cleaner look than simply adding normal text. Anti-aliased text works great for headings and other title text, and can definitely get your site looking more like the "Big Boys."

However, don't go hog wild and convert all your text to graphics. Not only does that make your Web pages much bigger, but it also ends up looking like "brochureware" rather than a lively Web site.

# Never, Ever, Ever, Ever Assume

You probably remember that silly little saying about what "assume" means? Well, keep that in mind as you design your site to rival the "Big Boys:"

- ✔ Never assume all your visitors are on high speed. Many will not be and won't think your super-size Flash control or Java applet is fun to download, no matter how cool it is.

- ✔ Don't assume that your visitor has the latest browser or latest plug-in. Many users stick with whatever was installed on their PC and the time of purchase.

- ✔ When you get a new 21-inch monitor for Christmas with 1280 x 1024 screen resolution, don't assume all your visitors received the same gift. Some will still try to come to your Web site with a puny 14-inch 800 x 600 monitor and expect to have the experience that you have.

# Chapter 17

# Ten SiteBuilder Tips You Really Need to Know

### In This Chapter

▶ Using SiteBuilder more productively

▶ Making your Web building more enjoyable

*I* love my dad, but the way that he uses his computer reminds me of someone who knows how to drive a car well but never bothered to take the time to learn how to turn on the stereo or open the trunk. (Sorry, Dad!) In other words, for the tasks he knows how to perform in Windows, he's an expert. But the moment he gets outside of that box, I get a phone call. In fact, if the phone ever rings past 11 p.m. in my household, I'll invariably answer, "Hi, Dad. What's happened?"

For the first 16 chapters of this book, you've been focusing your attention on "driving the car" — using SiteBuilder to build Web pages. However, in this chapter, you back up a little and look at the car . . . errr . . . SiteBuilder itself. As you do so, you explore ten tips about using SiteBuilder that can either help as you build your site or simply make your "driving" experience more productive and enjoyable.

## Using the Insert Palette

The Insert palette, shown in Figure 17-1, is a handy tool for inserting any kind of element into a Web page in SiteBuilder, from a basic text element to a Site Search add-on to an iframe. If you can add it to your Web page, you can find it in the Insert palette.

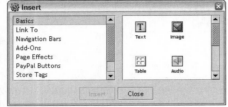

**Figure 17-1:**
The all-in-one inserter.

To access the Insert palette, click the Insert Palette button on the toolbar.

You never have to use the Insert palette, because all its functionality is available by using the standard menu or toolbar commands. However, it's particularly useful if you are adding several elements to a page at once or are wanting to simply look at what's available to add to your Web site.

The Insert palette is *nonmodal*, a techie term that simply means that you can leave the dialog box open while you're working with your Web page. Therefore, you can move the Insert palette off to the side while you design your page yet still have it available for you when you need to add new elements. Figure 17-2 shows how I use the Insert palette in this manner.

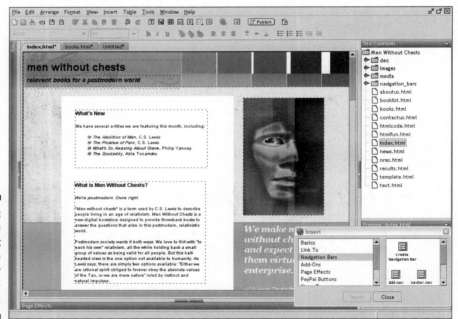

**Figure 17-2:**
Using the Insert palette inside your design environment.

To insert an element using the Insert palette, follow these steps:

1. **Click the Insert Palette button on the toolbar.**

   The Insert palette displays (refer to Figure 17-1). The elements are grouped by categories.

2. **Select the desired category on the left to display the elements within that grouping.**

3. **Double-click the element icon to insert it into the center of the active Web page in the Design pane.**

   Alternatively, if you want to position the element in a particular spot, you can drag the element icon from the palette window and drop it on a particular location on your page. When you release the mouse button, the element is inserted.

# Avoiding the Pain When Working with Panes

As Chapter 1 discusses, SiteBuilder divides its working environment into separate panes:

- ✔ A Design pane, for displaying the open pages you are working on

- ✔ Supporting panes, including the Help pane, Site Contents pane, Preview pane, and Page Effects pane

While the supporting panes are useful, you probably don't want to display all of them at the same time; they can take up a lot of space you might like to have for designing your Web page. Try the following techniques to get the workspace the way you like it:

- ✔ **Collapse and expand a pane:** Each supporting pane has a blue region on its border, as shown in Figure 17-3. By clicking this region with your mouse, you toggle the visibility of the pane: An expanded pane collapses, while a collapsed pane expands. The arrow on the blue region indicates whether the pane is expanded or collapsed.

- ✔ **Manually resize a pane:** While the blue region on the border is for expanding and collapsing a pane, you can resize it by dragging another part of the border and then releasing the mouse.

- ✔ **Restore the panes to their default position:** SiteBuilder saves the current state of the panes when you close the application. Normally, the saved state is helpful, because you can configure the environment exactly as you want it and have it stay that way. However, if you ever want to return the SiteBuilder environment to its original state, choose View➪Restore Default View.

Blue regions

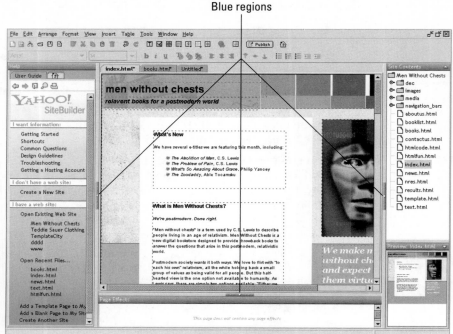

**Figure 17-3:**
Collapse and
expand the
panes in a
single click.

# Automatically Saving Your Work

Bad things can happen when you're working on your computer. A lightning storm kills the power. A bratty nephew is obsessed with your computer's Reset button. A buggy music player freezes your whole Windows session when you're in the middle of designing your site. To help prevent losing unsaved work when situations like these arise, I strongly recommend using the Automatic Save feature of SiteBuilder.

The Automatic Save feature is for emergency use only. SiteBuilder saves a background copy of your files for use only when SiteBuilder closes down unexpectedly. For normal use, you still need to save your files as you normally do.

To automatically save your work, follow these steps:

1. **Choose Tools⇨Preferences from the main menu.**

2. **Click the Automatic Save tab in the Preferences dialog box.**

   The Automatic Save tab appears, as shown in Figure 17-4.

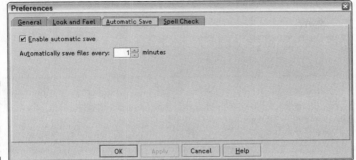

**Figure 17-4:**
Automati-
cally saving
your work.

3. **Check the Enable Automatic Save box.**

   This option is normally on by default, so you should simply need to confirm that the box is already checked.

4. **Enter the desired interval of time (in minutes) between autosaves you want SiteBuilder to work with in the box provided.**

   I recommend using 5 minutes or less.

5. **Click OK to save your preferences.**

# Working with Multiple Pages Open

By default, as you work inside SiteBuilder, the open pages you have display one at a time, with separate tabs shown in the Design pane for each open page. However, you can work with the pages in a side-by-side manner if you wish. To do so, click the Restore/Maximize button at the top right of the SiteBuilder window (shown in Figure 17-5).

After you enter the Restore mode, each page displays in its own window. You can move and resize these windows as you want within the SiteBuilder environment, as shown in Figure 17-6.

The most useful aspect of side-by-side view is that you can move a page element from one page to another simply by dragging it from one page and dropping it into another. This procedure is an alternative to the typical cut-and-paste operation.

Restore button

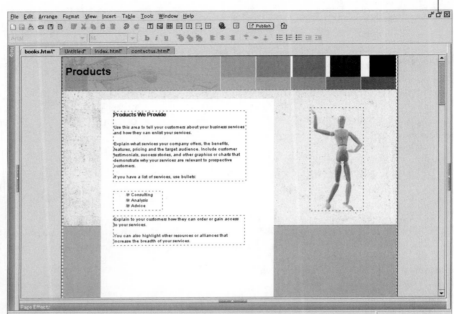

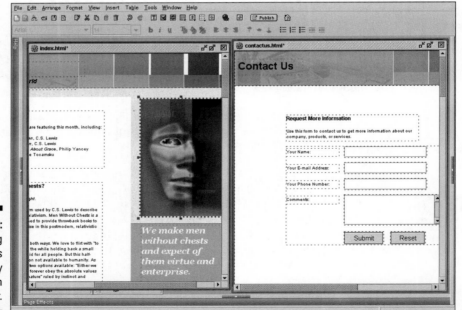

To return to the normal tabbed view, click the Restore/Maximize button on any of the page windows.

# Automatically Restoring Your Session

While SiteBuilder automatically loads your last opened site when you launch it, you can also have SiteBuilder reload the pages you had open during your previous SiteBuilder session. To enable this option, follow these steps:

1. **Choose Tools⇨Preferences from the main menu.**

   The Preferences dialog box appears with the General tab active, as shown in Figure 17-7.

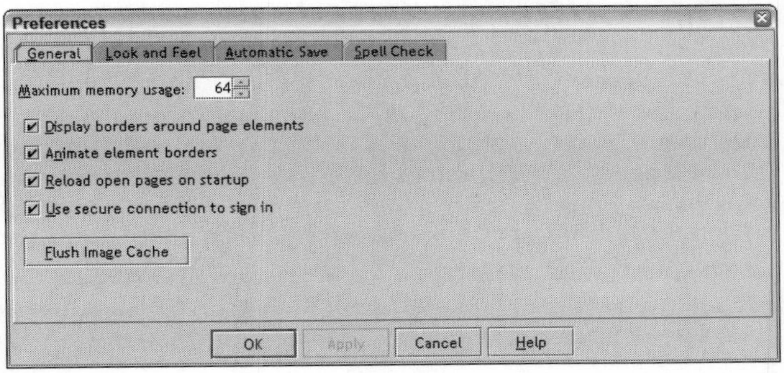

**Figure 17-7:**
Enabling
options
in the
Preferences
dialog box.

2. **Check the Reload Open Pages on Startup box.**
3. **Click OK.**

# Managing Multiple Sites

If you're working with more than one Yahoo! Web site and Yahoo! ID, you may occasionally find you need to sign into Yahoo! and SiteBuilder with a different Yahoo! ID.

The typical scenario is when you have published or interacted recently with the Yahoo! server with one Yahoo! ID and then go to open up another Web site that is managed using another Yahoo! ID and want to publish it in the same SiteBuilder session.

When this occurs, you'll want to change user IDs within SiteBuilder by following these steps:

1. **Choose File⇨Change User from the main menu.**

   The Sign In to Yahoo! dialog box appears.

2. **Enter the desired Yahoo! ID and password.**

3. **Click OK.**

   Your new Yahoo! ID is active through the remainder of the SiteBuilder session.

# Quick Access to the Yahoo! Web Hosting Control Panel

As Chapter 14 discusses, the Yahoo! Web Hosting Control Panel is your online "command and control center" for your Web site. The only downside is that you have to leave SiteBuilder in order to work with it in your browser. SiteBuilder at least enables that handoff to be seamless by providing access to the Yahoo! Web Hosting Control Panel through a menu command.

To access the online Control Panel, choose Tools⇨Web Hosting Control Panel from the main menu. SiteBuilder asks you to sign in Yahoo! using your Yahoo! ID and then opens up the Yahoo! Web Hosting Control Panel in your default browser.

# Embracing Gridlock

A key part of the page design process in SiteBuilder is the arrangement and organization of the elements on your page. However, because you are free to move and arrange elements anywhere you please on the page itself, sometimes being exact in your positioning is hard. Often, you end up eyeballing your Web page in SiteBuilder, and you think everything looks fine, only to have the elements be a pixel or two off here and there when you see it in your browser.

SiteBuilder optionally displays gridlines on your pages to enable you to precisely position elements on them. It's kind of like overlaying your Web page with that graphing paper you used to use in geometry class.

Gridlines show up on blank pages or pages with backgrounds. However, non-background graphics do cover up the gridlines. Therefore, if you're using a SiteBuilder template that uses graphics to cover most of the page area, you may not see the gridlines.

## Turning gridlines on and off

To turn on gridlines, choose Arrange➪Show Grid from the main menu. Figure 17-8 shows a page with the gridlines visible. A check box is added beside the menu item indicating its visible state. After the gridlines have been turned on, they remain on until you turn them off by choosing Arrange➪Show Grid again.

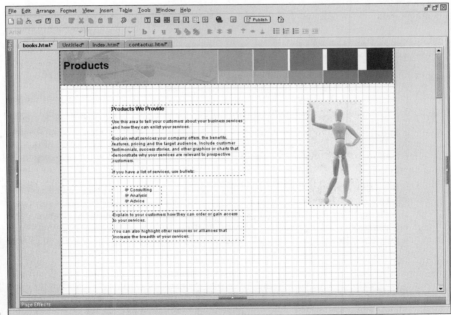

**Figure 17-8:**
Showing
gridlines in
SiteBuilder.

## Snapping to the grid

By default, you can move elements one pixel at a time anywhere on your page. However, if that's too wide open for you, and you'd rather have a little more control over where to position elements, use the Snap to Grid feature. When this feature is activated, you can only position elements on a gridline. Therefore, when you move an element, it goes from one gridline to the next, bypassing the pixels in between.

To turn this feature on or off, choose Arrange⇨Snap to Grid from the main menu.

## Adjusting the grid size

By default, the grid is divided into 15-x-15-pixel squares. You can adjust the size of the grid squares by choosing Arrange⇨Grid Size from the main menu. In the Grid Size dialog box, specify the desired number and click OK.

# Changing the Look and Feel of SiteBuilder

When I visit my parents once a year over the holidays, I sit down at my father's computer at some point. When I do so, I invariably realize that his Windows desktop looks the exact same way that it did the year before. In contrast, my Windows desktop looks different at least twice a week.

If I back up a little bit and look at all computer users, I suspect that my dad and I represent two different camps: the defaulters and the tweakers. The defaulters don't care about personalization or customization. They care only about using the computer for productivity purposes. In contrast, the tweakers love to personalize and customize their working environment to be more productive or fun.

If you fall into the tweaker camp, you will be glad to know that SiteBuilder allows you to personalize the look of the product itself, To adjust the look and feel, follow these instructions:

1. **Choose Tools⇨Preferences from the main menu.**

2. **Click the Look and Feel tab in the Preferences dialog box.**

   The Look and Feel tab makes an appearance, as shown in Figure 17-9.

**Figure 17-9:**
What kind
of mood
are you in
today?

3. **In the Interface drop-down menu, specify whether you want a more traditional Microsoft Windows look or a Metal look.**

4. **Enter the default font style and size for SiteBuilder.**

   This font setting is not for your Web pages; it's only for the SiteBuilder interface.

5. **If you chose Metal, then you can also specify the color theme in the Theme box.**

   Choose Steel, Amethyst, Sapphire, Emerald, Ruby, Strawberry Skies, Smoke, or Custom.

   The Preview area on the right updates to display the active theme look.

6. **Click OK to save your changes.**

# Previewing with Multiple Browsers

When you preview your Web site (by clicking the Preview in Browser button on the toolbar or by pressing F12), SiteBuilder opens the current page in your default Web browser. However, suppose you have the two major browsers — Microsoft Internet Explorer and Mozilla Firefox — both installed on your computer and would like to preview your page in each to ensure consistency.

Because SiteBuilder doesn't provide built-in support for local preview with multiple browsers, use this workaround instead:

1. **In SiteBuilder, click the Preview in Browser button on the toolbar or press F12.**

   The page displays in your default browser.

2. **In the browser's Address bar, select the URL and copy it to the Clipboard.**

3. **Open your secondary browser.**

4. **Click in the Address bar in your secondary browser and paste the URL.**

5. **Press Enter to navigate to the preview page.**

I recommend keeping the secondary browser open and pointing to the preview page. In this way, you can simply click the Refresh button each time you wish to preview the page.

# Appendix

# About the CD

## System Requirements

Make sure that your computer meets the minimum system requirements shown in the following list. If your computer doesn't match up to most of these requirements, you may have problems using the software and files on the CD. For the latest and greatest information, please refer to the ReadMe file located at the root of the CD-ROM.

- ✔ A PC with a 400MHz Pentium II or faster processor (1GHz Pentium III recommended)

- ✔ Microsoft Windows 98 or later (Windows ME/2000/XP recommended)

- ✔ At least 64MB of total RAM installed on your computer; for best performance, at least 128MB

- ✔ A CD-ROM drive

- ✔ A monitor capable of displaying at least 800 x 600 screen resolution

- ✔ At least 50MB of hard drive space (250MB needed to install all optional SiteBuilder templates)

- ✔ A modem with a speed of at least 14,400 bps

If you need more information on the basics, check out these books published by Wiley Publishing, Inc.: *PCs For Dummies,* by Dan Gookin; *Macs For Dummies,* by David Pogue; *Windows 98 For Dummies, Windows 2000 Professional For Dummies, Microsoft Windows ME Millennium Edition For Dummies,* or *Windows XP For Dummies,* all by Andy Rathbone.

# Using the CD with Microsoft Windows

To install from the CD to your hard drive, follow these steps:

1. **Insert the CD into your computer's CD-ROM drive.**

   Normally, a window appears with a button to install Yahoo! SiteBuilder.

   If no window appears, open the CD drive in Windows Explorer and double-click the `ysitebuilder.exe` file.

2. **Click the Install Yahoo! SiteBuilder button.**

3. **In the Yahoo! SiteBuilder Setup dialog box that appears, click the Next button to begin installation.**

4. **Follow the instructions provided in the setup wizard.**

# What You Find on the CD

The CD contains the full version of Yahoo! SiteBuilder 2.2, along with a complete bundle of SiteBuilder templates. For more information, visit the Yahoo! SiteBuilder Web site at `http://webhosting.yahoo.com/ps/sb/index.php`.

Be sure to check out the cool hosting offer from Yahoo! on the coupon found on this book's CD!

# Troubleshooting

I tried my best to compile programs that work on most computers with the minimum system requirements. Alas, your computer may differ, and some programs may not work properly for some reason.

The two likeliest problems are that you don't have enough memory (RAM) for the programs you want to use, or you have other programs running that are affecting installation or running of a program. If you get an error message such as `Not enough memory` or `Setup cannot continue`, try one or more of the following suggestions and then try using the software again:

✔ **Turn off any antivirus software running on your computer.** Installation programs sometimes mimic virus activity and may make your computer incorrectly believe that a virus is infecting it.

✔ **Close all running programs.** The more programs you have running, the less memory is available to other programs. Installation programs typically update files and programs; so if you keep other programs running, installation may not work properly.

✔ **Have your local computer store add more RAM to your computer.** This is, admittedly, a drastic and somewhat expensive step. However, if you have a Windows 98 PC, adding more memory can really help the speed of your computer and allow more programs to run at the same time. This may include closing the CD interface and running a product's installation program from Windows Explorer.

If you have trouble with the CD-ROM, please call the Wiley Product Technical Support phone number at (800) 762-2974. Outside the United States, call 1(317) 572-3994. You can also contact Wiley Product Technical Support at www.wiley.com/techsupport. John Wiley & Sons provides technical support only for installation and other general quality control items. For technical support on the applications themselves, consult the program's vendor or author.

# Index

# Notes

# Notes

# Notes

## USINESS, CAREERS & PERSONAL FINANCE

0-7645-5307-0

0-7645-5331-3 *†

**Also available:**

- Accounting For Dummies †
  0-7645-5314-3
- Business Plans Kit For Dummies †
  0-7645-5365-8
- Cover Letters For Dummies
  0-7645-5224-4
- Frugal Living For Dummies
  0-7645-5403-4
- Leadership For Dummies
  0-7645-5176-0
- Managing For Dummies
  0-7645-1771-6

- Marketing For Dummies
  0-7645-5600-2
- Personal Finance For Dummies *
  0-7645-2590-5
- Project Management For Dummies
  0-7645-5283-X
- Resumes For Dummies †
  0-7645-5471-9
- Selling For Dummies
  0-7645-5363-1
- Small Business Kit For Dummies *†
  0-7645-5093-4

## IOME & BUSINESS COMPUTER BASICS

0-7645-4074-2

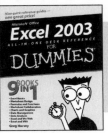

0-7645-3758-X

**Also available:**

- ACT! 6 For Dummies
  0-7645-2645-6
- iLife '04 All-in-One Desk Reference
  For Dummies
  0-7645-7347-0
- iPAQ For Dummies
  0-7645-6769-1
- Mac OS X Panther Timesaving
  Techniques For Dummies
  0-7645-5812-9
- Macs For Dummies
  0-7645-5656-8

- Microsoft Money 2004 For Dummies
  0-7645-4195-1
- Office 2003 All-in-One Desk Reference
  For Dummies
  0-7645-3883-7
- Outlook 2003 For Dummies
  0-7645-3759-8
- PCs For Dummies
  0-7645-4074-2
- TiVo For Dummies
  0-7645-6923-6
- Upgrading and Fixing PCs For Dummies
  0-7645-1665-5
- Windows XP Timesaving Techniques
  For Dummies
  0-7645-3748-2

## OOD, HOME, GARDEN, HOBBIES, MUSIC & PETS

0-7645-5295-3

0-7645-5232-5

**Also available:**

- Bass Guitar For Dummies
  0-7645-2487-9
- Diabetes Cookbook For Dummies
  0-7645-5230-9
- Gardening For Dummies *
  0-7645-5130-2
- Guitar For Dummies
  0-7645-5106-X
- Holiday Decorating For Dummies
  0-7645-2570-0
- Home Improvement All-in-One
  For Dummies
  0-7645-5680-0

- Knitting For Dummies
  0-7645-5395-X
- Piano For Dummies
  0-7645-5105-1
- Puppies For Dummies
  0-7645-5255-4
- Scrapbooking For Dummies
  0-7645-7208-3
- Senior Dogs For Dummies
  0-7645-5818-8
- Singing For Dummies
  0-7645-2475-5
- 30-Minute Meals For Dummies
  0-7645-2589-1

## INTERNET & DIGITAL MEDIA

0-7645-1664-7

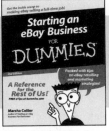

0-7645-6924-4

**Also available:**

- 2005 Online Shopping Directory
  For Dummies
  0-7645-7495-7
- CD & DVD Recording For Dummies
  0-7645-5956-7
- eBay For Dummies
  0-7645-5654-1
- Fighting Spam For Dummies
  0-7645-5965-6
- Genealogy Online For Dummies
  0-7645-5964-8
- Google For Dummies
  0-7645-4420-9

- Home Recording For Musicians
  For Dummies
  0-7645-1634-5
- The Internet For Dummies
  0-7645-4173-0
- iPod & iTunes For Dummies
  0-7645-7772-7
- Preventing Identity Theft For Dummies
  0-7645-7336-5
- Pro Tools All-in-One Desk Reference
  For Dummies
  0-7645-5714-9
- Roxio Easy Media Creator For Dummies
  0-7645-7131-1

* Separate Canadian edition also available
† Separate U.K. edition also available

Available wherever books are sold. For more information or to order direct: U.S. customers visit www.dummies.com or call 1-877-762-2974.
U.K. customers visit www.wileyeurope.com or call 0800 243407. Canadian customers visit www.wiley.ca or call 1-800-567-4797.

## SPORTS, FITNESS, PARENTING, RELIGION & SPIRITUALITY

0-7645-5146-9

0-7645-5418-2

**Also available:**
- Adoption For Dummies
  0-7645-5488-3
- Basketball For Dummies
  0-7645-5248-1
- The Bible For Dummies
  0-7645-5296-1
- Buddhism For Dummies
  0-7645-5359-3
- Catholicism For Dummies
  0-7645-5391-7
- Hockey For Dummies
  0-7645-5228-7

- Judaism For Dummies
  0-7645-5299-6
- Martial Arts For Dummies
  0-7645-5358-5
- Pilates For Dummies
  0-7645-5397-6
- Religion For Dummies
  0-7645-5264-3
- Teaching Kids to Read For Dummies
  0-7645-4043-2
- Weight Training For Dummies
  0-7645-5168-X
- Yoga For Dummies
  0-7645-5117-5

## TRAVEL

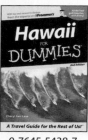

0-7645-5438-7

0-7645-5453-0

**Also available:**
- Alaska For Dummies
  0-7645-1761-9
- Arizona For Dummies
  0-7645-6938-4
- Cancún and the Yucatán For Dummies
  0-7645-2437-2
- Cruise Vacations For Dummies
  0-7645-6941-4
- Europe For Dummies
  0-7645-5456-5
- Ireland For Dummies
  0-7645-5455-7

- Las Vegas For Dummies
  0-7645-5448-4
- London For Dummies
  0-7645-4277-X
- New York City For Dummies
  0-7645-6945-7
- Paris For Dummies
  0-7645-5494-8
- RV Vacations For Dummies
  0-7645-5443-3
- Walt Disney World & Orlando For Dummies
  0-7645-6943-0

## GRAPHICS, DESIGN & WEB DEVELOPMENT

0-7645-4345-8

0-7645-5589-8

**Also available:**
- Adobe Acrobat 6 PDF For Dummies
  0-7645-3760-1
- Building a Web Site For Dummies
  0-7645-7144-3
- Dreamweaver MX 2004 For Dummies
  0-7645-4342-3
- FrontPage 2003 For Dummies
  0-7645-3882-9
- HTML 4 For Dummies
  0-7645-1995-6
- Illustrator CS For Dummies
  0-7645-4084-X

- Macromedia Flash MX 2004 For Dummies
  0-7645-4358-X
- Photoshop 7 All-in-One Desk
  Reference For Dummies
  0-7645-1667-1
- Photoshop CS Timesaving Techniques
  For Dummies
  0-7645-6782-9
- PHP 5 For Dummies
  0-7645-4166-8
- PowerPoint 2003 For Dummies
  0-7645-3908-6
- QuarkXPress 6 For Dummies
  0-7645-2593-X

## NETWORKING, SECURITY, PROGRAMMING & DATABASES

0-7645-6852-3

0-7645-5784-X

**Also available:**
- A+ Certification For Dummies
  0-7645-4187-0
- Access 2003 All-in-One Desk
  Reference For Dummies
  0-7645-3988-4
- Beginning Programming For Dummies
  0-7645-4997-9
- C For Dummies
  0-7645-7068-4
- Firewalls For Dummies
  0-7645-4048-3
- Home Networking For Dummies
  0-7645-42796

- Network Security For Dummies
  0-7645-1679-5
- Networking For Dummies
  0-7645-1677-9
- TCP/IP For Dummies
  0-7645-1760-0
- VBA For Dummies
  0-7645-3989-2
- Wireless All In-One Desk Reference
  For Dummies
  0-7645-7496-5
- Wireless Home Networking For Dummies
  0-7645-3910-8

0-7645-6820-5 *†

0-7645-2566-2

**Also available:**

- Alzheimer's For Dummies
  0-7645-3899-3
- Asthma For Dummies
  0-7645-4233-8
- Controlling Cholesterol For Dummies
  0-7645-5440-9
- Depression For Dummies
  0-7645-3900-0
- Dieting For Dummies
  0-7645-4149-8
- Fertility For Dummies
  0-7645-2549-2

- Fibromyalgia For Dummies
  0-7645-5441-7
- Improving Your Memory For Dummies
  0-7645-5435-2
- Pregnancy For Dummies †
  0-7645-4483-7
- Quitting Smoking For Dummies
  0-7645-2629-4
- Relationships For Dummies
  0-7645-5384-4
- Thyroid For Dummies
  0-7645-5385-2

---

## DUCATION, HISTORY, REFERENCE & TEST PREPARATION

0-7645-5194-9

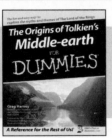

0-7645-4186-2

**Also available:**

- Algebra For Dummies
  0-7645-5325-9
- British History For Dummies
  0-7645-7021-8
- Calculus For Dummies
  0-7645-2498-4
- English Grammar For Dummies
  0-7645-5322-4
- Forensics For Dummies
  0-7645-5580-4
- The GMAT For Dummies
  0-7645-5251-1
- Inglés Para Dummies
  0-7645-5427-1

- Italian For Dummies
  0-7645-5196-5
- Latin For Dummies
  0-7645-5431-X
- Lewis & Clark For Dummies
  0-7645-2545-X
- Research Papers For Dummies
  0-7645-5426-3
- The SAT I For Dummies
  0-7645-7193-1
- Science Fair Projects For Dummies
  0-7645-5460-3
- U.S. History For Dummies
  0-7645-5249-X

---

# Get smart @ dummies.com®

- **Find a full list of Dummies titles**
- **Look into loads of FREE on-site articles**
- **Sign up for FREE eTips e-mailed to you weekly**
- **See what other products carry the Dummies name**
- **Shop directly from the Dummies bookstore**
- **Enter to win new prizes every month!**

† Separate Canadian edition also available
* Separate U.K. edition also available

Available wherever books are sold. For more information or to order direct: U.S. customers visit www.dummies.com or call 1-877-762-2974.
U.K. customers visit www.wileyeurope.com or call 0800 243407. Canadian customers visit www.wiley.ca or call 1-800-567-4797.

# Wiley Publishing, Inc.
# End-User License Agreement

**READ THIS.** You should carefully read these terms and conditions before opening the software packet(s) included with this book "Book". This is a license agreement "Agreement" between you and Wiley Publishing, Inc. "WPI". By opening the accompanying software packet(s), you acknowledge that you have read and accept the following terms and conditions. If you do not agree and do not want to be bound by such terms and conditions, promptly return the Book and the unopened software packet(s) to the place you obtained them for a full refund.

1. **License Grant.** WPI grants to you (either an individual or entity) a nonexclusive license to use one copy of the enclosed software program(s) (collectively, the "Software") solely for your own personal or business purposes on a single computer (whether a standard computer or a workstation component of a multi-user network). The Software is in use on a computer when it is loaded into temporary memory (RAM) or installed into permanent memory (hard disk, CD-ROM, or other storage device). WPI reserves all rights not expressly granted herein.

2. **Ownership.** WPI is the owner of all right, title, and interest, including copyright, in and to the compilation of the Software recorded on the disk(s) or CD-ROM "Software Media". Copyright to the individual programs recorded on the Software Media is owned by the author or other authorized copyright owner of each program. Ownership of the Software and all proprietary rights relating thereto remain with WPI and its licensers.

3. **Restrictions on Use and Transfer.**

   (a) You may only (i) make one copy of the Software for backup or archival purposes, or (ii) transfer the Software to a single hard disk, provided that you keep the original for backup or archival purposes. You may not (i) rent or lease the Software, (ii) copy or reproduce the Software through a LAN or other network system or through any computer subscriber system or bulletin-board system, or (iii) modify, adapt, or create derivative works based on the Software.

   (b) You may not reverse engineer, decompile, or disassemble the Software. You may transfer the Software and user documentation on a permanent basis, provided that the transferee agrees to accept the terms and conditions of this Agreement and you retain no copies. If the Software is an update or has been updated, any transfer must include the most recent update and all prior versions.

4. **Restrictions on Use of Individual Programs.** You must follow the individual requirements and restrictions detailed for each individual program in the "What's on the CD" appendix of this Book. These limitations are also contained in the individual license agreements recorded on the Software Media. These limitations may include a requirement that after using the program for a specified period of time, the user must pay a registration fee or discontinue use. By opening the Software packet(s), you will be agreeing to abide by the licenses and restrictions for these individual programs that are detailed in the "What's on the CD" appendix and on the Software Media. None of the material on this Software Media or listed in this Book may ever be redistributed, in original or modified form, for commercial purposes.

5. **Limited Warranty.**

   **(a)** WPI warrants that the Software and Software Media are free from defects in materials and workmanship under normal use for a period of sixty (60) days from the date of purchase of this Book. If WPI receives notification within the warranty period of defects in materials or workmanship, WPI will replace the defective Software Media.

   **(b)** WPI AND THE AUTHOR(S) OF THE BOOK DISCLAIM ALL OTHER WARRANTIES, EXPRESS OR IMPLIED, INCLUDING WITHOUT LIMITATION IMPLIED WARRANTIES OF MERCHANTABILITY AND FITNESS FOR A PARTICULAR PURPOSE, WITH RESPECT TO THE SOFTWARE, THE PROGRAMS, THE SOURCE CODE CONTAINED THEREIN, AND/OR THE TECHNIQUES DESCRIBED IN THIS BOOK. WPI DOES NOT WARRANT THAT THE FUNCTIONS CONTAINED IN THE SOFTWARE WILL MEET YOUR REQUIREMENTS OR THAT THE OPERATION OF THE SOFTWARE WILL BE ERROR FREE.

   **(c)** This limited warranty gives you specific legal rights, and you may have other rights that vary from jurisdiction to jurisdiction.

6. **Remedies.**

   **(a)** WPI's entire liability and your exclusive remedy for defects in materials and workmanship shall be limited to replacement of the Software Media, which may be returned to WPI with a copy of your receipt at the following address: Software Media Fulfillment Department, Attn.: *Yahoo! SiteBuilder For Dummies,* Wiley Publishing, Inc., 10475 Crosspoint Blvd., Indianapolis, IN 46256, or call 1-800-762-2974. Please allow four to six weeks for delivery. This Limited Warranty is void if failure of the Software Media has resulted from accident, abuse, or misapplication. Any replacement Software Media will be warranted for the remainder of the original warranty period or thirty (30) days, whichever is longer.

   **(b)** In no event shall WPI or the author be liable for any damages whatsoever (including without limitation damages for loss of business profits, business interruption, loss of business information, or any other pecuniary loss) arising from the use of or inability to use the Book or the Software, even if WPI has been advised of the possibility of such damages.

   **(c)** Because some jurisdictions do not allow the exclusion or limitation of liability for consequential or incidental damages, the above limitation or exclusion may not apply to you.

7. **U.S. Government Restricted Rights.** Use, duplication, or disclosure of the Software for or on behalf of the United States of America, its agencies and/or instrumentalities "U.S. Government" is subject to restrictions as stated in paragraph (c)(1)(ii) of the Rights in Technical Data and Computer Software clause of DFARS 252.227-7013, or subparagraphs (c) (1) and (2) of the Commercial Computer Software - Restricted Rights clause at FAR 52.227-19, and in similar clauses in the NASA FAR supplement, as applicable.

8. **General.** This Agreement constitutes the entire understanding of the parties and revokes and supersedes all prior agreements, oral or written, between them and may not be modified or amended except in a writing signed by both parties hereto that specifically refers to this Agreement. This Agreement shall take precedence over any other documents that may be in conflict herewith. If any one or more provisions contained in this Agreement are held by any court or tribunal to be invalid, illegal, or otherwise unenforceable, each and every other provision shall remain in full force and effect.